FREELY ASSOCIATED

FREELY ASSOCIATED

Encounters in Psychoanalysis

with

CHRISTOPHER BOLLAS
JOYCE McDOUGALL
MICHAEL EIGEN
ADAM PHILLIPS
NINA COLTART

edited by

ANTHONY MOLINO

FREE ASSOCIATION BOOKS / LONDON / NEW YORK

Published in 1997 by
Free Association Books Ltd
57 Warren Street, London W1P 5PA
and 70 Washington Square South,
New York, NY 10012–1091

ISBN 1 85343 384 5 hbk; 1 85343 386 1 pbk

A CIP catalogue record for this book is available from
the British Library

Produced for Free Association Books by
Chase Production Services, Chadlington OX7 3LN
Printed in the EC by J.W. Arrowsmith, Bristol

Contents

INTRODUCTION

In recent years, the genre of the interview, or what I prefer to call
the "conversation," has enjoyed a renewed appeal, especially
where the exploration of psychoanalysis and the work and thought
of its most innovative theorists are concerned.* The genre's rele-
vance, and the particular needs it addresses, are underscored by
Adam Phillips, in a chapter entitled "Telling Selves," from his book
On Flirtation: Psychoanalytic Essays on the Uncommitted Life (Faber
& Faber, 1994). In this essay, Phillips laments the paucity of
available life stories from within the ranks of psychoanalysis:
"There are surprisingly few occasions – or rituals – in which people
are expected or invited to tell the story of their lives from wherever
they think the beginning is; or to tell the even odder story that is
their dream." Similarly, in an interview presented here, psychoanalyst and Jewish mystic Michael Eigen explains: "Nowadays, I
think of psychoanalysis as an aesthetic, as a form of poetry. You
have all these psychoanalytic poets and singers trying to express
their aesthetic experience ..." It is these two perspectives, at the
interstices of intellectual and personal history, and of imaginings
and aesthetic experience, that have gone largely ignored in the

---

* I am thinking, primarily, of Karnac's *A Skin for Thought: Interviews with
Didier Anzieu* (1990); of Guilford's *Psychoanalysts Talk*, a collection of
interviews with twelve world-renown psychoanalysts organized around a
single case history (1994); of NYU Press' 1988 *Women Analyze Women (in
France, England and the United States)*, and of Thomas Ogden's *Subjects of
Analysis* (Jason Aronson, 1994) the concluding chapter of which presents
a conversation on analytic theory and practice between the author and
Stephen Mitchell. Prior to this volume, in 1995, Free Association Books
also entered two significant volumes (by Bob Mullan) into the growing
literature of this genre: *Therapists on Therapy* and, more notably, *Mad to
be Normal: Conversations with R.D. Laing*. To this list we may add, alongside my earlier *Elaborate Selves* (Haworth, 1997), Suzi Gablik's *Conversations Before the End of Time: Dialogues on Art, Life and Spiritual Renewal*
(Thames and Hudson, 1995) and Linda Greenspan's *Genius Talk*
(Plenum, 1995).

study of recent psychoanalytic theory. To this end, I've conceived of the vehicle of the conversation as more than the exploration of a singular experience. Hopefully, the conversations here collected – with five of the most engaging and essential "psychoanalytic poets and singers" working and writing today – move beyond the biographical to illustrate connections between life experience, culture and the production of knowledge in an increasingly complex world.

Ultimately, this book has a simple aim: to provide, in a single collection, an overview of the lifework and thought of five of the most insightful and provocative thinkers in contemporary psychoanalysis. Conducted and compiled over the course of two years, from December 1994 to January 1997, each "conversation" has as its nucleus a thematic concern – reflecting my own idiosyncratic reading of an author's work – from which centrifugal energies radiate into less focused, but equally illuminating, areas of general interest to readers engaged in/by psychoanalysis. Each conversation, in turn, is preceded by an "impresssionistic" sketch of sorts – that is, by a similarly idiosyncratic exercise in which I try to capture and reflect a mood, a reflexive moment, an indelible impression, that helped structure and define for me the contours and content of five encounters I will long remember fondly.

Clearly, the criteria at work in the selection of the five analysts contributing to this volume were, to a great extent, subjective ones. Over the years, experiences of pleasure and wonder, of jealous admiration coupled with fantasied elective affinities of taste and sensibility, and of transferences that any worthwhile reading experience awakens and engenders, all constellated for me in the process of reading Bollas and Coltart, Eigen, McDougall and Phillips. But aside from these subjective considerations, there are two other unequivocal "facts," if you will, that legitimate this singular grouping. One is reflected in the very title of the collection. For the analysts here presented are, in a way, all "freely associated." All either identify with, or have gravitated around, the British Independent tradition. Across generations, and the divides of oceans, from New York to New Zealand, D.W. Winnicott is one figure they all acknowledge and admire. In this sense, then, there is the associative bond of a common ancestry and intellectual heritage. A more immediate consideration is the fact that all five of these analysts have a great – as well as an occasionally public – respect for one another's work. Phillips' respect for Eigen, for example, is most readily evidenced by his compilation of *The Electrified Tightrope*, a book of Eigen's selected writings. Bollas is known to have been instrumental in bringing the work of Nina Coltart to the attention of American audiences. McDougall and Eigen are linked in a different way: for all of the differences inherent in their origins and cultural sensibilities, both openly acknowledge their debts to Bion and Lacan. In sum, there is already an ongoing conversation – sometimes subterranean and intertextual, at other times openly celebratory – that interlaces the writings of these important figures. One of my intentions, then, in bringing these analysts together in this volume, was to highlight the context of this broader conversation. In this way, and in the shared spirit of "Beyond Psychoanalytic Sects," the closing essay of McDougall's most recent book, *The Many Faces of Eros*, I've also conceived of *Freely Associated* as a way of countering the contentious and sometimes fratricidal quality of discussions in contemporary psychoanalysis. I have done so, however – or at least so I hope – without indulging or fostering anything of the very kind of gratuitious, self-congratulatory sectarianism that can be so sadly prevalent in our midst. If any inkling of such an attitude should spill from these pages, the responsibility is entirely my own. (I should specify, in any case, that all of the interviews have been reviewed by my interlocutors, both immediately after transcription and, subsequently, for approval – together with my introductory "sketches" – upon completion of the editing process.)

Finally, albeit obviously, I would hope that the five conversations here presented also reflect the significance generally attributed to each of these figures in the world of contemporary psychoanalysis. Few figures are as compelling, when it comes to the depth and vigor of their theoretical contributions; and yet few figures, I would suggest, are so relentlessly committed to bringing the riches of theory to bear on the nitty-gritty demands of clinical practice. Fewer still write with such a capacity for aesthetic engagement as to provide, together with intellectual nourishment, inexhaustible sources of delight. Bollas' fertile theorization of the vitality of objects, and elaborations of unconscious experience; McDougall's daring insights into the psyche/soma, and into the archaic links between sexuality and creativity; Phillips' insistence on the value of stories and, more centrally, on the conversational dimension in psychoanalysis; Eigen's groundbreaking explorations into mysticism and psychosis; Coltart's adventure into Buddhism and retrospective glances over the history of psychoanalysis ...

These are only some of the hallmarks that distinguish this free association of eminent thinkers and clinicians. It has been my pleasure, and indeed an honor, to have elicited their reflections over the course of the past two years. My hope, needless to say, is that the pleasures can now be shared.

I take this opportunity to renew my thanks to Christopher Bollas, Nina Coltart, Michael Eigen, Joyce McDougall, and Adam Phillips for their generous and gracious collaboration. I also wish to acknowledge the Haworth Press for permission to reprint my conversations with Bollas and Eigen from my earlier *Elaborate Selves: Reflections and Reveries of Christopher Bollas, Michael Eigen, Polly Young-Eisendrath, Samuel & Evelyn Laeuchli, and Marie Coleman Nelson*. Among the many other people who helped make this volume possible, Paul and Lucinda Williams, Pina Antinucci-Mark and her family, Fred and Linda Feirstein, Jeffrey Rubin, Susan Larkin, Wesley Shumar and Christine Ware all stand out for their friendship and support, across two continents, three countries, and at least a half-dozen cities. Finally, my deepest gratitude goes to two very special people, who strongly believed in this project from the start: to Gill Davies, my editor at Free Association Books, and to my loving wife Marina, to whom I dedicate this volume.

ANTHONY MOLINO
Vasto, Italy, May 1997

EDITOR'S NOTE (July 3, 1997).

The manuscript of this book was delivered to the publisher just a few weeks before the sudden death of Nina Coltart on Tuesday, June 24, 1997. In fact, it was forwarded to Gill Davies in early June, only a few days after I'd received from Dr. Collart a letter confirming her final review and enthusiastic approval of the interview. Together with Gill Davies, the decision has since been made to keep the preceding introduction unaltered. I have, however, withdrawn the original "sketch" of my encounter with Dr. Coltart that was to accompany the interview. Reflections of a different sort now seem in order. Also, at the request of Nina Farhi, a colleague and dear friend of Dr. Coltart, a postscript now follows the interview. As Dr. Farhi personally asked Gill Davies – friend, publisher, and longtime pen-pal of Dr. Coltart – to write the postscript, it is my honor, in this moment of sadness, to endorse such a timely and fitting request.

CHRISTOPHER BOLLAS

When I interviewed Christopher Bollas in his London home in the winter of 1995, it was the first time I'd been to England. And, much as I'd been forewarned, the weather was typically damp and cold and grey, with a prickly form of precipitation in the air that had the irksome quality of condensing around one's head and ears. When I arrived in the vicinity of Bollas' house, legs weary and chilled to the bone, I was already battling a numbing fever. Not the best way, surely, to present myself at the doorstep of a man widely regarded as one of the foremost psychoanalytic thinkers and writers of our time. So, with flu symptoms further compounding my original, deferential hesitation, I pushed up the hill to 42 Mount View Road, fantasizing outcomes, mostly catastrophic, to the work that lay ahead.

In the eternity of the dreary, one-block walk between my bus stop and now-dreaded destination, I would have been well served had I recalled the words of Adam Phillips, who in his book, *On Flirtation*, writes of Bollas: "(He) gets us close to the ordinary but absolutely elusive experience of making a dream." There was, indeed, something absolutely dreamlike about that walk, as if my body had somehow become suspended in a bleak and timeless space. Of much greater consequence, however, was the dreamwork to follow, around the amazingly ordinary exchanges that took place within the modest and comforting surroundings of Bollas' home and office.

Settled and warmed by a cup of tea, I spent the next four hours mindless of my body and its ills. The sense of suspension persisted, but in a transformed state. I began to understand why Bollas, who years earlier had inspired the idea of this collection, would only agree to an interview within the familiar confines of his own space. As he'd told me before, it had to do with a penchant of his for reverie: an atmosphere of fluid, unconscious germination, not unlike, again citing Phillips, "the sleep-walking à deux" of the psychoanalytic enterprise. Something similar, I believe, was unfolding, and enfolding me. As Bollas reclined and dipped into a treasure chest of memories and other psychic objects, the serene wealth and elegance of his answers made for an atmosphere of absorbing ease. So much so that twice in the course of our time together, we both forgot the presence of the tape recorder, and failed to heed the clicking sound signalling the end of the tape. On one such occasion, it was only after a half-hour that we realized that an answer of his had radiated into an essay, and been lost. Just like that, in much the same elusive and ever-so ordinary way in which a dream is made.

The following interview, which took place in London on January 9–10, 1995, explores themes taken up by Bollas, mostly in *Being a Character.* His latest books, *Cracking Up* and *The New Informants*, were published soon after our conversations.

AM: *In his book* The Postmodern Condition, *Jean-François Lyotard, citing the work of Wittgenstein, writes: "The social subject itself seems to dissolve in this dissemination of language games. The social bond is linguistic, but is not woven with a single thread. It is a fabric formed by the intersection of at least two (and in reality an indeterminate number of) language games, obeying different rules ... (T)he principle of unitotality – or synthesis under the authority of a metadiscourse of knowledge – is inapplicable." In a similar vein, much of your work on the self also goes against the grain of any unitotality. And yet in an earlier book,* Forces of Destiny: Psychoanalysis and Human Idiom, *you put forth what you call a theory for the* true *self. Is there a contradiction here? As clinician and theorist, how does Christopher Bollas understand the self?*

CB: In *Cracking Up* there's a chapter on this thing called *self.* Winnicott's concept of the "true self" and what we mean by the self are not the same. The true self was just his way of designating the presence of spontaneity: the true self as gesture. The false self, the only other "self" he wrote about in relation to the true self, indicates its presence through compliance: it describes a reactive attitude. My belief is that we have a sense of self that exists within an illusion of integration: an illusion essential to our way of life. Even those who see themselves as radical deconstructivists cannot, and do not, live a life without that illusion.

Michel Foucault has also written about postmodernism and, more or less directly, about psychoanalysis, in the contexts of his "histories" and "archaeologies." In line with his thinking, where he argues for "the insurrection of subjugated knowledges," *of what he calls anti-sciences, where and how do you situate your writing? Can psychoanalysis be something other than what Foucault calls a totalitarian theory?*

Already Freud's *Interpretation of Dreams*, in his writing of his self-analysis, and the reporting of his dreams to interpretation – in what was so remarkable an event, and so very fertile an occasion – doesn't support a totalitarian structure. If, like Freud, psychoanalysts write openly, if they provide enough detail, if there's enough saturation with the unconscious, then any reader will re-read and re-write a text in such a way as to undermine any thematic totality. It is those psychoanalytical writings, written with a greater degree of unconsciousness, that are, to my way of thinking, the more interesting. I include in this area the writings of Jacques Lacan, for example, where something primitive, something mythological and elusive persists, that leads one to imagine them, and open them up in so many directions. Harold Searles' writings are unconsciously rich. Each psychoanalyst must, no matter whether he or she does it consciously, re-invent psychoanalysis for themselves. It's those analysts who show the re-invention that sustain a level of creativity that's essential to the development of thinking. One can see this in certain contemporary analysts, like André Green, Adam Phillips, Michael Eigen, Harold Boris, James Grotstein, Joyce McDougall. All these people are recasting psychoanalysis, and re-creating it.

Along these lines, is there an element of a "project" in your work?

I can answer that question only toward the end of my life, when I look back. I don't wish to develop a "Christopher Bollas theory"; nor do I wish to re-use or echo terms which first served simply to establish a point I was intent on making in a single, earlier essay.

Speaking of archaeology, Freud had already used it as a metaphor for psychoanalysis. In your book, Forces of Destiny: Psychoanalysis and Human Idiom, *you seem to be inviting something new when you write: "Perhaps we need a new point of view in clinical psychoanalysis, close to a form of person anthropology." In a postmodern world, where the self, for one, is described as fragmented, decentered, discontinuous, multiple ... take your pick! – what would a "person anthropology" entail?*

It would be an analysis of any individual as a privately evolved but structured culture. It would mean that those signifiers that were currently important to an individual could be deconstructed; or, to think, when analyzing someone for the first time, that we're to enter a foreign country. It's like going into a different culture with a different language. Psychoanalysis then becomes in part a process for the translation of a person's different and changing perspectives, a way of deciphering all the many rules of foreign lives, of private cultures ...

In Forces of Destiny you take issue with D.W. Winnicott's notion of the true self, where he links it with the id (in juxtaposition to the false self and its connection to the ego). Yet you rarely speak of a false self; it seems, rather, that there exist only degrees of realized potential of true self, owing to the interplay of trauma and what you later, in Being a Character, call "genera." Is this so? And if it is, why resort to adjectives like "true" and "core"?

I resort to them because I come from a particular intellectual and analytical tradition, and have felt it important to indicate those origins. As for Winnicott, I think my critique of the link you mentioned was an incomplete critique. I think I understand why Winnicott linked the true self up with the id, as he was trying to get to something viscerally powerful and primitive. He did not want it linked to the ego because of that. On the other hand, I believe the organizational density of the true self, what I call *idiom*, is too intelligent a phenomenon to be, as it were, ascribed to the id. As a seething cauldron of primitive urges, the id did not, at least in the Freudian structural theory, have the kind of thick intelligence to it that I think exists for the true self, or indeed for idiom. Conversely, when Freud theorized the unconscious ego, he got to something which had that kind of dense intelligence to it: something that really has to do with the aesthetic organization of the self, or with the self as an aesthetic organization. Ultimately I think it is understandable why Winnicott linked his idea of the self with the id; but too much of his concept of the true self would still have to find a place in Freud's theory of the primary repressed unconscious, or later, of the unconscious ego. So, it was a failed effort, I think, to link it up to the structural theory.

Your reflections on the self, on idiom, have taken you to explore the realm of "character," a word which appears prominently in the title of your last book. It's not a concept usually invoked by psychoanalysts ...

I think that "character" is an aesthetic. If our way of being refers to our very precise means of forming our world, both internal and intersubjective, then each of us is a kind of artist with his or her own creative sensibility. We know that the distinctiveness of that creation is the particular form we have brought to it. We will share many contents with other beings; we share many phenomena in common, but we render them differently, and it's the rendering of a life that is so unique to us.

It is a pleasure to express and articulate the self: there's an erotic dimension to that kind of representation. Indeed I think Freud's theory of the instinct with its source, its aim and its object is an arc ... a pure arc ... without any actual "other" present in a way. But it's almost a pure arc of the pleasure of representation, because the erotics of the instinct drive is not simply in its final gratification through an object: it's the entire process ... In order for there to be the reduction of excitation, for there to be pleasure, representation is needed.

My own view is that in the formation of character we similarly have that arc: except I would say that, instead of there being a pure line from source through aim and object, there are many lines that fragment and break, in something like a vast symphonic movement which is, in and of itself, a pleasure. It is not the end point, not what we find at the end, not the objects that reduce the excitation, that constitute the pleasure. The pleasure is in the entire movement: which nonetheless remains something far too complicated and condensed, too thick, to be reduced to a single meaning, or even to two or three meanings, or two or three interpretations.

What about Winnicott's distinction between the optimal progression of an ordinary human life and what he views as the superior development of the creative artist or artistic personality?

I think by "ordinary" he means a return to the unformed existence of an unconscious. Certainly I think psychoanalysis, if it proceeds via the medium of free association, engages the analysand in a process of expression that leads consciousness to realize how extraordinary unconscious life is; in that respect, we must live dangerously, because we do take risks by allowing our unconscious life its freedom. It takes risk to speak what one thinks freely. Therefore, an analysand who is operating within the milieu of free association is living dangerously. And I believe there is a great deal to be gained from that kind of risk: not only is the free-associating analysand creating his analysis, he's creating his life. This is true to the extent that one is not operating through a process of carefully constructed narrative, which then leads the analyst to an equally carefully constructed interpretative narrative, i.e., interpretation of the transference, and so on and so forth. It leads to something more dense and unconscious ... more frightening, in a way, for both the analyst and analysand, in a sort of pleasurable way ... One does not often know consciously what to make of this, even though one has quite an acute sense that these movements are essential, intriguing, mysterious, developing ...

There was an enormously small word in your last answer of some consequence. You said: "if a psychoanalysis proceeds via free association ..." That seems to imply that an analysis could proceed differently.

There is a fundamental divergence between analysts or schools who see the analysand's free expression of thought and feeling as a priority, and those who don't. There are, in a certain sense, two paths. Along the first, this fundamental expression would have to take priority over the psychoanalyst's interpretation: without this freedom of mood, of thought, of feeling, without this density, the analysand is not going to issue a license to the unconscious; he or she is not going to find a voice in the context of an analytical situation. For the analyst, this means remaining quiet when he or she can see certain things operating within the transference. The analyst's silence, then, is in the interest of that movement, of that evolution in the analysand which gives rise to meaningful, if limited, self-reflections, to self-generated insights. To insights, mind you, which proceed not only from the psychoanalyst, but from within the patient: insights which over time establish an intriguing relation between the analysand's production of his or her own existence, between the creation of a life through free association and the unconscious movement that informs those insights.

That's one theorization, one path psychoanalysis has taken. On the other path, which is very different but very popular at the present time, is the patient who speaks about his or her life to an analyst, who then translates that speech into a metaphor of the patient's relation to the analyst; or of a part of the patient's self in a here-and-now relation to a part of the analyst. This is something which is not difficult for well-trained psychoanalysts to do, and in my view is also very interesting and meritorious in some ways; but it offers psychoanalysts the opportunity to resolve the ambiguities of a session's unconsciousness through a kind of reliable interpretation of events as they see them taking place. This, I believe, forecloses free association in the analysand, although one could argue that the process is split off within the patient, experienced somewhere but not uttered. Still, the difference between that analysand and the one who's freely speaking is enormous. Well, this difference poses a problem. I have no idea what will happen but, perhaps as time goes on, there will be two substantially distinct traditions in psychoanalysis, and people choosing to have an analysis can have one or the other, and will then know more or less what country they're entering.

It would seem that each of those paths carries with it, perhaps unconsciously, a very different sense of what a psychoanalytic cure would entail.

The highly interpretative analyst is very embracing, and promotes a cure by object relationship, by narrative restructuring. Of course, in the best of times, the interpreting analyst is in fact illuminating important pathological structures, important transferential anxieties; and therefore there is enough truth to his exercise for it to be meaningful for an individual. A lot is gained in this kind of an analysis; if it were a complete waste of time people wouldn't stay with it. They might be drawn to it but wouldn't stay with it for such a long time. But unfortunately, there is as much lost as there is gained in this kind of an analytical procedure. What's lost is something truer to life, because in a life we don't have accompanying us, day-to-day, an interpretative companion. We do not have an analyst alongside us interpreting the interactive meaning of every one of our gestures. And so I don't see how, in the end, that kind of an analysis fits in with a human life. However interactive we are, we're living in a fundamentally solitary space where we will always be generating meanings unconsciously, and only partially understanding ourselves. It is, therefore, the first path of analysis I identified that I believe takes into consideration the full nature of a human life: in that it aims to increase unconscious creativity and to situate unconsciousness, or the interpreting part of the self, in a meaningful but modest relation to creativity; whereas the other form of an analysis operates under a very particular illusion that a partnership, between a purely interpretative self and a purely unconscious self, will exist throughout a human life.

Again on the true self, you write: "A genetically biased set of dispositions, the true self exists before object relating. It is only a potential, however, because it depends on maternal care for its evolution." This could read like an essentialist argument, one that some orthodox Jungians might favor. Was that your intention?

No, though I don't disagree it's an essentialist position. I am arguing that we begin life with an essential core, with a nucleus of logic ... with logical nuclei ... or, let us say, with "positions" waiting to come into existence, that we somehow have to account for. How can each infant be so different from any other infant? *Forces of Destiny* had on the cover sets of human fingerprints. So what is the psychic correlate of the human fingerprint? I think there is something psychically as irreducibly different about each newborn as the irreducible difference of a fingerprint. And because I don't know where this intuition comes from, I rest back in the area of genetic predisposition. Of course there is a fetal existence, the incredible evolution before birth when the fetus is influenced by the world and engaged in relation to the inside of the mother's body, and to objects beyond the inside of the body. Already then the "something" that we are is in the beginning of a process of fragmentation, of a creative fragmentation that depends on both its own creativity, as well as on the mother's and the father's medium of care: on whether objects are provided for the infant and child to use and through which to disseminate themselves.

In what you call a person's "idiom moves," objects in the environment function both as receptors for our projective identifications and structuring agents of the mind. What is the relationship, or perhaps the difference, between these idiomatic expressions of the self and the symbolic elaboration that is the task of genera?

I think at any one moment in time, whenever we approach an object, we can say we're either going to use it for its projective potential or for its evocative integrity to structure us differently. There is a different, fundamental orientational attitude in the subject's use of an object. In the process of our own inner unconscious evolutions, we will be using objects either to contain parts of ourself or parts of the other, or in order to break us up via the structuring dimensions that are inherent to the object's integrity. In other words, more to fragment us than to contain the break. In that way, I suppose, where the elaboration of the self is concerned, the movement of genera depends upon whether at any moment in time we're deploying the objects in our environment, or whether we ourselves are seeking to be redeployed: whether we're putting ourselves somewhere through the deployment of objects, or whether we ourselves are seeking to be thrown into a new organization.

Any child, then, who is privileged to evolve by virtue of maternal and paternal care will have as an unconscious principle the formation of genera and the evolution according to those formations ... Psychic genera cannot emerge within the subject unless there has been substantial support for the evolution of the subject's idiom, which is a sort of fundamental paradigm for the genera of the self.

In your writing the subjective realm of human experience is paramount, from the womb to the grave. I'm reminded of Victor Turner's etymology of the word experience, *where he derives it from the Indo-European base* per-, *meaning "to attempt, venture or risk," which also yields the word* peril. *In an essay of Turner's on the anthropology of experience, he identifies the Germanic cognates of* per *in the German words "fare," "fear," and "ferry"; while the Greek* perao *relates experience to "passing through," with all the attendant implications of rites of passage. In your elaboration of the strivings of the self and the workings of genera, you seem very much attuned to this tragic quality of much of our existence, as the etymology of the word* experience *indicates.*

I like this deconstruction. In a way, the Sophoclean tragic vision is of violent action that breaks things up, followed then by reflection, seeing and sizing up what's occurred. This Sophoclean vision, cast in Oedipal terms, is of devastation, and involves the realization of the unwitting dimensions of the devastation. Put in terms of the Oedipus, we could argue that the entire process is true of the nature of life itself: that consciousness is blind to unconscious development, and that unconscious development is radically destructive.

You could say: "But what is it destroying?" Perhaps it destroys all mothers and all fathers; perhaps the evolution of any self destroys what was formed for us earlier by the mother, or by the father. Perhaps any evolution is going to break the desires of the other. It is then that we create our destiny, and live it. There are objects of desire and objects of hate, objects of intimacy and corpses of the expelled; and then, when we look back, in a Sophoclean way, one could say: "My God, what have I done? Only now I understand it all." And we see that progression as a tragic one, or as the ordinary way in which life is lived, as something unavoidable. Thus, in the notion of existing, or of experience, are the concepts of a ruthless breaking, of an opening up, of a dissemination, of a perilous venture. And, in addition, of something which borders on a kind of reflective faith: a kind of belief, upon reflection, that what's taken place was unavoidable and essential.

Thinking back at your discussion of the erotics of self-representation and the aesthetics of the self, are these pleasures simply breaks or interludes in the context of this greater tragedy? How do the tragedy and pleasure play off each other?

I think representation is a pleasure; therefore, the representation of Oedipus, the Sophoclean presentation itself, is a pleasure. Whatever the contents of the tale, whatever the story, its telling is always a pleasure. This is why I think, in the end, that Freud's theory of the dream as a wish fulfillment is true: not because the contents of the dream fulfill a precise wish of the dreamer, but because the representation of the dream, its creation, the very act of dreaming, is the fulfillment of the wish. The wish is to represent. So what we do or say is always a pleasure in that sense. Yet the fact that something is pleasing to the subject does not mean that it's good; it doesn't mean that it's going to be morally admirable. The pleasure could be awful, it could be terrible: but it would be, nonetheless, in the service of desire.

Postmodernism contends that "the center does not hold," that the function of narrative – as one way of identifying or cohering around a center – has essentially been lost. Psychoanalysis seems to oscillate between the free-associative dimension you've emphasized and what you're now identifying as the pleasure of the narrative. Still, I've found that a sense of history is missing more and more in the tellings of patients. There seem to be fewer and fewer stories to tell; and the stories people do tell are often altogether devoid of pleasure. This quality, in my experience, almost takes on a pathological dimension. Is this something that you see as a generalized contemporary malady, or is it something that the very nature of psychoanalysis exacerbates?

That's a very interesting question. I've not really heard it put like that before. I agree, there is less pleasure in the historical rendering of the self, or the rendering of the self in history than certainly there was in the past. I'm limited here by my American life, because I lived in the U.S. until I was thirty, during the rise of Erik Erikson's work, when the taking of the history and the giving of the history were very important.

Certainly I've understood the phenomenon in terms of the European migrations to America: once one has left one's place of origin for a new country, what one subsequently does becomes in effect a personal account of heroic evolution. The birth of the hero comes with crossing the seas, as Otto Rank said. But the crossing of the ocean, the rebirth on the new continent, and the subsequent evolution of the self, all give rise to a very neat narrative progression, with its emphasis on accomplishment, and so on. A myth, I think, Americans find very palatable. In the world of psychoanalysis and psychotherapy, American clinicians were very keen to hear the history of the patient, even if the person had been born and raised in the United States. Something of the myth of the hero was an important part of American consciousness. Today in the U.S., that is less the case than it was twenty or so years ago, and I think it no doubt has something to do with the failure to imagine a country capable of giving a new birth to the self, a capacity held to be true in earlier decades. That imaginative possibility has broken down, and therefore a certain relation to the history of the self is now more problematic.

Only occasionally, in your work, is there a mention of Freud's idea of the death instinct, whereas its correlative of the life instinct is given ample press, as evidenced by the emphases on idiom *and* genera. *How do you envision Freud's grand instinctual dualism? And would you grant it a kind of biological status, or does it serve primarily as a metaphor for the inescapable tensions we all confront?*

I think of it as a principle. The death instinct, like the life instinct, articulates or explains certain fundamental attitudes in relation to life itself. That is, if one is going to make use of life, and of all that goes into a life, as an object, we can speak of the life instincts operating; if a person withdraws from life as an object and shuts the self down, then I believe we can talk about a death instinct. Freud's theory of the death instinct, which fundamentally has to do with the decathexis of the object and a retreat into a narcissistic position, is a theory which makes eminent clinical sense to me. One can see it with certain patients who refuse and have retreated from object usage.

Emphasis on the creative endeavour of each indiv. trying to find his own definition? rich use of objects to achieve this [handwritten annotation]

However, to give Freud's portayal of these superordinate moving categories an allegorical power, such that we are driven by life instincts or death instincts, is not something I'm comfortable with. Different from Freud's, Melanie Klein's theory of the death instinct seems more configured around the infant's projection of persecutory factors. Though I find this interesting, I also do not agree with the extent of her allegorization of these two forces in the subject's attitude toward life itself. It's gone too far, and doesn't make sense to me.

You write in Forces of Destiny *of "a virtually legal imperative to pursue desire, ... of the ruthless pleasure of the human subject to find joy in the choice and use of the object. Indeed, there is an urge to use objects through which to articulate – and hence be – the true self, and I term this the destiny drive." What do you see, then, as the relationship between Freud's pleasure principle and "the destiny drive"?*

I think they are very similar. I think the pleasure principle generates the destiny drive. All that I'm adding to Freud's pleasure principle is an aesthetic dimension, an aesthetic aim. The pleasure of intelligence that forms the link between an urge, the aim of the urge, its object and the gratification of the precise pleasure of the self. That structure, that aesthetic dimension, is a crucial part of the selection and use of an object, which I see as part of the subject's destiny drive.

I imagine it is the case with everyone who practices psychoanalysis that one's own analysis has had profound effects on one's life and obviously on one's thinking. Would you be able to say anything about that?

Well I had three analysts, the first when I was a student at the University of California. He was a Mexican who, to the best of my knowledge, originally had a Kleinian training and then, after coming to North America, was training classically. My second analyst, during my training period in England, was Pakistani, from the Independent Group, and was analyzed by Winnicott. And my third – one should never say final analysis! – my third analysis was with an Italian. So all three people were from different cultures, with entirely different ways of viewing life, although each one was operating, in his best moments, in a way that conveyed a sense of the universality of psychoanalytical methodology. So I was always, in some ways, in the same place. I was always somehow within the same method, though there were three different drivers, three different people who operated and interpreted.

Obviously one is profoundly affected by one's analyst, but the last person who really knows in what way he or she has been affected is the analysand, precisely because of the nature of the transference and, arguably, because of the need for true unconscious participation to be unconscious. So, I have only glimmers of the ways in which each of these analysts has influenced my way of practicing. And although I was influenced by the best of their work, there are certain ways in which they got me wrong, or said things that were poorly constructed, or took certain positions that I learned from, because I knew they were mistakes. I think I learned from their mistakes as well as from their more creative, technical dimensions.

Is it safe to assume that all three of these people had a language other than English as their mother tongue? I find that rather peculiar.

They all had a language other than English as their mother tongue. I haven't thought about this until your question, but I think each of them also had built into him what I would call a generative hesitation. That is, I was not immediately sensible to any of them, but there was built into their speech, into their form of address, a form of translation which slowed down the process. I think this was enormously helpful to me, because the last thing I needed was quick response, or premature interpretation or precocious comprehension. And indeed I suppose I was eventually drawn to the Independent Group because of the high priority placed on analytical quiet, on the essentials of reverie and the permission not to speak, which was part of that group's technique. My first analyst too, though originally Kleinian, certainly gave me very considerable amounts of time to find myself internally before I spoke, and then to lose my self through speech in ways which were intriguing.

Did it ever happen that because of this intrinsic and fundamental language bridge you had to cross, your own sense of being comprehended was compromised? Was this generative hesitation of theirs paralleled by any hesitation of yours?

Oddly enough, no. I think this may have something to do with the fact that my father is French. His first language was French, his second language was Spanish, and English was his third, no, his fourth language. He knew French, Spanish, Italian and then English. But the three analysts that I was fortunate to have were all intelligent, gifted people who tolerated not knowing, and who gave themselves plenty of time. When they did speak, they all tended to do so with lucidity, putting their thoughts into language in ways I found creative.

Perhaps one of the interesting facets of translating, not consciously but unconsciously, from a mother tongue or a father tongue to a third or fourth language, is that what one says is always going to be rather idiomatic in its expression, always rather inventive, in its arriving in the moment. I quite liked the odd ways, sometimes, in which my analysts put their thoughts. I liked the invention that took place in language. It had a certain sincerity to it, a certain truth, a lack of guile, a kind of refreshing affection.

Any effort of thought into speech, any real effort, is very intense; it's hard work; and when my analysts made their interpretations, what often impressed me was the intensity and concentration, the sheer effort of putting something into language that had not before been put into language until that moment. And the fact that they were not of the same tongue as was I meant that we couldn't have commonly assumed cliches. There wasn't what I'd call the "lazy" element of language. I think I benefited from that; in fact, I know I did.

I'm thinking of your writings, of your acknowledged de-emphasis of interpretation, and your parallel emphasis on nonverbal forms of knowledge, on intuition. To what extent may these attitudes of yours have derived from the experience of your own analyses?

If I were to go back through my books, there's one correction I would like to make, regarding the unnecessary rivalry between verbal and nonverbal, between the uninterpretative and the interpretative. I would want to go back and, in the interest of accuracy, give a higher priority to the function of interpretation than I originally gave in my writings. I think there is a link between language, between speaking and internal inspiration. Whatever one's intuition is, one does not ultimately know what one thinks until one speaks, and therefore interpretation creates perspectives that are intimately linked with the unconscious work taking place inside. I think, regrettably, that I underplayed that aspect of analysis.

Has this shift been reflected in your own clinical practice? Do you find that you interpret more now than you suggest in your writings?

No, I think I always have interpreted more than I was able to bring about in my writing. Actually, it's not that I've interpreted more, but that interpretation was more important to me and to my analysands than I managed to communicate in my written work. Writing in the 1970s about clinical work, I underemphasized interpretation because unfortunately, in Great Britain at the time, it was the view of the Kleinian group in particular that only through interpretation could one gain access to the patient. So I was inside a political and polemical world at that time, and unfortunately went too far to the other extreme.

I gather from the biographical hints in your own work that you came to psychoanalysis from literature. Could you chart that itinerary?

I came to psychoanalysis when I was an undergraduate at Berkeley, at a point in my life when I was very distressed. I needed help, and so I went to the Student Health Service, and by chance was assigned to see a psychoanalyst. I had been studying history, and had come to read psychoanalysis because I was working on seventeenth-century New England village life, and was very interested in the Puritan mind. But my introduction to psychoanalysis was really through my own psychotherapy. As an undergraduate, then, I studied with Fred Crews; he invited me to his graduate seminar on literature and psychoanalysis, where I became more interested in the intellectual dimensions of psychoanalysis.

After graduation I worked at the East Bay Activity Center in Oakland, with autistic and schizophrenic children. Working with them I found the mystery of their illnesses so compelling and intellectually challenging that I knew I wanted to continue with that sort of work. I didn't know at the time how I could do it, because I didn't want to study psychology, and I didn't want to study medicine. As I was very keen on literature and wanted to go to the University of Buffalo, I went there to study literature and psychoanalysis. It was through the Department of Psychiatry that I was able to continue with clinical work; they created a little niche for me, and eventually we helped form together a university program in psychotherapy for people in the humanities. When I had to choose, ultimately, between being a professor of literature and clinical life, there wasn't any difficulty for me. I knew I wanted to train to be an analyst. I wanted to train in Great Britain, where I was accepted for training and came over in 1973.

Sometimes, when I read your work, the words use of the object echo with a ring of self-serving ruthlessness, where arguably the self being served is only served at the expense of other human beings, of other selves. Is it your position that your writings are intrinsically divested of ideological, moral or ethical implications? I can't help but wonder if the language itself is somehow a by-product of the "ruthlessness" of the 1980s, and of the social and economic policies of that period ...

One of the difficulties in writing about "ruthlessness" was the fact that in the 1980s, the term had a very particular moral significance – and correctly so. It was paradoxical that, at a time when the concept of the id – of that which grasps and takes for ruthless, amoral reasons – had departed psychoanalytical writings and been replaced by too sanitized a language, I was, in a way, reintroducing the idea just as a certain type of greed was operating in a ruthless way in the culture at large. This is something I was aware of, and was not all that pleasing to me. But nonetheless, I spent a lot of time on those essays, going over and over them to try to make clear what I was writing about. In effect, whether we like it or not, if we cannot be ruthless in the primary, instinctual sense, in the sense of the infant's need to feed, if we cannot follow that early urge ... I don't believe that the true self, or object usage, will arrive. Indeed much of psychic conflict has to do with different forms of antipathy towards urges and drives and so on. But where ruthlessness is concerned, I address it on purely psychological, and not moral, terms.

A focus of Being a Character, *already prefigured in* Forces of Destiny, *is your concern with the creative personality; with the fashioning of a life as a work of art. You point out how so much of this effort has to do with the maternal provision of an illusion of creativity in infancy, from which the child secures a sense of somehow engendering the object world. But you also stress repeatedly, albeit in passing, the function of what Peter Blos calls the "pre-oedipal father." What about the infant's generation of and introduction to the object world, via the ministrations and presences of both parents?*

We are now having to try to define what we imagine to be the infant's experience of the father. My own imaginings incorporate many of the well-known psychoanalytical views of the place of the father: the father as the embodiment of reality beyond the couple; the father, in the Kleinian sense, as the embodiment of the phallic entry into the mother's body; the father as inter-generational presence, and so on. But to these ideas I would add the "textural" difference of the father from the mother, or the "feel" of the father: the father who embodies a different odor, a different smell, who has a different way of holding, of carrying the child; who has a different way of breathing, of walking, a different tone of voice. Qualities which, for our purposes of discussion, I would say embody the masculine. The father is the embodiment of the masculine, much as the mother is the embodiment of the feminine. And I think, at both a biological, sensual level and at a higher level of imaginative distinction, that the mother and the father are enormously different; and that the infant, therefore, is, as it were, carried by two different persons. Arguably, the presence of agreeable difference – of difference not in the violent sense, not in the sense of having either gender eradicated – is an essential part of the child's development of creative opposition.

Blos talks about the early father's role as being essential develop-mentally in breaking the somewhat symbiotic bond to the mother and instituting that sense of difference. Would you say something similar?

Lacan takes that position as well, I think, in his concept of the Name of the Father, invoked to separate the infant from the mother. Yes, this I think is a widely held European view. I think in European psychoanalysis there is a consensus that the father has an important function in separating the infant from the mother. One could call this a kind of early Oedipal formation based upon the father's desire, as it is imagined by the child. In it, the child, so to speak, imagines the father's entry in order to properly create the separation from the mother later in the Oedipal period.

Before addressing the question of the contemporary fate of our cul-tural superego, I wonder how you see the origins of the personal superego? Given what you just said, if you take Freud's classic Oedipal conflict on one end, and Klein's much earlier developmental configuration of the superego on the other, how do you see the father's role in the formation of the superego?

I believe Klein and Freud are talking about two different mental structures; though they both use the term "superego," they're not talking about the same mental structure. On the one hand, Freud's idea makes enormous sense: that in identification with the father, the child takes in and psychically transforms the actual other into an imaginary companion, as part of a tripartite structure between the instinctual urges and the ego-self's presence. It makes sense if we look at it as the first moment, or moments, in the rise of a judicious self-awareness, in which the child is actually weighing up, *in consciousness*, the play of the different elements of the self that get mediated by the ego: of instincts and paternal prohibitions, of paternal views and so on. This theory of the superego, then, has much to do with the arrival of consciousness, of a sort of self-reflectiveness or awareness. But above all else it addresses the child's mediation between the different forces of the mind, the different elements that go into a self.

On the other hand, the Kleinian superego refers to persecutory anxieties the infant projects into the object, which is then imagined to be harmed by those very projections. It has a principle of retalliatory law, an intention to harm the infant. So there is an initial anxiety, perhaps an initial drive, increasing greed and envy in this area, which intensifies the attack on the object and then leads to this kind of projective circle I've just defined. Now, I do believe this is a factor in all infant life, but that it's more decidedly present in infants where there's been a breakdown in the infant–mother relationship. To such a child the persecutory anxieties become more predominant. I do not think this is linked to the father, as such; this is not part of superego formation. This is part of the formation of consciousness, but is not the moment in which self-awareness arrives in the infant. What Freud envisioned, and how he saw the superego played out within the context of the family, is a very different imagining, of a very particular way, that the child has of conceptualizing himself.

Quoting you: "I think that one of the tasks of an analysis is to enable the analysand to come into contact with his destiny, which means the progressive articulation of his true self through many objects." Very simply, how does psychoanalysis accomplish this?

By supporting the patient's right to free association. Through free associating the patient unconsciously selects objects of desire and articulates, through these objects, evolving self experiences. Now, some patients have a very real difficulty free associating; for some initially it's impossible, and therefore the analytical task through interpretation and other means is to try to free this person up so that he or she can actually speak more freely, in order to develop a form of unconscious creativity. Once that occurs, once the analysand is freely associating, then he or she is quite naturally picking objects up. We're talking here, of course, of mental objects: of objects that come into mind through which nascent self-states are released into articulation.

Is it free associating, ultimately, that you see as being the curative or reparative factor even in dealing with the scars that result from the early breakdowns or failures in environmental provision?

I certainly think that the capacity to freely associate is the most important curative dimension of the psychoanalytical treatment. It is the medium, in my view, through which analysands can articulate themselves, reflect on what they mean by what they say, and ultimately develop a good enough intrapsychic relation between the unconscious part of the self – which is ultimately beyond knowing – and consciousness which wishes to know something and to make something out of unconscious processes. This I think happens through the process of free association, which is a kind of intermediary between purely unconscious phenomena and lucidity. In short, free association is the presence of the true self in a session.

In this light, what about the dialectic of transference and counter-transference? As forms of knowledge encapsulated outside of words, in the realm of the psyche-soma, how can their dynamics "provide" for destinies to unfold? Could you relate some clinical examples?

As I said a moment ago, it's through free association that the destiny drive has its purest form or path. But patients also use their analysts, or they use part of the analyst's personality, quite unconsciously, I believe, in a way that this usage remains unconscious even for the analyst himself. Through the use of an analyst, the patient can elaborate, or give rise to and articulate, different parts of the self.

This, I think, is where there are very profound differences among patients who do not make a lot of sense when looked at according to psychoanalytical psychodiagnostics. For example, one can be working with a narcissistic analysand or a borderline analysand. The two can have similar pathologies. With the borderline there can be a movement between claustrophobic anxieties and agoraphobic anxieties, a back-and-forth oscillation; with a narcissistic patient there can be a kind of autistic, enclosed dimension to his or her object relating. One can see these shifts in both, but with one of these individuals there may be a much greater use of the analyst. For example, one borderline patient might be relatively nonverbal, relatively dead; another might be more verbal, describing different experiences with very different shades of affect that in turn elicit different feelings, different associations, or different responses from and inside the analyst. In the latter situation the psychoanalyst is being used much more complexly; the patient's degree of object use is much richer. Both patients are the same psychodiagnostically, but when it comes to the use of an object, the object is being used very differently.

This kind of transference, which Winnicott only implied in his concept of the use of an object, is not something to be found in the psychoanalytical literature. There one customarily finds references to fairly clear coercions, or fairly clear projective identifications, which have a particular sort of effect upon a clinician: inevitably, the outcome of the pathology. The logical extension of Winnicott's thinking, where the use of an object is concerned, is to look not so much at the pathology of the analysand, but at what outside the area of the illness are the capacities of the personality in relation to the other. That is, how can this personality use the other? This makes all the difference in the world so far as the ability to make use of life as an object is concerned.

Thus, we can take a borderline personality like Sylvia Plath, who had a tragic life and committed suicide ... And yet, at the same time, she wrote some of the world's greatest poetry, with a capacity to relate to her cultural objects that was quite profound. Another borderline personality, not a poet, who was restricted in many areas, might not make use of any objects and would have an even less enriched life. Sylvia Plath was mentally ill, as indeed are all borderline personalities, but unlike some, she also made use of life: which perhaps is one of the reasons why we look to her as such a tragic figure. If her life had been an irremediable write-off, if she had been a total loss to herself and all others, then individuals reading her works and reading about her would not feel such a loss. But it's because she enriched herself and others through her use of the object world that to see her kill herself, we feel an even greater loss. Because this was not a dead soul. There are some patients, unfortunately but true enough, whose lives are so bleak, who are so profoundly without creativity, so unnourished by any part of their life experience, that one can feel in the countertransference that one is not being used as an object, one is not being utilized unconsciously. With such patients, there's very little life present; whereas in other persons, with similar structural difficulties and with similar pathologies, there is a more complex and enriched use of the self.

You mentioned a type of patient who presents him- or herself as dead, and often stays that way for very long, excruciating stretches of time. Technically, where free association is not within the patient's repertoire, do you just wait out that person, or that self state?

I don't have, as I expect you'll appreciate, categorical, technical moves. Inevitably, my response would rely entirely upon who that particular patient is, where that particular patient was in the analysis, what understanding if any I had of what the aim was of that deadness. There are certain situations in which I will be quiet and say very little, if anything, in an hour, or in the course of days. But there are other occasions when I will be talking to the patient, telling him or her what I think this means, what is happening. In the best of times, psychoanalysts hopefully find themselves approaching a problem with a particular patient differently than they would any other patient. Our own technical interventions, I think, are thus part of the unconscious work occurring usually, spontaneously and freely within us.

In your concluding chapter to Being a Character, *you talk surprisingly about the "necessity" of a false self; how there is something intrinsic to psychic life that seems to require it. You almost seem to suggest that to fully develop the true self, or to elaborate one's idiom, could lead one to the limits of madness. Could you address this idea?*

The false self allows each person to construct a ready-made means of negotiating with the conventional object world, while preserving the complicated movements of the true self in the unconscious. Winnicott said there was a *necessary* false self in relation to the object world.

Is there an echo here of the conservative nature of the life instinct?

Perhaps there is ... and certainly there is an echo, really and simply, of going back to Freud's theory of unconscious functioning. In remaining true to Freud's theory of the unconscious, we operate as highly complex creatures. The simple operation of condensation or displacement in unconscious life is so thick, so obviously beyond consciousness, that were we to be continuously reminded of our complexity, we would be confronted with a form of madness. We forget, we simply forget about that complexity. In a way we forget about ourselves; and in forgetting about ourselves, we allow the self or selves to get on with their own perambulations, evolutions, interests, curiosities, and so on ... And we benefit from that kind of forgetting.

Much like Lacan, you too seem involved in a "return to Freud" that continually mines his findings to rethink his concepts. There is a vitality, in your writing, that in a way returns the unconscious to ontological status. How does Christopher Bollas understand, or imagine, the unconscious?

When I was re-reading *The Interpretation of Dreams* some years ago, I was struck by the fact that in Chapters 4, 5, and 6, we have the clearest, most lucid charting of the way the unconscious works in psychoanalysis. I was immediately struck by how all of Freud's subsequent theorizings on the unconscious, particularly in Chapter 7 of *The Interpretation of Dreams*, in his metapsychological papers, and then with the structural model, were all much less adequate, much less clear. In those chapters of *The Interpretation of Dreams*, together with his books *Jokes and Their Relation to the Unconscious* and *The Psychopathology of Everyday Life*, Freud indicates how the unconscious works. He shows through examples condensations and displacements, substitutions, assimilations; he illustrates the dense texture that is the unconscious process of an existence.

I was taken by how the dream, as a nighttime representational event, as the mid-point in a total process originating within competing daytime psychic intensities, worked to discharge the excitements and the energies of those very intensities – but without discharging their meaning! I was taken by how, the next day, the breaking up of the dream text occurred, through the process of free association, which in turn breaks open this condensation, and leads to a kind of intense outward movement. That whole arc, that whole evolution, is a remarkable example of how we live unconsciously. It's a process I've verified in my own life, as well as in my work with patients, charting the flows and ruptures of my own psychic intensities.

I came then to believe that Freud's theory of the dream's evolution, of this nighttime event which carries with it the history and experiences of the preceding day, the history of the infant or child, and which brings all this into a text that's broken up through free association ... I came to believe this entire process takes place on a much smaller scale, one might say on a less unconsciously creative scale, during our every day. This realization led me to imagine self experience in ways which, through re-reading Freud, I feel are closer to the way we truly are: that is, at any one moment, under the influence of our entire history. But then something new occurs. We meet up with an object which evokes an intensity within us: not because the object has some inherently meritorious dimension, but because it has to do with our own self. Something I see when walking along a street generates an intense moment for me that it wouldn't for you, or for anyone else.

This reaction, then, obviously has to do with one's subjectivity. But without the object there, without the integrity of *that* object, the reaction is not going to happen. Freud, for example, sees a botanical monogram in a bookstore, an object with quite a powerful evocative capacity to it. At that moment of perception a kind of nucleus is made, and a gravity befalls Freud. We could say this is a type of genera, newly formed. Then, for Freud as for us all, upon the moment's being experienced, upon the completion and fruition of that intensity, certain things will come into consciousness and begin to break up that moment, through the trains of thought that had compacted into its evocative quality. We are then off in a thousand different directions, until the next such psychic intensity. Now, I realize this is too schematic, too simplistic. Intensities are occurring inside us all the time. We can remember an intensity from the day before or a few hours before ... we don't have to be experiencing an actual object for all this to be taking place. But if we can begin to see this phenomenon as a kind of universe of stars ... as limitless, gravity-laden intensities that somehow endure and convey themselves, then I think we have a rather accurate metaphor of what we are and how we think: a metaphor that makes room for both our conscious and unconscious minds.

Where a pathology or a neurosis is present, would you agree that the number of objects that might evoke these intensities in the course of a human life is somewhat limited? And is there invariably a limit to the

*number of objects that even a healthy personality can be "intensed" by,
so to speak?*

That's a good question; I only wish I knew the answer. Individuals
who are ill, who are foreclosed for different reasons, will have a
narrower range of objects. They will therefore have fewer generative, evocative experiences of the object. It doesn't mean, however,
they're going to have fewer psychic intensities: they could have
more psychic intensities than another individual. But they will
have fewer generative experiences of the object world. No doubt,
in order to protect ourselves against the intrinsic complexity of our
capability, we choose to limit the field of the evocative, because
otherwise it could be too intense an existence. Certain friends of
mine, for example, who are poets, tend to maximize their percep-
tions of the object world and thus invite quite powerful evocative
moments. They live a life of continual surprise, whereas I myself
am too cautious and conservative a person to want to live that
stimulated an existence.

*Your emphasis on the object's evocative qualities reminded me, indi-
rectly, of Lacan's idea of the signifying chain. What has been his
influence on your work? Unlike Wilfred Bion and Winnicott, whose
provisions come across as maternal, indeed as transformational objects
or transitional spaces, throughout your oeuvre, when it comes to Lacan
I sense a more "ghostly" presence. Why is that?*

It's not simply Lacan. I think it's the French, and French
psychoanalysis, which I feel very close to. I've read in translation
some of André Green's works, as well as Pontalis and Smirnoff,
but I have a less consciously foregrounded use of French thinking than I do of British thinking. About Lacan, I did not like his
work to begin with. I was unsure whether this was a person who
was to be "believed." There were grave questions in my mind
about whether he was writing in good faith or bad faith, but I
benefited from close friends who had studied his work or knew
him personally, most importantly Stuart Schneiderman. So I
have read Lacan and find him increasingly relevant, but in ways
I'm afraid I just don't know.

*When I originally asked the question about Lacan, in my notes I
had next to the word "ghostly," in parentheses, the word "fatherly,"
followed by a question mark. When I conceived the question, I didn't
know your father was French ...*

That was immediately how I understood your question, you see! I think that I'm very influenced by my father and his way of thinking, by his whole frame of mind. He thinks, and has lived his life (he's still alive), as a French person does. His world is so much a part of me, so unconsciously absorbed, that it makes the French and their thinking very familiar. I feel in some way as if these are the people from whom one learns. But I don't speak or read French adequately, and that makes for a complex relation to French intellectual tradition. On the one hand, I would like to know more than I do, but I'm restricted by my own inadequacies, as far as the language is concerned.

Your idea of "futures" harkens back to the earlier reference of the postmodern "selves." The plural is one you yourself often use, as the idea of the self's multiplicity has recently been making a lot of noise: Stephen Mitchell and Jane Flax have both written extensively on it, theorizing multiplicities that James Glass, on the other hand, sees as an unwarranted, and indeed pernicious exaltation of the stakes that inform multiple peronality disorders and schizophrenia. What do you mean when you write of "selves"? How do they manifest in the course of a given treatment? And where do you stand in the current debate?

It depends upon how the term's being used, on what we're addressing or attempting to articulate. We are "selves" because in the course of time, of a human lifetime, this self that we are has many representations of itself, along with many representations of the object. In one day alone we go through many different self states, which by itself implies a plurality to our experience of our own being. And it's not an occasional plurality: it's a structure. We're fated to be multiple; to have, in a sense, a multitude of self and object representations. At the same time, I believe that all of us have – if we're fortunate enough – a feeling of unity: a feeling of there being one "self," even if we were to argue against that possibility. In the spirit of your polarization of the argument, I think that both positions are correct. One without the other is either too simplistic or too dangerous: we are both multiple and one at the same time.

So we do have a sense of a self. In an essay from my book *Cracking Up*, I argue that we have within us a sense of a nucleus that gives rise to our particular aesthetic in being. We have a sense of our own self-authorship, of something that is irreducible and that determines us. It is my point, in that essay, that though we may never know what that "something" is – in theology some might say it's "God" – that sense is a kind of organization that somehow determines us, that drives or predisposes us. But I can't say I have a great interest in this particular debate, even though I am sympathetic with those who regard this celebration of multiplicity as too "over-the-top"; I agree that it is, that it's too celebrated as a kind of accomplishment. We seem to go into fashions where there are these polarizations of one side of a binary process, and I think we are now over-privileging the multiple.

You quote Madame de Stael: "The greatest things that man has done, he owes to the painful sense of incompleteness of his destiny." Is there an echo here, of a Lacanian dialectic of desire and "lack"? Or does "the incompleteness we all must endure" refer to something else?

I think it refers to being a psychoanalyst at work with a patient. To the fact that, as a psychoanalyst, one launches the most intense process of self discovery that we have yet fashioned in Western culture, and that this process can be generated and cultivated by two people working together. And yet, at the end of the day, it raises more questions than it answers. I have to live all the time with my own sense of incompleteness as a psychoanalyst, and my analysands' sense of the incompletion of their own analytical lives ... I'm now fifty-one, and probably more aware than before of what will inevitably be the incompleteness of a life. One can only know, only see, so much. It's not as if there's not a lot more to be seen or known, even within oneself ... But we're too unconsciously productive to ever be able to fully grasp ourselves ... In that sense we can't get hold of ourselves.

Last night I had the occasion to hear an interview with Allen Ginsberg. After starting off by revisiting states or stages of Ginsberg's life that might have been reflected by the poet's changing appearance over the years, the interviewer ended up by asking: "Who is the real Allen Ginsberg?" To which Ginsberg replied: "Well, they all are, and none of them are." He went on to relate his experience as a practitioner of Buddhist meditation, and spoke primarily in terms of a Zen orientation. When Christopher Bollas writes about the true self, is there at any level a correspondence with the self that Zen purports to influence?

If so, it is not intentional. But it certainly has come to my attention, predominantly from people who are Zen Buddhists, that some of what I say resonates with some of their own beliefs. When writing, as in *Being a Character*, about the unconscious as a form of fragmentation, of a psychically intense experience, as a process of deep or thick experience that radiates out and dissolves the intensity, or through which the intensity is dissolved, Zen practitioners have told me that what I'm trying to convey is close to the notion of that which is gained through the dissolution of the ego: a view which, when I first read about in Zen Buddhism in the 1960s, I always thought was nonsense, because I understood it in terms of ego psychology at the time. Nowadays, I understand a little bit more about the idea; that is, that a form of consciousness must dissolve in order for a type of freedom to occur within the subject. In that limited area, then, I reckon there is some overlap between what I'm saying that what Zen Buddhists have maintained and believed for a very, very long time. But, as I'm not versed in Buddhist thought, I'm not in a position to comment on confluences in any depth.

Complementary to your notion of destiny is that of "futures," what you call "imaginary objects that are visions of potential use." "Fated futures," you write, "carry the weight of despair" – where you acknowledge the stifling effects of oppressive sociocultural contexts alongside customary environmental and parental trauma. Could you reflect for a moment – perhaps much as you have in chapters from Being a Character *on "The Fascist State of Mind" and "Generational Consciousness" – on the "futures" that inhabit our present socio-cultural, or "postmodern," contexts? What do you see them carrying, into the twenty-first century?*

For a black child living in Detroit, in a large family without a father present, and with a mother overwhelmed, perhaps on dope, seeing twenty-year-old blacks being killed, and few surviving into their thirties ... One would say there's very little in that child's future. There's very little in what he or she can imagine about a future that will facilitate the radical imagining of a self: this is essential, in my view, for any person's envisioning or appropriation of a future, and for its use as an object. Among middle-class people, each generation violently destroys the previous generation's ideals and objects; it is through this process of destruction, then, that each generation constitutes its own objects, through which to envision its own future. And it is in this respect that a generation gets hold of its future and uses it as an object.
Much of the literature today, on the so-called lost generation,

is a literature written by people in mid-life or older, in which there's a kind of anticipatory grief over what today's youth will not get. I'm suspicious of that kind of writing. I think it reflects more of the generational crisis of the baby-boomers themselves, a generation of great ideals that is now facing its demise and having a very hard time dealing with the losses that are part of that evolution. What's happening, I think, is that this group is projecting its own despair, over its own mortality, into the next generation; so that the adolescents of today, and those in their early twenties, are unconsciously meant not to have as good a future. I don't believe this will be true. I think that young people today, from what I can see, are generating their own idioms: musically, in fashion, in literature ... and I see no indications that they are bereft of a capacity to envision their futures. They don't imagine themselves in their futures in the ways we imagined ourselves.

When Sputnik went up in 1957, all Americans thought that they were immediately part of a march into the future, called upon to save their nation twenty years hence. And there was an enormous fuss made over our generation, as the one that could save the generations then in power. This made for an over-investment in the politics of future, and in the future of a self imagined through politics. Today, of course, there is enormous despair in the United States and in other countries amongst people of our generation over the so-called failure of politics.

If my generation is critical of contemporary youth, over how they've lost their ideals, have no political aims, or don't seem particularly interested in "doing" anything, I'd say that criticism is an unfair and inaccurate portrayal of contemporary youth who generally seem to have a more modest idea of what is realizable and can be accomplished in a life. They're not all marching off to Harvard or Yale or looking to get MBAs ... and I think it's altogether for the better. They're less likely to be materially as well off as our generations were, or so we're told, and so their imaginings of their future seem more modest. But by "modest" I don't mean less creative: it may well be a more creative generation than ours was.

In this context, you end your chapter on the destiny drive with a lovely meditation on the richness of the term "personal effects," and with a mention of the analyst's related work in discerning the analysand's culture. We're back, it seems, in the realm of an anthropology of the person: among objects, structures, and relationships that echo for me Gaston Bachelard's idea of a "poetics of space." Would you comment on this?

I'm pleased you bring Bachelard into this conversation. He is someone whom I read in the late 1960s and was very important in my development. I loved *The Poetics of Space, The Poetics of Reverie* and his other books. I think he's had an effect upon my imagining of psychoanalysis, and on the way I think of people. Roland Barthes was also very important to my way of thinking. Some of his early books were very crucial to the way I imagined my patients, if I think of the ways in which he deconstructs cultural objects to reveal mythopoetic thoughts; I found intriguing, for example, his idea of the way a culture thinks through its commodities. And I believe it's not too difficult to move from his analysis of such phenomena to any patient's discussion of an object in a psychoanalysis. These objects are saturated with private meanings and idiomatic significations.

In your own work you've hinted at some of the "personal effects," at some of the personal and cultural objects that fill "your house," so to speak. What are some of those around which your experience has crystallized?

It's hard for me to know, because I think those individuals whose works influenced me – whether in literature, film, music, or painting – are usually not persons whom I formally turn into objects of prolonged study as such. Ironically, I probably spent more time with certain writers and thinkers whom I believe I should come to terms with, whom I should address or make use of, than those who really and truly affect me. Of these I am less aware. So I have, for example, felt I *should* work with the thoughts and theories of Wilfred Bion. Working with Bion's writings has been important to my own way of thinking, but he's not a pleasure to read. I don't find him such an agreeable spirit, if I can put it like that. His language is, to me, colorless and without poetry, without vitality. But at the same time, he is a profound thinker, and I made a decision that I had to come to terms with him.

Of those people who have really and truly influenced me, most are from outside of psychoanalysis. Some, like Gustav Mahler, or Kant, I cannot even say in what way ... Mahler has influenced for me a vision of the self, or a vision of life; for several years I listened to his music, read the scores, listening and reading at the same time ... But I couldn't possibly say how that has affected me. More recently, I saw DeKooning's exhibit in New York three times; the first time was so overwhelming I had to leave halfway through. Then I returned the next day and saw the exhibit through, and then returned again two days after that. I suppose I spent about seven or eight hours at this exhibition; and I know for sure I have not been so moved by an object in a long time.

I think DeKooning's way of painting captures something about the nature of the unconscious; there's something about his expression of textures, of thought and ambition and endeavor, and about the way he erases ... The way he scrapes off certain lines, certain figurations that are then painted over ... but the erased lines are still there somewhere ... Something about his vision, his vision and re-vision, really spoke to me. What he taught me, in a way similar to Freud's theory of deferred action, is that the unconscious is not just an envisioning, but a re-visioning; and therefore, while one is writing one's self, one also edits and cuts and pastes and reviews, again and again and again. I think this was a very profound "discovery" on DeKooning's part. One has to put it that way. It's in Freud, but DeKooning actually, literally, illustrated the discovery. So in all I've been very affected by this, and seeing that exhibit has changed my whole way of thinking about life. But will I cite DeKooning in my next book? It's unlikely ... It would seem odd, out of place ... perhaps even a bit precious ... And I wouldn't know where to place him.

There were two other influences I thought you would have mentioned. What about Melville, and Henry Moore?

There are writers who have been lifelong companions, and Melville is one of them. Like all American school children, I read his works when I was very young. I grew up by the sea. As an eleven-year-old I was once swimming off the coast, about a hundred meters off shore, when a very small California gray whale – which didn't seem small to me at the time! – passed right by me. I recall thinking that a reef that had usually been in its place had unrooted itself and was moving toward me ... So I therefore had a very particular love of whales from that moment on, because I thought my life had been spared. In an analytical vein, when I was later doing my dissertation on Melville, I was unaware of the link to my own boyhood experiences. But Melville's fiction I always found very intriguing. One has in the very early novels, in *Omoo*, or *Typee*, a sort of adventure story, a young person's novelistic moment, novels of travel. In his subsequent novels his writings deepen, as more and more repressed phenomena from his own life start to emerge. And then you get to the profound engagements in works like *Moby Dick* and *Pierre*. The parts of the self have by then shaken him deeply, and writing becomes a means of survival. And to his great credit, mind you, he negotiates and resolves a crisis in such a way that he no longer has to write.

As long as you're asking about whom I've read and has influenced me, I've always read Camus. And there was a period of time when I was very influenced by the plays of Ionesco and Durrenmatt. I loved Ionesco particularly; I loved the surrealistic imagination in his plays. In the early 1970s, in London, I taught Modern European Philosophy to a group of very gifted American undergraduates; I taught Hegel and Heidegger, works like *The Phenomenology of Spirit*, and *Being and Time*. Reading Heidegger was a very important moment in my life, and changed my way of thinking in my twenties. I had been influenced by Heinz Lichtenstein, a psychoanalyst in Buffalo, whose essays were later collected in a book called *The Dilemma of Human Identity*. Lichtenstein had studied with Heidegger, and really had Heidegger in him. And as his own psychoanalytical vision had been informed by Heidegger, when I taught *Being and Time* it was, in a way, Heidegger taught through Lichtenstein.

Henry Moore? I would be hard-pressed to say in what way sculptors like Moore, Gabo or Barbara Hepworth have influenced my vision of life. I actually met Naum Gabo, and learned a lot from his writings about sculpture. I knew Bernard Leach, who was one of Great Britain's great potters. He was a deep and profound man, and any visit with him was a very special occasion.

Let's follow on this train of thought. Freudians aren't wont to speak of myths generally, outside of Oedipus. Yet in Melville you've mentioned one of the greatest modern myth-makers. How has, or what sense of, myth has informed your thinking?

I think anyone who grows up by the sea forms a type of myth about the meanings of his or her childhood, that invariably incorporates the order between two entirely different worlds: the terrestrial world and the sea. Being on the boundary of two very different worlds, to be a participant in both, in different ways, to grow up in that place, naturally lends itself to constructing myths out of it. My schoolmates from Laguna

Beach have all, I think, constructed quite powerful myths that involve a kind of story or legend of the self alongside the sea, and of how one carries the sea within. I still am very close to my school friends. We see each other every year ... I'm now referring to people I was with in elementary school and in high school. I know each of them has that part of their life formed into a myth that is always with them, in one way or another.

You are, after all, an expatriate. Is there something about the sea, for you, that inspires both daring and nostalgia?

I think that anyone going out to sea as a child, or who is part of a culture that goes to sea, lives in an intimate relationship to that which gives life and takes life. I used to assist as a lifeguard during days when there would be a very powerful surf, with very big waves. And of course I would be part of rescuing people who were close to death, close to drowning ... In that kind of situation you also see people who have drowned. So as a child and an adolescent I saw people who were killed by the sea.

Perhaps one of your most fertile and arguably long-lasting contributions to theory is the idea of the transformational object. How did you come to elaborate the idea, and to what extent was it informed by your clinical work and observation?

I first wrote about it in my notebooks in 1973, and it was a reflection of my own experience of being in analysis for the first time: of what it feels like to speak oneself and then to be understood in a very particular way, and for that understanding to change one's perspective. It was the generative dimension of that ordinary aspect of a psychoanalysis which got me to thinking, among other things, what kind of object accomplishes that? Or, in the sense of an object relationship, who is that? Later, when I first began doing analysis in 1974, as I was very aware that my analysands would be experiencing me as a process of transformation, as well as of the difficulty of an adequate transformation, I then developed a different view of technique, and of the crucial nature of wording a person to themselves.

Following up on this, we talked earlier about the dream, especially where your own "return to Freud" is concerned. You've gone beyond, however, a broad textual re-evaluation of The Interpretation of Dreams *and of the theory of the unconscious Freud propounds there. The dreamwork, and the dream space, have become in your work not only metaphors but models for both psychic life and the very dialectic of psychoanalytic practice. What about dreams, dream space, and the dream that we are?*

A session is a potential space. As the patient talks, the psychoanalyst associates. Both participants are engaged in a process of free association along the lines of the dream work as defined by Freud. In this respect, both persons are dreaming each other through the workings of substitution, assimilation, condensation, displacement, etc. They may actually form something like a text, as in the analyst's making of an interpretation. Whether or not it is an inspired interpretation, or an inspired comment, whether it comes out of the dreaming between the two of them or not, always remains to be seen. Very often interpretations are matters of routine; whether transference interpretations or not, they may often recur in the analyst's mind. One could say then that interpretation may not come out of the dreaming: the dreaming continues but it doesn't give rise to the comment.

But sometimes what an analyst says to a patient is actually and distinctly different. It's new, it's inspired, and both patient and analyst know it to be so. And I think both know it to come out of the interplay between them. But perhaps precisely because it's inspired and condensed and overdetermined, this kind of interpretation usually has a short shelf-life. The patient makes use of it quickly, unconsciously, and it's then broken up, disseminated, and like a dream it unravels.

I think the dream is the heart of psychic life, and if our patients didn't dream and remember their dreams, if there weren't the possibility of dreams being told, I don't think there would be a thing called psychoanalysis. We simply wouldn't have it. And I agree with Winnicott that the dream really and truly is the pure unconscious, which makes its presence very important to the kind of work we do.

Would it be correct to say that you view the dream as a locus that replicates, on a daily or nightly basis, the containing function of the mother's unconscious for the infant? You also speak of it as a place where the self is "loosened," as it were, allowing for what you call "a plenitude of selves" ...

J.-B. Pontalis makes this point. And I agree, that the dream space inherits the place in which the mother functions in relation to the infant. So to dream, to bring oneself together in that kind of place, is based on a kind of memory of being brought together by maternal holding and maternal reverie. The process of dreaming is therefore, intrinsically, a recurring, regressive, refinding of an early type of object relation that was profoundly transformative.

Clinically speaking, if a patient routinely reported nightmares or disturbing dreams, would you see this as an indication of faults or failures in that person's earliest environments?

I think invariably so. It's very interesting that most schizophrenic people find their dreams terrifying. Many schizophrenics report no dreams at all, and have managed to eliminate dream life, or at least any contact with their dream life. We can speculate, then, in an individual for whom dreaming is nightmare, that there has been a breakdown in early maternal holding. This is not to say the mother fails the infant, because many things can go wrong from the infant's side of the equation that make it impossible for any mother to effectively hold the child. But something has gone wrong, and therefore there is not an experience of good-enough reverie in the mother.

What about the place of dreams in clinical practice, in the actual course of a psychoanalysis? Does their unfolding point invariably to the healing effects of treatment, in a somewhat sequential way, or do they function differently, differentially?

I think one can determine psychic change from dreams. That is, one can tell when a patient has changed in and through the dream, or when the dream registers the change. Take, for example, a patient who never dreamt about her children, and for whom her children were of no psychic significance whatsoever because of a profound pathology of a narcissistic type. When she first included one of her children in a dream, this indicated psychic change; and it was evidence of a change in relation to all of her children. She had created room within herself not simply for the child, but for someone whom she could nurture, whereas in most of her dreams she'd been searching for the nurturing other and unable to hold onto a capacity for nurture. So dreams do register important psychic change. Personally, however, I have never had the luxury of reading through the notes of an analysis and systematically study the history of its dreams, in order to be able to comment on whether or not that important private literature is indicative of a very precise kind of evolution and development.

There's a word you use in Being a Character, *in the essay by the same title, that I wasn't familiar with. "We are inhabited by the revenants of the dream work of life ..." I'm left with echos of remnants and reverie, of covenants ...*

What I meant by *revenants* are the phantasmatic, the phantasmagoric residues of our dream works, and so of our life as well. It's a word that carries the outcome of our own private unconscious creations.

When we first contemplated this process several years ago, the lone condition you stipulated was that we record the conversations here in London, in your space, because you needed to provide for what you called "reverie." What is reverie for you?

There are always levels of thought, levels of engagement, levels of response to a question, levels of thinking about something. I can think off the top of my head ... I can provide a certain level of response to what you might be discussing, or to what a patient might be saying to me. But for reverie to take place, I have to be able to drift inside myself ... in a more associative way ... in a less quickly reactive manner. I also have to be relaxed within myself for this to take place, and speaking to you here as opposed to speaking to you just after travelling on an airplane allows me to get to a different level of thinking. It's always a frustration for me when I travel to other countries, as I am never able to get to a level of thought that I value very much. I think it's one of the reasons that I love doing psychoanalysis, because it's a real privilege and pleasure to be working with people within a methodology that frequently allows for this experience of reverie.

In an earlier conversation, Marie Coleman Nelson and I explored the possible impacts, on both the unconscious and on psychic development, of the techno-culture in which much of Western consumer culture exists: a culture, for example, where ancestral notions of time and space have practically collapsed, and the fertile confusion of tongues that was Babel is being superseded worldwide by an electronic culture of prefabricated images. What do you see as being in store for our species, as language becomes more and more homogenized, less creative, and as our visual capacity becomes increasingly prominent?

The younger people I see in treatment are indicating a frustration with homogenized imagery and cultural symbols. For example, rap music which is violent, sexist, almost anti-melodic, is exceedingly popular amongst middle-class children all over the world. I take this to be a good sign, a good indication that a revolution of sorts is taking place in consciousness.

These kids do not want to be part of an anodyne world, laundered of the visceral dimensions of an existence. I'm not pessimistic about the cultural future of our civilization. I actually think our generation – I'm speaking now of people in their forties and fifties – has been less creative than it could have been, and it's ironic because it's an unusually self-preoccupied generation: in the sense of the history of generational consciousness, we've been more aware of ourselves as a generation than other previous generations, but not more creative and, if anything, somewhat less creative. If one looks at music, or to fine art, literature or philosophy ... if one looks around for very creative people who are in their forties or fifties, there simply aren't many. This wasn't the case with earlier generations. I believe we have been in a kind of cultural wasteland of our own creation, something our own generation has created with a certain abandon. I don't understand it myself, but it's there to be seen. And I don't think it's going to last very long. I don't see this period of the Miramax world, let's say, of the homogenized, cinematic productions that have had a culturally devastating effect on European film industries, as proving to be the end of Western culture, or of the generation of meaning in Western culture. We've seen bits and pieces of this, but I think there are also signs of ferment and creative destruction amongst younger people.

As you've occasionally tackled questions pertaining to the relationship between psychoanalysis and culture, I was wondering how you view the rabid rise of fierce and violent nationalisms and religious fundamentalisms around the world. Today's news alone highlights the ongoing Bosnia tragedy, Cecenian uprisings, fundamentalist crusades in Algeria and Palestine, and even here in Western Europe the increasing intolerance of immigrants – a topic Julia Kristeva took up in Strangers to Ourselves. *Is this something psychoanalysis should also be concerning itself with?*

I think psychoanalysis should enter public discourse. I think it has a great deal to offer to a public understanding of destructive processes, and it's a great shame that it has been as little utilized as it has. I was at a recent reunion of the Free Speech Movement in Berkeley, where seminars and discussions on the 1960s were taking place. One of the noticeable absences, in terms of critical perspective, was the psychoanalytical view of culture and social movements, and of the link or relation between violent destruction and economic deprivation. This is less so in Europe, where people make use of psychoanalysts. I am part of a Labour Party think-tank, in which there are two other psychoanalysts, and ten or twelve social theorists and media thinkers. I think it's important that these circles want to have psychoanalysts present, and want us to be part of the cultural deconstruction of contemporary culture.

But getting to the heart of your question, I think that the world has always been a terrible place in many respects. And it's an unfortunate but essential part of every human life that, unless one is immediately and directly affected by extreme political privations, there's some distance we can put between ourselves and the world. One can go through childhood, adolescence and youth without being too aware of this. But by middle-life, one becomes more and more aware of the world at large, of the processes occurring in and around the world, by which one is not immediately and directly affected, and this recognition brings to mind just how disturbed world affairs are. Yet how is the situation in our world now worse than it was in the nineteenth century or the eighteenth century? Certainly the capacity for destruction is greater, the ability of groups to destroy their societies has been increased by technological developments, and mass communication makes it possible for a man like Saddam Hussein to dominate a large country because he can control it through the media and communication networks. In the nineteenth century, arguably, it would have been harder for someone like him to do this. So, in that respect some things are worse; but I don't think that the world is decidedly more venomous, more malicious than it's always been. It's always been awful.

You've suggested that you don't think the world is any more of a horrible place than it's always been. Yet throughout the West there's a growing concern with what is arguably a significant increase in crimes committed by juveniles. Aggression seems more and more unbridled among the young, and in our societies gener-

ally: to the point that a sense of evil, which you have written about, seems to have become more pervasive, more concrete, less of a metaphysical concern ...

I don't think the young are more violent than they were. What they have now that they didn't have before is access to lethal weapons. Access to guns has made the American adolescent in some cities a more dangerous person than he was before. Street violence, street aggression is fairly high in Great Britain, which goes contrary to the notion of this being a gentle country. It's not. But English persons tend not to be armed, and guns are quite rare.

Amid the general consensus that violence is on the increase, I've often wondered if a sense of group solidarity, of communal values or ideals, is disappearing. With this in mind, I was wondering if psychoanalysis ought to confront the question of whether our dominant models of the superego (Freud, Klein) need rethinking. Are they too proving inadequate in an age when sexuality, arguably – and I'm not sure you agree – is not the unspeakable, culturally repressed force that Freud first unearthed?

I believe that sexuality is still *the* unspeakable repressed force, and I would take the politically correct movement in the United States, and the fate of certain persons who are right now incarcerated because of that oppression, as evidence of my contention. In the United States there is an epidemic of belief in sexual molestation. Persons accused of molestations are in jail, and we now know many of them are innocent; still, they remain in jail. In religiously fundamentalist families, or in their secular equivalents, one finds situations where there is not a high degree of sexual molestation but a great degree of oppression, where sexuality and aggression are concerned. When children from these families reach adolescence, one of the ways they can imagine sexuality and aggression is through fantasies of violence and of sexual perversion. So, taking adolescent girls, for example, one way they can imagine and talk openly in their family about their sexuality is by putting it in someone else and demonizing it. Then it gets attacked but represented at the same time. So, towards the end of the twentieth century in the United States, there is, from my point of view, a resurgence of the hysterical personality, of hysterical complaints and a mood of hysteria. I would say, then, that sexuality, for its oppression to lead to these rather bizarre forms, is still very much a sufficiently dangerous phenomenon. But I think your question had to do with a breakdown in values in the U.S., as this connects with something gone wrong in the formation of the superego ...

Thinking back at that marvelous essay of yours "Why Oedipus?," one thing I've noted is that you do seem, in your own reflections on the superego within the context of the Oedipus myth, to attribute a shifting but significant power to the group, as embodied in Sophocles' play by the chorus. If this is the case, where can we nowadays locate the voice, the principle, the authority, if you will, of the paternal function? In our own social context, where, in what group, can we locate that function?

I think it's crucial here that we keep in mind Winnicott's concept of the superego, which Adam Phillips writes up brilliantly in his book *Winnicott*. Winnicott argues, in essence, that the child's sense of what is right emerges out of its experience of being with the mother and the father; he argues, in essence, that the child has an intrinsic sense of right and wrong. This sense is not something internalized, so to speak, by virtue of a reluctant moral appropriation that results from a pure identification with the father; nor, indeed, is it a begrudging accomplishment of Klein's depressive position: i.e., the achievements of a somewhat expedient requirement to maintain the loved object at the same time that it's discovered to be a hated object. Personally, like Winnicott, I think that the child has his or her own intrinsic sense of right and wrong. This doesn't mean that knowing what's right leads the child to behave correctly: one can, in fact, often see a child acting mischievously, looking carefully at the parents, not because he wants to find out if what he's doing is right or wrong, but in anticipation of a certain censorious response from the parent – precisely because he knows that what he's doing is wrong! In a child's participation in culture, he comprehends pretty quickly what is good behavior and what is bad behavior. This development is a part of human nature, in a very similar way that the experience of anxiety, or the experience of guilt, or the experience of despair are all natural.

The Oedipal period, then, in which the threesome assumes significance, inaugurates the child's negotiating new difficulties with the mother and father. This is the period when a boy will go through his castration complex, or the girl goes through hers, and each negotiates their appearance of mutilation, and all else that goes into this incredible period of a life. My point in "Why Oedipus?" is that there is a stage beyond this, a stage that's always existed but only becomes increasingly apparent with a latency or school-aged child. When the child goes to school, and when taking part in the group feels all right, the child is in essence carrying part of the family structure, of the Oedipal structure, inside the self. He or she may in fact be imagining the loving mother and the loving father. And yet children's own families are, to their surprise, not powerful or strong enough to sustain the family laws, habits, and idiomatic features away from home; children find that these laws don't always print out onto culture at large, where they meet a different world. They not only find that the world is different, but that each of their peers at school has different families, and that together they're all part of what is in effect a very large group. It's this participation in the group which radically challenges family structures.

And that actual group, moreover, is coincidental with the arrival of an internal group of objects, where the child's self and object representations of the mother and father, of the self and others, is impressively multiple. And because of this multiplicity of structures, this development dissolves the primacy of the dyadic and triadic structures. It does not erase them, however; so that we can and do return in our lives to dyadic and the triadic structures: to the former, for example, by having a relationship, and to the triadic through the creation of a family of one's own. These are, I think, essential transformative retreats from the fact of a human life: from the fact of the actual group, and from the internal group of objects which had earlier dissolved the more simplifying structures. But I think in part we're talking about these issues out of the spirit of your comments regarding the world at large. Is it not a more dangerous place? Is it not a less culturally generative space? From my point of view, it is simply a realization about what is always beyond our families and our private lives. Out there is a world of a large collection of peoples, of countries, of forces which is beyond our thinking, beyond our organization.

In a different vein, you've spoken often of the "integrity" of an object. What do you mean by an object's "integrity" – a word that itself connotes a certain moral value or quality? What determines an object's integrity?

I simply mean the structure that any one object possesses. Mozart's 40th Symphony, as an object, is different from his 25th object

Symphony ... and it certainly differs from a Bruckner symphony. So that each time one hears that symphony, each time one approaches that object, it has a recognizable integrity to its structure that can't be changed. It can be interpreted differently by different conductors, but there's a reliable, integral feature to it. When we choose an object, we very often pick something that will process us, and the integrity of the object is an important part of the gain to be derived from that object's selection. Psychoanalysis has tended to focus too much on the projective uses of an object, on what we can put into it; it thus has tended to regard objects as sorts of neutral or empty spaces to receive our contents.

For example, in psychoanalysis we speak of the mother and the father as if there were no intrinsic distinctions between mothers and fathers, when of course we know there are enormous distinctions. But we can't make room for those distinctions when it comes to theories of projective and introjective identification. Allow me to correct myself a bit: we can with introjective identification, but we can't so much with projective identification. And we don't need to really: those theories are important and exist in their own right outside of their particular frame of reference. But at the same time, when we make use of objects, when we select a book to read, or a novelist to explore, we're going to be processed by the integrity offered us by that object: namely, by its structure, which differs from that of other objects. That's what I'm really focusing on.

But in a culture where bombarding images mediate, and often condition and define the experience of objects, can we still speak of their integrity? I'm thinking, at a very basic level, of how Madison Avenue manipulates our desire, and through its selling of sex, for instance, can distort, thwart, or even pervert our expectations – indeed, our experience – of the opposite sex ...

Our experience and use of objects is always vulnerable to an interpretive appropriation of those objects by powerful movements or authorities outside our realm. So I don't think, for example, that Madison Avenue's interpretation of our sexual objects is more oppressive than the interpretation given to objects by a seventeenth-century minister in New England, who dominated the village and indicated to all and sundry how they were to interpret their environment, or their sexual objects, and how they were to understand their desires. However, there's already a difference between life in an early seventeenth-century

New England village and life toward the end of that century in a New England village. The difference is not that the people were any less sexual or less sexually specific in the early seventeenth century, and therefore more liberated in terms of sexual desire in the late seventeenth century. The difference of course was in the mentality. Toward the end of the seventeenth century there was a greater degree of toleration of human preferences, and a less effective oppression created by the church. That's where matters were different.

So in contemporary terms, I don't think the oppressiveness we live in will end people's subjectivities. The politically correct movement, combined with the ability of the media to generate a kind of homogenized vision of life, will not stop people from reading, from writing music, from painting. Their forces are not going to stop civilization. But there is a mentality in these forces which makes the quality of our life different, and thus restricts us. This we must oppose ... Hence the spirit of your questions. In that sense, I agree: there is something to be opposed. But if you're asking me is this the end of culture, my answer then is no. We have been here before, and we will be here again. Hopefully, though, it doesn't have to happen in the lifetime of every generation. But if we could go back through the preceding generations, we might hear how each generation had a similar experience fo the world. Again, it has to do, I think, with the sense of decline that takes over each dominant generation, and its surrender of power to the new generation. It's about the sense of failure, the sense of despair, that arrives over what wasn't accomplished.

Looking back at your concept of the evocative object, you make a distinction between what you call a "mnemic" object and a "structural" one. Can you clarify the distinction?

The structural object is close to what I later call the "integral object," which I've written about in *Cracking Up*. The mnemic object is an object that is significant because it has received prior projective identifications on the part of the individual. In *Being a Character*, for example, I pointed to a swing that has particular significance for me. However, a swing is also a structure, it does something ... This comes close to the concept of what the integrity of the object is, and of how it will have its own particular effect upon my self. So we can use objects both mnemically and structurally. Another example: Schubert's *Unfinished Symphony* was the first symphony I fell in love with as a child, one I'd also purchased through the Columbia Record Club. In that way it's mnemically powerful for me: it brings back memories of my life at that time. At the same time, it has an independent structure to it; it has its own integrity independent of my projections. And I can also appreciate it as a piece of musical composition in its own right, and thus see the difference between it and Schubert's other symphonies. Thus we will sometimes choose objects for their structural capability that may have no mnemic significance for us whatsoever. If I choose, for example, to go sailing or boating, I pick an object that is part of a process that engages me, but is not mnemically significant for me.

In your opening chapter of Being a Character, *you make a peculiar reference to what you call your "postmodernist cousins." Who are they, and why do you call them "cousins"?*

I'm very aware that my own particular development as a psychoanalytical theorist has gone along postmodernist lines in some respects, and I think many of your questions and comments are quite correct in placing me within a certain intellectual tradition. I'm also aware of being influenced by some of the works of Jacques Derrida, for example. And having done my training in literature at the University of Buffalo in the 1960s, where there were many soon-to-become postmodernist thinkers, one couldn't help but be influenced by postmodernist thought. There are, however, some ways in which my thinking is not postmodernist. You pointed out, for example, what you regarded as a certain kind of essentialism in my thinking, with which I would agree. So I see my own positions as a theorist containing substantial contradictions. And although I can understand why I'm seen as a postmodernist writer in some ways, I would also say that I'm an essentialist in others: hence I could not say of Derrida, or of someone such as he, that he is a brother. But I can see that he is a cousin! There are familial connections, although not always direct ones.

Reading your work as an oeuvre that has paid such focused attention to the subject–object relationship, a flash came to me of the title of a book that was very important in my formation, Martin Buber's I and Thou. *Is there a space where human objects – be they evocative, or objects of desire – or even the "ordinary" object world, say, of Zen experience – can engage us as subjects, and collapse the dualism of subject and object?*

No, I don't think so. I don't think we can be engaged by the human other in such a way that they cease to be an object for us. In our psyche we will always be unconsciously or consciously objectifying them. But the "other," the human other, in particular, does have a profound subjective effect upon us: in the sense that our subjectivity is restructured by their processional effect. I tried to get to that side of the equation of object relations by conceptualizing the other as a process, as a transformational object. And I do have a project to try to delineate and differentiate, among the internal objects we hold in us, those that are fundamentally a result of our own work, and those that might be more fundamentally the work of the other upon our self. But I haven't yet reached that point in my writing.

When you say that objectification of the human other is inevitable, do you mean something more than that it can't help but be the recipient of our projections and transferences?

I simply mean that we form the other as a mental object. For however actual, however substantial, however intimately and profoundly sensitive the other is, and for however much they embody the "otherness" of the other, we always destroy that sense through our formation of a mental object: as when we change the other according to our own desire, or our own subjectivity. And it is in that act that we always reconstitute the other inside our self.

And yet you do talk and write about the encounter of unconscious subjectivities in the process of analysis. About how, at the level of the unconscious, we can be subjects to one another ...

I understand more precisely your focus now. Both persons affect one another, subject-to-subject, at that unconscious level of inter-affectiveness or interrelating. There really will be direct processional effects ... one upon the other ... unconscious to unconscious, according to the laws of unconscious condensation, displacement, substitution and so on. However, each person will at the same time be objectifying that experience: that is, bringing it up into mind both unconsciously and consciously, so that those objectifications of the subjective dimension will always be retranslated and re-formed by the subject. Then as time passes .. we're not talking about a long period of time, it could be even a matter of minutes ... there are subsequent re-editings and changes of that initial

engagement. That's why I like DeKooning's theory of the unconscious, because I think the initial moment does get erased and
changed and then changed again, until the revision itself is
changed and edited.

There's a marvelous phrase in Being a Character *that I'd like you to
talk about. In the essay that gives its title to the book, you write,
apropos the ego-psychological ideal of adaptation to reality:* "It seems
to me equally valid that as we grow we become more complex, more
mysterious to ourselves and less adapted to reality." *A sentence like
that could drive legions of therapists crazy!*

Another way of looking at it would be to say that reality is increasingly less available for adaptation. Apropos of your earlier questions of the disturbing changes in the world, my response in part is
that it's not just that the world is changing, but that we're changing too. This is usually the sort of perspective of a person in
mid-life, or later; but it's one in which you realize that the world is
so complex a place, how could one possibly adapt to it? So, what is
reality? Assuming one could even find it, how would one adapt to
it? I know what ego psychology meant. I know that it was talking
about the broad structures of a life: marriage, children, professional life, the ability to manage the problems that come with each
phase in a life cycle, and so on. Certainly the concept of adaptation is a useful one, but it's also exceedingly restrictive and, as a
view of what takes place in the course of a human life, I think
unfortunately and substantially wrong. That is, as we get into mid-
life in particular, we enter a phase of the life cycle in which we
become increasingly aware of how complex life is; of how in some
ways it can't be adequately thought. Life is too complicated to be
thought out. And it's not just life as a phenomenon: life, whatever
it is, is beyond our thinking. Political affairs are in some ways too
complex for a single thinker to think out ... or to be content with
his or her thinkings. Each of our own lives is so complicated. There
are so many strands of interest, of convergence and interpretations, that at any one moment in time we ourselves are, as conscious individuals, beyond our own individual efforts of thought.

This, I believe, is humbling. I believe it leads us towards more
modest senses of what we can accomplish in life. Another way of
looking at this attitude would be to see it as part of an effort to
promote a vision of the end of an analysis. What is the frame of
mind of an individual towards the end of his or her analysis? I
don't think psychoanalysis has offered visions of the self after a

psychoanalysis is concluded. It's left us with metaphors like "integration," "adaptation," "depressive position," and so on, which are accurate so far as they go, but in and of themselves are rather meager in comparison to the complexity of a life, and how one looks upon and relates to that complexity.

What are your hopes for psychoanalysis? Are we a dinosaur close to extinction? Or is there room for us not only to survive but to thrive in contemporary society?

Psychoanalysis just has to survive "the psychoanalytic movement." If it survives psychoanalysts and their schools, then it will grow and develop. But this remains to be seen.

WORKS CITED

Bachelard, G. (1969). *The Poetics of Space* (tr. by M. Jolas). Boston, Beacon Press.
—— (1971). *The Poetics of Reverie* (tr. by D. Russell). Boston, Beacon Press.
Buber, M. (1970). *I and Thou* (tr. by W. Kaufmann). New York, Scribner.
Freud, S. (1900). *The Interpretation of Dreams*, in J. Strachey, ed. *The Standard Edition of the Complete Psychological Works of Sigmund Freud*, 24 vols. London, Hogarth, 1953–73, S.E. 4–5.
—— (1901). *The Psychopathology of Everyday Life*, vol. 6.
—— (1905). *Jokes and Their Relation to the Unconscious*, vol. 8.
Hegel, G.W.F. (1977). *The Phenomenology of Spirit* (tr. by A.V. Miller). Oxford, Oxford University Press.
Heidegger, M. (1962). *Being and Time* (tr. by J. Macquarrie and E. Robinson). New York, Harper.
Kristeva, J. (1991). *Strangers to Ourselves* (tr. by L. Roudiez). New York, Columbia University Press.
Lichtenstein, H. (1983). *The Dilemma of Human Identity*. New York, J. Aronson.
Lyotard, J.F. (1984). *The Postmodern Condition*. Minneapolis, University of Minnesota Press.
Melville, H. (1959). *Typee, a Real Romance of the South Sea*. New York, Harper.
—— (1969). *Omoo, a Narrative of Adventures in the South Seas*. New York, Hendricks House.
—— (1971). *Pierre, or, The Ambiguities*. Evanston, Northwestern University Press.
—— (1981). *Moby Dick, or, The Whale*. Berkeley, University of California Press.
Phillips, A. (1988). *Winnicott*. Cambridge, Harvard University Press.

CHRISTOPHER BOLLAS: Selected Bibliography

The New Informants (1995, with Donald Sundelson). London: Karnac; Northvale, NJ: Jason Aronson, Inc.

Cracking Up (1995). London: Routledge; New York, Farrar, Straus & Giroux (Hill & Wang).

Being a Character: Psychoanalysis and Self Experience (1992). London: Routledge; New York: Farrar, Straus & Giroux (Hill & Wang).

Forces of Destiny: Psychoanalysis and Human Idiom (1989). London: Free Association Books; Northvale, NJ: Jason Aronson, Inc.

The Shadow of the Object: Psychoanalysis of the Unthought Known (1987). London: Free Association Books; New York: Columbia University Press.

JOYCE McDOUGALL

When Gill Davies, my editor at Free Association Books, informed me last spring that Joyce McDougall would be around the corner from my Philadelphia home, in New York, for a few days in April, I could do little to hide my dismay. With less than a month to prepare for an interview which had been projected for the same time, a year later, in Paris, I found myself shuffling my already hectic schedule, but also lamenting the dissipating prospect of revisiting Chartres, the Seine, and a special group of people and places whose lustre had been subtly tarnished by time, and the insidious dimming of memory. It had been nearly ten years since my lone visit to France, and it was difficult, all of a sudden, to give up the incubating delights of a trip long planned and anticipated. But my dismay notwithstanding, and as necessity would have it, there followed a preliminary exchange of faxes and phone calls, the latter mostly via answering machines, through which Dr. McDougall and I began to arrange our stateside, whirlwind rendezvous.

"Dr. Molino? Oh, hello. Did I wake you? I am terribly sorry. I thought I'd get your answering machine ..." It was 3 a.m. in Philadelphia when a buoyant, unfamiliar voice burst through my bedroom phone. I'd never spoken with Dr. McDougall before, but in a comical, albeit maddening way, she had made for the most spontaneously successful of introductions. In one fell swoop she both addressed me as an equal ("Most analysts I know turn their phones off at night," she apologised, with just the right hint of good-natured embarrassment ...) and established a mood of playful familiarity – aided, no doubt, by the very awkwardness of the *faux pas*. By the time we'd finalized the arrangements for our interview and, like people meeting on a blind date, got down to the business of determining just how we'd manage to recognize each other, "Joyce" then put the finishing touch on a wonderfully wacky call: "I'll be the woman with the rose in her mouth! ..."

It was then, after we'd hung up, that I began to understand the inspiration, the force, behind such classic works as *Theaters of the Mind* and *Theaters of the Body*. I sensed, if you will, the characterological genius that had enriched psychoanalytic thinking and practice with the metaphor of the internal stage. And, finally, it was thanks to that charming moment of histrionic flair that I began to reflect more deeply on the metaphor's own richness. For in the analyst's dual role as spectator and fated director of countless ensembles in search of an author, there persists – as Joyce McDougall knows well – a living sense of the original Greek word *theatron* defined by Webster's as "akin to thauma." Akin, that is, to something of a miracle.

The following interview took place in New York City on April 21, 1996, shortly after the publication of McDougall's most recent book, *The Many Faces of Eros.*

AM: *You open your book,* Theaters of the Mind, *with a quote from the French comedian, Raymond Devos: "One always hopes to become someone only to find out in the end that one is several." To what extent has your own history and resultant bilingualism, as a New Zealander transplanted to Paris, informed both your sensibility and your theoretical perspective on multiplicity?*

JMcD: Maybe it starts with an early interest in theater and only later a fascination with the internal theater of the psyche. When I was a child my father and grandfather used to tell stories of the theater pieces that Pater (as we always called my grandad) wrote to be performed in the little country school of which he was the headmaster. My grandfather, George William Carrington, had emigrated as a young man from England in dramatic circumstances, because the London family (so my aunt informed me) had lost all its money in the Canadian Pacific Railway crash, thus forcing Pater to leave his art studies and go to work in a bank. He was so unhappy he decided to emigrate to New Zealand. There he discovered that he had a sufficiently good educational background to be allowed the charge of a little "one teacher school". (There were many such schools in the outlying country areas of New Zealand.) So, at the end of every school year, my grandfather put on a musical theater show for which he wrote the play, the songs and the music, and every child in the school had a role in his play.

Young Mr. Carrington's school show became well known in the community and one year a friend invited Sarah Jane Martin (who was destined to become my grandmother) to see the play. She was apparently entranced, and when the headmaster bowed at the end of the show and thanked the audience for their applause, Sarah Jane Martin announced to her friend: "That's the man I'm going to marry!" As she was that kind of woman, she married him! She truly loved him and swore that she would devote her life to him and to his lost career as an artist. In her mind he should give up teaching and go back to painting. But this project took many years to come to fruition. Meanwhile the couple had six children, and at the end of each year, each one in turn played a role in the school show. My father, who told me many stories of this period in his life, recalled that one of his earliest memories was having to play the role of "the lost child." He was barely three and remembered that, half asleep, he was propelled onto the stage where he had to call out "Mummy, Daddy. Where are you?" I loved these stories, of course, and apart from my father's memories, I would try to imagine my grandad's theater and ponder the different roles and selves that people might play.

Mater's dream eventually came true when my Uncle Cedric, the youngest son, bought a farm and Pater, although he had to help with milking the cows, could at last spend many hours each day painting. He painted hundreds of pictures and in fact became one of New Zealand's most renowned artists. I was lucky enough to see a retrospective of his life's work just three years ago, when I was back in New Zealand on a short visit.

What a treasure chest of memories!

Yes indeed, although it wasn't until somebody asked me in an interview not long ago where my interest in theater came from that I realized it had begun in childhood. Then, of course, there were my father's "war stories" about his adventures during the First World War, and his meeting my mother in England during leave from the Western front. The result of their romantic encounter was marriage as soon as the war was over, when he brought her back – like a proud prize of war – to New Zealand. So I think my interest in selves, and theater as such, arises in part from family legends. In high school I eagerly joined the "Shakespeare Club" and took part in many Shakespeare readings. Later, when I began my studies in psychology at Otago University, I became an active member of the Drama Club. But my interest was not in acting – my greatest desire was to produce plays (like Pater), and each production was most exciting to me. What I found particularly exciting was getting people to let their own inner selves join with their role until the character became a part of them. In a way, I suppose, I was already doing something like an analyst tries to do. I don't know if that answers your question about theater ...

It does. To add to it, though, can you say a bit about your bilingualism?

With English-speaking parents in an English-speaking country of course I only spoke English, with the exception of two years of high school French. Little did I imagine that one day I would be living in France! After graduating from Otago Girls' High School I was accepted at the Teacher's Training College, and there too I was an active member of the Drama Club. In fact it was during a theater performance of *Night Must Fall*, in which I played the leading female role, that I met Jimmy McDougall who had the leading male role – and we eventually married. We decided to leave New Zealand with our two children when we were still in our twenties. My dream was to have a personal analysis as well as the hope that eventually I might be able to train as a psychoanalyst in England. Jimmy McDougall, whose field was in worker's education and university extension work, hoped to go further in his specialty in London. So we sold everything we owned and arranged our passages to England. There were no air flights in those days: the children and myself came by boat, where we were in "B Deck" (Economy Class) ... and for six weeks, we voyaged under the water ... I remember we used to watch the fishes through our portholes. Jimmy McDougall, like all young New Zealanders in those days, worked his way over on another boat, as second vegetable cook, and arrived eight weeks after myself and the children. Once in London I wrote to everyone whose books I had read – Anna Freud, Winnicott, Robert Moody and others, and eventually I was invited to meet each of these prominent people. My encounter with Anna Freud was particularly meaningful because I was interested in training for child psychoanalytic work ... I am getting around to telling you why I speak French and how I became a French analyst, but it's a long story ...

Take all the time you need ...

Well my visit to Miss Freud at Hampstead Gardens still stands out in my mind. She was living in the house where Freud found refuge in the last years of his life, and his widow, Marta Freud, was still alive ... this was in 1950 ... The first thing Anna Freud asked me was, "Wherever did you hear about my father?" I said "but Miss Freud, I went to the university in New Zealand and of course we studied your father's works." "Oh," she said, "nobody talks about my father in the university here in London." I was astonished. How could a "Kiwi" know more than a student in London? She seemed very pleased to hear that her father's books were known and studied in my country ...

I could also have told her that at sixteen I had already read *The Psychopathology of Everyday Life*, and that what I'd learned was sufficient to make me decide that I did not want to go to Medical School as others in my family circle had done. Instead I made up my mind then and there that I would study psychology ... So I told Miss Freud that I wanted to apply for the child psychotherapy training and she said 'But have you any experience with children?' I said, 'Well, I have a little girl and a slightly bigger little boy.' She informed me that I would have to begin a personal analysis which of course I was eager to do. And I received word within the next two weeks that I had been accepted as a student. Our little family of eight or nine candidates in training met for seminars four nights a week. You were supposed to really study! But it was exciting and challenging. Just as soon as I managed to get a job I began my analysis with Dr. Pratt, whom I chose because he was a member of the "Middle Group." By the time Jimmy arrived I'd found a little apartment in a Victorian "row-house" as well as schools for our children, and was already short-listed for a job as clinical psychologist at the Maudsley Hospital, in the children's department. As the leading psychiatric hospital in London, Maudsley was a rich experience: I heard lectures from many interesting people – analysts of different schools of thought, like the French psychiatrist and analyst Henri Rey and the Jungian analyst Gordon Prince. It was a stimulating intellectual world and I believed my dream was coming true – to do child psychoanalytic training and continue training for adult work later. But Jimmy McDougall found no work in London other than several hours a week lecturing for the BBC, broadcasting to the armed forces in Europe. He became terribly depressed. For a year and a half he struggled on, applying for jobs everywhere. Then suddenly he was offered a challenging post in the Diplomatic Corps with UNESCO's "Fundamental Education" department – but it was in Paris! ...

So I'm at last answering your question about my bilingualism. Halfway through my training at the Hampstead, here was Jimmy in France and happy at last. Of course I had to tell Miss Freud – and she looked incredulous. "You're not leaving the course are you?" I said "Well, Miss Freud, it breaks my heart to leave the course. But my husband's been here a year and a half with no job offers. He's already in Paris." "But there's no child training in Paris." "I know, Miss Freud ... but maybe I can take something of what I have learned here if I'm accepted by the Paris Psychoanalytic Institute." "No," she said "I would not want this to be a stepping stone to some adult institute." I didn't really know what to say next, so I came up with: "Well you know the children do need their father." "Ah yes, your little children – so you do have to go," she said ...

Anna was of course aware of her tender devotion to her own father, and even if she was not impressed by the fact that I was separated from my husband, she did feel that children need their father. So ... I found myself in Paris, obliged to do my psycho-analytic training in a language that I hardly knew how to speak.

Could you say more about your training in England?

The Hampstead training opened up for me a new world of knowledge. It was thoroughly classical of course ... There was much friction at that time between Anna Freud and Melanie Klein, and we were not encouraged to go to any Kleinian lectures. I remember the jokes that circulated ... such as ... the Kleinian analysand who rings his analyst because his car has broken down saying "I'm sorry, I'm going to be half an hour late for my session but just start anyway!" This was a hit at Kleinian technique – about which I knew very little at the time. And I'm sure equally comical stories were being told in Kleinian circles about the Hampstead group. However, in my second year I began to go regularly to the Tavistock Clinic for different seminars that were being offered: advanced use of the Rorschach, group techniques, etc., and was able through contacts at Tavistock also to get stimulating insights into Kleinian theory ...

Still, the most important influence on my thinking was Winnicott. I went to his open lectures and his consultations at the Paddington Green Children's Hospital. He liked having students around him, and his technique was fascinating. One delightful story that was very typical of him: a cockney woman had brought along her little boy of about three and a half and said, "Doctor, we gotta see you. We saw our doctor and he said we gotta come here. He's got a problem." "Oh," says Winnicott, "he won't shit? How long is that he won't shit?" "Three weeks, doctor, he don't shit." Winnicott looks at the little boy and gives him paper and pencil and says, "Would you like to draw something?" The boy makes endless rounds while Winnicott asks the mother to talk about her family life. And at a certain moment he said, "And how many months pregnant are you?" She looked astonished, "I ain't told anybody I'm pregnant." He says, "But you are, aren't you?" "But nobody knows, not even my husband." (As I remember, I think she'd kept her pregnancy secret because she feared her husband might want her to get rid of the baby.) "Nobody knows but me." Winnicott then waved toward the little boy and said, "But he knows." He then asked the boy, "Wouldn't you like to know more about that baby that mummy's got in her tummy?" And the little boy, still drawing circles nods, and says, "Yeah! I would." Winnicott turned back to the mother saying "it's up to you whether or not you tell your husband, but do talk to your little boy about the baby." The following week she came back and immediately announced "Oh Doctor – he shit and shit and shit." Incidents like this made Winnicott so endearing, to me anyway.

What a marvelous story ...

To my mind he was a marvelous person – but of course he was severely criticized by many of the London analysts who didn't approve of his ways of working, or appreciate his creativity. Yet he himself sought for harmony; he tried to bring people together: for example he tried to reconcile the Anna Freudian and the Kleinian groups ... but ended up antagonizing both!

What about your training in France?

When I got to France I discovered that, effectively, there was no regular child psychoanalytic training at the Paris Psychoanalytic Institute, as Anna Freud had predicted. However I applied for the adult training and was accepted in spite of the fact that I hardly understood a word of French. Then, once accepted as a candidate, I introduced myself to Dr. Lebovici, who was a child psychiatrist and the leading figure in child psychotherapy at the Paris Institute. One day he said "Oh by the way, I'm looking for an analyst for a little American boy. Can I give your name?" I said I would be very pleased. So this little boy, Sammy I'll call him, came along and the work we did together eventually became a book ... In English it's called *Dialogue with Sammy*, and Winnicott wrote the preface for the English edition. Of course the French colleagues were astonished to hear that I saw this child four times a week ... because at that time they were only seeing children once a week or even once a fortnight ... psychotherapy rather than psychoanalysis ... but I didn't know this. I just followed on from what I'd learned in London. And I learned a lot from Sammy, too! He needed me to write down everything he said ... and if I stopped writing, he would whack me ... so I wrote fast. Otherwise, he was destructive and aggressive in different ways and twice tried to set fire to things in my consulting room. But as long as I was writing everything down and noting his commentaries on his drawings, he was less agitated. Then I would read the notes back to him at the next session, and that way I could get him to listen to my interpretations and that's also how the book came to be written. And I was always grateful to Lebovici who, after three months where I felt I understood nothing of what was happening in Sammy's analysis, invited me to come and present my work with Sammy to a group with whom he met every week. I said I would be very happy to do so. So in my terrible French, every week, I would give a breakdown of my day-by-day account of Sammy's four weekly sessions. The members of the group all talked so fast that I had difficulty in following their commentaries, but I felt less alone in this unchartered psychoanalytic voyage with such a difficult little partner ...

Finally, then, when Sammy left to return to the States, Lebovici suggested that the work should be published if I would agree to translating Sammy's and my "dialogue" into French. This was done with the help of a bilingual student who put it into reasonably good French. Nothing of the kind had ever been published in the psychoanalytic literature. Later, Melanie Klein published her "Narrative of a Child's Analysis," but *Dialogue with Sammy* preceded it. Of course, it came out first in French. Winnicott was very interested in it when I sent it to him and was helpful in getting Hogarth Press to publish it in English.

I later found that my fellow students knew nothing of the work of Winnicott, Klein, Bion and so on. I was instrumental in bringing different London analysts to Paris to talk to us about their work. I invited both the Anna Freudians and the Kleinians as well as analysts from the Middle Group – today known as the "Independent Group" – to talk about adult or child training. The French students were very thrilled and eager to help with this project. And of course one of the first people we invited was Winnicott.

Did analysts from other Paris Institutes come to these lectures?

At the time there was only one psychoanalytic institute in France. Before being accepted as a candidate I had to be interviewed by four different people, one of whom was Lacan.

Really?

Yes, he was still there, but the Paris Society was on the brink of civil war. There were fierce arguments and accusations flying around – so different from the British whose warring schools of thought were in the same violent opposition but expressed their disagreements more covertly, and of course kept the British Society together. Some months after my arrival in Paris the animosity reached such a pitch that everyone was told to choose either to stay with the Institute or to break off and form a Society around Lacan. Of course most candidates chose according to the choice their own analysts made. If you were in analysis with Jacques Lacan, then you followed him. If your analyst was on the side of the Institute Director, Sacha Nacht, then you tended to follow suit. It had already been heartbreaking for me to leave my London analyst, so I was most concerned about any risk of losing my Paris analyst, Dr. Marc Schlumberger. Meanwhile we had to make up our minds and I didn't know how to choose, since my analyst, being very classical, wasn't going to tell me what his position was. He said I must decide for myself. I didn't know which way to go while the other candidates were all wildly beating the drums for their analysts – if they knew what their decision would be.

At the same time I tried to find out what exactly were the crucial differences between Nacht and Lacan. I kept suggesting to my fellow students that we should start a "Middle Group" as had been done many years before in London. Middle Group students did one supervision with a Kleinian and one with a classical Freudian. My colleagues laughed at me when I suggested we might envisage a Lacanian Group, a Classical Group and a Middle Group. This British compromise just didn't make sense to the French. "No way!" they all said. "How naive can you get!" Anyway, that was the era into which I plunged, and it was quite some time before I sorted out the clinical and theoretical differences between the two schools.

So how did you manage to extricate yourself from these passionate standpoints?

Well, I decided to ask both Lacan and Nacht if they would grant me an appointment to explain their personal viewpoints. Both graciously agreed. On being shown into Lacan's waiting room I found four people in each corner, and I realized for the first time what the "classical" group were criticizing – that several analysands received appointments for the same time but none

quite knew when their turn would come. I tried to find a fifth
corner in which to wait my turn. Suddenly Lacan opened the
door and called out, "Où est la petite anglaise?" As I stood up he
came toward me and took me in by the hand. The other four
looked at me strangely. Then Lacan said, in somewhat broken
English, "Tell me all." I asked what he wanted to know but
added, a little anxiously, that I had really come to learn something from him regarding the split in the Society ...

... *sounds more like an injunction than an invitation* ... *"Tell me
all."?!*

Yes, rather. And then Lacan went on to ask me what I was
lacking. I didn't know much at that time about his concept of
the *manque-à-être* otherwise I might have found a more
sophisticated response. Instead I replied rather foolishly that
what I lacked most of all were psychoanalytic books in English.
He said: "I have many books here and you can come and read
them in the evenings." He then laid his hands on my knees in a
rather seductive (or perhaps fatherly) way, and said: "Everyone
will come to me. Everybody. Because I have the answer." He
made a gesture as though the answer were behind his left shoul-
der. He went on to explain in a messianic way that he had
something very special to offer, that he had great news for
psychoanalysis and that everybody would come to learn from
him. I had anticipated that he would talk to me about psychic
structure and paternal law but he was more like an overflowing
breast ready to feed the world. I left feeling a little disturbed by
his excitable discourse. The next day I went to see Dr. Nacht.
There was no one else in the waiting room, he took me on time,
and said: "What do you want to know?" I said: "I've seen Dr.
Lacan and I'd like to know about your point of view also." He
said: "You'll see! I'm going to get social security benefits for the
Institute, and government support from the Health Department
... there will be a mental health clinic on full social security as it
is in Anglo-Saxon countries. You will be wise to stay here, you'll
see." I left Dr. Nacht in as much confusion as I had felt on
leaving Dr. Lacan. "My goodness!" I thought – neither of them
talked about psychoanalysis ... nor told me anything about their
theoretical standpoints or their clinical approaches that might
help me understand their divergences. To make a long story
short, I discovered from a colleague that my analyst was staying
with the Institute. So I too stayed with the founding Society.

It sounds like you were an object of desire for both ...

Well, we all were. Many students, like myself, did not want to lose the benefit of Lacan's inspirational teaching even if his clinical concepts of "logical time," short sessions and so on, awakened a certain mistrust. But I, along with many others, like my good friend André Green, continued to go to Lacan's lectures. At first there were meetings in bistros and at the homes of different students who had followed him. It was a very inspiring period ...

Albeit marked by schisms ...

Oh, yes. But this is the history of psychoanalysis too. There are schisms everywhere. I used to think it was only the French. But I now find in whatever country I'm invited to lecture that, if the analytic community has not already split into two groups, then it is about to do so.

But to have one's origins so marked by that fracture ...

Yes, it was a shattering experience – but even though I stayed with the original Society I followed all of Lacan's lectures, and did so for years to come. I found his concepts thought-provoking and most influential with regard to my own thinking. But I couldn't practice the way he did. Although Lacan denied this, there was rather a gap, in my mind, between his theory and his way of practising. But I learned a great deal from him.

Could you say more about the gaps, as you saw them, between Lacan's practice and theory?

I went to Paris full of what I'd already learned in London, from the Hampstead, a very classical Freudian background: fifty minute sessions, careful analysis of the transference and so on. And more particularly I was impressed with all of Winnicott's ideas ... as well as what I had read of Bion. In Paris, Lacan was the charismatic figure that Winnicott was in London – and I was immediately struck by the differences between them. Lacan favored splits and divisions ... whereas Winnicott was always trying to bring groups to understand each other and work together. Winnicott believed that you had to work at creating a containing space in which people would feel safe and slowly develop a sense of trust. Lacan on the contrary warned that the patient must never feel at ease; he must not delight in complaining or exploring his emotional states, and should be under constant pressure, knowing that the session might terminate at any minute. He seemed to advocate closing the session whenever any transference affects were mentioned, or if the analysand became too emotional. This was an entirely different way of creating the atmosphere of the session. It seemed to me, coming from the Winnicottian–Freudian background, that Lacan was favoring some kind of artificial trauma. Mind you, he backed that up with many different theories, though sometimes I thought he created a theory for every one of his weaknesses ... but he was a stimulating thinker, and as any great thinker, forced you to do a lot of intellectual work. Even if you come up with ideas that in the long run differ from those of the person who's inspired you, you've made a worthwhile intellectual voyage. Melanie Klein's work does this to me as well. It's stimulating and even if you don't agree with it all, it's well worth struggling to grasp its essentials ... and I found the same with Lacan. I had a dream of trying to bring Melanie Klein's and Lacan's teachings together, because they seemed poles apart. For example, Klein emphasized particularly the essential role of the primitive mother, whereas Lacan laid particular emphasis on the essential role of the father.

Of my questions on the self and multiplicity, one actually relates to Lacan. In this day and age, it's hard to talk about a split or decentered self, or subject, without referencing Lacan. I was wondering what connections, if any, there are between Lacan's understandings and your own ...

I took in Lacan's conception of the decentered self, the barred Subject and so on, but it was a highly intellectual approach which focused more on the construction of subjectivity as such, and at no point did Lacan illustrate his theories with any clinical examples. Instead he used graphs and mathematical formulas to convey his meaning. At first I found these confusing and devoid of emotional empathy with the patient. But I struggled along, as we all did, to master his way of conceptualizing.

Can you say more about the French atmosphere at that time?

I found the French intellectual atmosphere extremely invigorating, but this created a problem too because, in a way, the intellectuals ran away with psychoanalysis in France. "Freudism" became a popular university course – which had never happened in England. In a sense, of course, analysis never took on in England. There's still only one major institute – although the Kleinian and post-Kleinian movement has had considerable influence throughout the analytic world. In England practically all analysts, though they may affirm that they are not Kleinian, are marked by Kleinian thinking – much as the Lacanian movement stamped all of French psychoanalysis. Even those like myself, who would not claim to be Lacanian analysts, were immensely influenced by Lacan. These influences mark the analytic thought of a country – just as here in New York everybody was influenced for decades by the ego psychology school of Hartmanian inspiration.

One shared feature I've noted between your work and Lacan's is your common emphasis on the defense mechanism of foreclosure ...

I learned a lot from him on that, as well as on the structure of psychotic defense mechanisms in general.

... In Lacan's framework, if I'm correct, the defense is central to his understanding of the psychoses – to the extent that it bars access to the phallus as the paternal signifier. In your work, instead, it's often identified as the hallmark of psychosomatic disorders ...

Well that's my own theoretical notion. Many years later I began to see how the Freudian theory of foreclosure – "repudiation from the psyche" is the way it's translated in English – could be applied in other than the specific ways Lacan indicated. For example, I never found Lacan particularly inspiring in attempting to understand the mysteries of the psychosoma and psychosomatic phenomena. He seemed to want to incorporate his understanding of the soma into the theory of verbal signifiers, which seemed to me to be confusing and didn't sufficiently emphasize the difference with neurotic hysteria. I was more helped by Bion's theory of bêta functioning in trying to conceptualize the psychic organization that lay behind psychosomatic disorders. Of course Lacan's theory of foreclosure, as applied to psychotic organizations, was helpful when I came round to conceptualizing what I called "psychosomatosis": I was dealing with psychosomatic sufferers who seemed eminently normal, in no way psychotic. But I realized that this was a pseudo-normality and, with time, I came to refer to these patients as "normo-paths." One could say that the body is delusional in that its functioning doesn't make biological sense. It's a crazy body that will suddenly throw out all its contents, as though it had been poisoned, as in ulcerative colitis; or that refuses to let the breath out, as in asthmatic states.

Yet in the absence of any physiological problem the soma is obviously obeying some signal from the mind. That's why I came round to coining another term for which I've been much criticized – archaic hysteria – which as the term suggests is a body–mind response that is considerably more primitive than classical hysteria. The latter is built out of words in response to what is felt to be forbidden, such as the enjoyment of normal adult privileges: the right to sexual and love fulfillments, to narcissistic enjoyments in professional or personal fields and so on. This is true of all neurotic organizations, whereas psychotic symptoms are con-cerned with the right to be alive. Many of the conflicts in people with psychotic organizations are similar to those that we find in the deep psychic structure of polysomatizing patients or those with severe psychosomatic disorders. Nevertheless I must reiterate that everybody somatizes under stress, analysts as well as analy-sands ... I talked about this in *Theaters of the Body*.

Over the years, you have come to establish yourself as perhaps the foremost psychoanalytic thinker on matters concerning psychosomatic illness. How did this fascination originate, and how did it later evolve into a major professional preoccupation?

I wouldn't say that I am the foremost psychoanalytic thinker in that field – also I was not particularly interested in psycho-somatic phenomena for the first twenty years of my analytic practice. It's only since I published *Theaters of the Body* in 1985 that people attribute this reputation to me. I tried to forge new concepts based on my clinical experience, some of which challenged the concepts of established psychosomaticists. Nor do I feel that psychosomatic phenomena are a major professional preoccupation for me. Following the publication of *Plea for a Measure of Abnormality* and *Theaters of the Mind* people thought I was a specialist on the subject of perversions and sexual deviations. Latterly I heard that I was a specialist on "creativity and its problems" because of some recent lectures and my chapters on creativity in *The Many Faces of Eros* !...

Actually in that book I do have something new to say about psychosomatic disorders. I tried to go a little further in the section on "Sex and the Soma" than I had been able to do in *Theaters of the Body*. Just as I tried in the chapters on "Deviations of Desire" to go beyond my earlier concepts concerning sexual deviations. All these interests continue, but probably what intrigue me most at present are the mysteries of creativity – and its inhibitions.

If I might insist, for a moment, on the matter of treating psychosomatic illnesses: what are the particular or most salient countertransference issues that you've had to contend with, and how have they affected your experience and your body?

I think it's because we all try to identify as deeply as possible with what our patients are experiencing ... For example, if I have a patient who suffers from asthmatic or other respiratory problems, I try to imagine what it must be like not to be able to breathe, or not to be able to let your breath out; or with ulcer patients I try to feel what it must be like to be attacked by gastric ulcers. In a sense I try to decode what the stomach or what the bronchial tubes are communicating. And eventually I attempt to put my understanding into words, following on my introjective identifications with my analysands ...

Sometimes, even as I open the door to my waiting room, I get an immediate impression that is translated somatically – when for example I see a patient whose shoulders are hunched up, I feel hunched up too and guess that my analysand is trying to stifle aggressive thoughts – or perhaps warding off a fantasized attack. I've noticed with my ulcer patients that my stomach might gurgle a lot, while I sometimes want to cough when my asthmatic patients are talking about their bronchial spasms, or feel itchy when they talk about their eczema. When I try to decode what the skin is communicating, what the bronchial tubes are screaming about, and so on, you might say it's a form of hysterical identification. On the other hand I don't think we run the risk of reproducing these illnesses in ourselves, any more than we catch the neuroses or the sexual deviations of our patients. But we must attempt to capture the potential meaning of somatic communications. It took me years before I was even able to "hear" the soma speaking, and help my patients to find words that might replace the need for the psychosomatic expression. That's when I discovered that behind their apparently normal facade such analysands were facing psychotic anxieties – terrors of the body or the self dissolving.

This would seem to be coincidental with your theorizing of archaic hysteria ... a notion, you said, which has come under criticism. Can you say more on the matter?

Archaic hysteria? ... well, many pyschosomaticists claim that psychosomatic symptoms have no underlying symbolic meaning – which I put into question, at least insofar as my own analysands are concerned. One of our leading Parisian psychosomaticists, Pierre Marty – whose lectures and recordings of interviews with psychosomatic patients I followed with great interest – always said the psychosomatic symptom was "*bête*": that it had no psychological significance. Instead he posited a slow somatic disorganization, whereas I found with my patients that there was an underlying significance of a protosymbolic type of which we were frequently able to reconstruct the meaning. Perhaps as a result of these efforts, many of my analysands did lose psychosomatic symptoms of many years standing. But no doubt it's a different clientele from that of the psychosomatic centers. Those seeking analysis come with psychological problems, not somatic ones – so they are already open to questioning their unconscious thoughts and fantasies. "Who am I?" "What do I not know about myself that I need to discover?" and so on. Whereas people sent to a psychosomatic clinic by their doctors tend to say: "Well, I have a gastric ulcer, or asthma or ulcerative colitis or psoriasis ... apparently it's psychosomatic. Can you help me?" It could happen that they have no interest whatsoever in exploring what goes on in their minds ... so my analysands are not typical of psychosomatic patients in this respect. They come to analysis because of neurotic or character problems, whereas they frequently take their somatic symptoms for granted, not imagining that these could have any psychological significance.

That comes later?

Yes, sometimes much later, although I have learned over the years to say during initial interviews: "You have told me many things about yourself – and what about your physical health?"

In reading any number of your cases, the theater of the body seems always in season. What is it about the particular ways in which psychosomatic patients have presented themselves to you that engages you so profoundly?

Probably because the body's ways are mysterious. But I don't feel that this particular research engages me profoundly. Basically I've always been interested in anything that tends to escape the psychoanalytic process. This began with my interest in sexual deviations that patients didn't talk about, because they were afraid that analysis might cause them to lose their sexual orientation or pattern. This of course is understandable: people don't want to lose their expression and pattern of sexual relations. So I'd try to understand what was being excluded from the work. I was aware that something was being acted out – that is, outside the analytic sessions. What does this dream mean? What are these thoughts about? What is this analysand finding difficult to discuss? I discovered early on that people with addictions often hide the fact – for fear of losing their recourse to disperse mental pain. So, my interest in understanding the meaning of sexual deviations then led to the symptomatic area of addictive sexualities and to addictions in general.

... I remember my surprise when a young woman who had been coming to analysis four times a week for more that two years suddenly let it drop that she drank three or four glasses of cognac every night because otherwise she could not sleep. I asked her if this were her only means of assuring sleep and she recounted that she also took sleeping pills and various forms of psychiatric medication. She'd never talked of any of these dependencies before – she wanted to protect her access to these forms of artificial paradise. I realized for the first time that there were many hidden scenarios being acted out of which I knew nothing, and I began to understand why our analytic voyage seemed to be stagnating. This is the patient I called "Olivia" in *Plea for a Measure of Abnormality*. She taught me a lot, and from there I became interested in understanding people suffering from tobacco addictions, alcoholism, bulimia and the like, because they are a constant source of hidden symptomatology which is being discharged in an act instead of being contained and thought about – or talked about – in the analysis. Character patterns too fall into this category, since people take their way of being for granted; these, however, can also be forms of acting out that create a slowing up of the analytic process. Finally I began to realize that psychosomatic symptoms are another set of phenomena that escape the analytic situation.

From what I've gathered in reading your work, you don't seem to attribute the kind of perjorative connotation to acting out that many analysts do.

Not all acting out is deleterious. Some such behaviors are quite healthy. But they need to be talked about, and the reasons for which they have not been mentioned are also important. Some patients don't even want the analyst to know they're making progress – often because they're afraid we'll lose interest in them ...

I'd like to return for a moment to the symbol of the phallus, mentioned earlier while discussing Lacan's notion of foreclosure. In your work, you take issue with the position of certain feminists who see the symbol as the expression of a repressive phallocratic order ...

Yes, well of course Freud was rather phallocratic – it was a prominent symptom of his day and age. Nevertheless I prefer to make a distinction between the phallus as a symbol – the symbol of unity for both sexes – and the penis as a part-object. This distinction was first developed some thirty or more years ago by a French analyst called Bela Grunberger. He wrote some of the earliest papers on the salience of narcissism and the importance of understanding the role of what he termed narcissistic needs, as well as studying this level of relating in the psychoanalystic encounter. He talked of the phallus as the symbol of narcissistic complementarity for the two sexes. I'm sure you know that the phallus in the ancient Greek rites is always erect. The ithyphallic symbol does not have the same significance as the sexual organ. Lacan also came to refer to the phallus as the symbol of desire and therefore to be distinguished from the penis as a genital. I can understand the objections made by the feminists in regard to Freud's papers on femininity and female sexuality, but these have attracted criticism for decades now. However, the confusion between the phallus and penis may be an unfortunate one for clear thinking.

What struck me, in trying to elaborate for myself the feminist critique, is that the phallus – while a symbol of fertility and unity for both sexes – can only refer to the vagina's complementarity of the penis ...

Yet the erect penis, i.e., the phallus, is also a response in relation to the vagina and the woman's desire for penetration ...

Precisely. But the phallus, in its very quality of being erect, can still only evoke the vagina. It's almost as if the vagina's anatomical invisibility can only complement the masculine organ ...

The fact that the vagina is invisible perhaps explains why the part-object penis, and not the part-object vagina, is used as the symbol. I believe that in certain cultures there are symbols for the vagina or the feminine internal body – perhaps in matriarchal societies? Nevertheless, the feminists have many reasons to take issue with Freud, apart from the use of terminology.

You've anticipated my next question. Where do you situate yourself, vis-à-vis the feminist presence within the broader context of contemporary psychoanalysis?

Within the context of contemporary psychoanalysis we still find many male and female analysts following Freud's simplified view of female psychology and the structuring of femininity. I've described my point of view at length in *The Many Faces of Eros*, so I'll just make a brief summary.

In spite of Freud's brilliance, his dominantly phallocratic attitude prevented him from being able to think about femininity and female sexuality outside the constraints of the Victorian era. In most other respects he defied Victorian conventions. Nevertheless he discovered the unconscious and the meaning of hysteria through his work with women. But alas, he took the Victorian woman as the model of all femininity. And in his final paper on femininity he is downright denigrating: "women have no moral sense, they've never contributed valuably to civilization, to art, literature or music" ... and so on. This is extraordinary when you think of the number of famous women in Germany during Freud's epoch – painters, musicians, writers, whom he must have known about. I think he was afraid to allow himself to identify too deeply with the woman. He understood clearly that dimension of his primary homosexuality that related to his father. But he could not accept the complementary part of primary homosexual feelings – as I conceptualize these in *Eros* – which relates not only to a wish to possess and be possessed by the same sex parent, but also to the wish to be the opposite sex parent. Freud well understood the former but totally overlooked or ruled out the other wish of every little boy – to be feminine. I think it was Kardiner who recounts in his "Analysis With Freud" that at one point he remarked that Freud was like a wonderfully kind mother-figure. Freud replied that this was absurd because he felt so masculine! He somehow rejected this part of himself – a dimension we all have – which of course is the wish to have and to be everything.

To get back to your own work. Within the context of contemporary feminism, how do you situate yourself?

I'm very sympathetic to the feminist movement. It was a totally necessary revolution. When I went to France, I was scandalized to learn that many women in important positions were paid less than men for the same work. Also, women got the vote very late in France. Coming from New Zealand where women had had the right to vote for almost a century, and where there was recognition of equality for equal work, I was shocked to find this was not the case in England or in France. I read the work of Betty Friedan and others and was most enthusiastic about their writing. Having always considered Freud's theories on female sexuality as disastrously biased I also became interested in the whole problem of male envy. I'm not going to attempt a "wild analysis" of Freud, but it seems probable that he was somehow frightened by the wish to be and possess any female dimension.

Along these lines, much of your work is built upon the founda- tional yet lifelong tension between the two poles that you call the impossible and the forbidden – between Narcissus and Oedipus, or what in your words constitute "the ineluctable framework from which our personal identity is constructed." Can you elaborate on this tension, and on the processes inherent in the construction of a sense of identity?

Well, I'm particularly interested in understanding the narcis- sistic levels of relationship, and the archaic structures that underlie and precede the phallic-Oedipal level of psychic organization. It is these primitive levels that I try to hear, in trying to conceptualize all that lies beneath the good, classical, neurotic level of disturbance ...

Where the impossible is concerned, it comprises the narcis- sistic wish to be and to have everything – the denial of otherness and the wish to remain indissolubly attached to the Other, the mother of infancy – in which one is omnipotent, and all wishes

are magically fulfilled. This impossible desire underlies the conflict of many psychotic people. Then, following the drama of
otherness, comes the drama of monosexuality, and here we enter
into the realm of the forbidden.

*At a recent conference I attended, one of the panelists, a man,
remarked: "The most important human being in the world, is the
newborn female child." What would Joyce McDougall say in
response to such a remark?*

I'd wonder why he said it. I agree that the newborn female
baby is very important, but so is the newborn male baby.
Perhaps the panelist was trying to swing the pendulum the
other way, as a way of asking why we always put the little
male in advance ... Or maybe he was thinking that the future
of the race lies in the hands of the mothers, and therefore in
the early psychic experience of the baby girl? Of course, the
female child is already destined to transmit the culture to the
next generation. But we have to allow for the importance of
the father's role as well. This would be my criticism ... the
little female is going to transmit the culture, but the way in
which she will transmit it will depend also on her relation to
and esteem for the father of her children – as opposed to the
woman who is herself a "phallocrat." The father's role also
includes helping his children out of their baby-like dependence
on the mother, and bringing them another view of the external
world. The children's respect for both sexes will also depend
on the father's breadth of vision in this respect. For all these
reasons we might say that the baby boy also holds in his
hands the cultural transmission that his children are to receive
from him.

*This connects, in a way, to my original question on the forbidden
and the impossible, to the extent that there is an aspect of your
work which we might, for lack of a better word, call "Lacanian"
... in the sense that father, too, is in the picture from the start,
albeit communicated and mediated via the mother ...*

Yes, absolutely ... the way in which the mother relates to the father
affects the baby even before its birth. To abstract one from the
other is a denial of both external and psychic reality. If a mother
doesn't take into account – or even attacks – the child's relationship to its father, that child may be faced with a sad situation in

later life. Of course Freud's solution to what he regarded as the neurotic state of being female was motherhood. But motherhood also implies fatherhood. Fathers are just as interested in their babies as mothers and babies are obviously fascinated with their fathers. And, of course, fathers may cause as many problems as mothers for their progeny.

I'm often amazed at how, in many training institutes, the father only materializes around age three or four ... it's almost as if the pre-Oedipal sphere comes to connote an exclusive mother–baby relationship.

Yes, that's crazy, isn't it? The mother is constantly transmitting to her baby her relationship to the father and to the male world. Early on the baby understands it's not the only object in mother's life, that it's not "mother's penis," to use one of Freud's unfortunate metaphors. A baby's best guarantee for healthy development is to have two parents who love and respect each other.

In fact, you come to suggest, in one of your more celebrated case histories, that where the father is impoverished or absent, the baby may well end up as the "cork in the chasm" ...

Yes, exactly. It feels lost faced with the role it may have to fulfill for the mother. It does not know how to situate itself. To have a genuine sense of one's individual identity and one's sexual identity we need two parents and the possibility of identifying with both, as well as coming to accept that one is the child of this couple and that he/she will never be the narcissistic completion of either parent. Should a child be led to believe that he/she is the only love object of either father or mother, then this child runs the risk of a pathological outcome.

You write about the Impossible and the Forbidden as a drama that confronts us eternally. It seems there's something of a Kleinian dynamic to the drama, as it oscillates back and forth between symbiosis and otherness – akin, in a way, to Klein's developmentally distinct but similarly polarized moments of the paranoid-schizoid and depressive positions.

Yes, although here I'm probably more influenced by Bion than Klein – though of course Bion was a post-Kleinian thinker. His work is actually a theory of thinking. This is where Bion's

thought approaches Lacan's. And Bion's hypothesis of alpha and
bêta functioning are, for me, valuable concepts. Bêta functioning
is in relation to what Freud called "thing-presentations," and is
allied with what I call the Impossible. Although these theories
were useful in trying to understand further the organization of
psychotic thought and problems of pathological narcissism, I was
able to use the concept of bêta elements to better conceptualize
psychosomatic phenomena.

... To the extent that psychotic and grave narcissistic distur-
bances may be rooted in the schizoid-paranoid position, this
could be appropriately assigned to the desire to achieve the
Impossible. And no doubt Klein's concept of the depressive
position accords with what I have described as the series of
mourning processes required to reach the more neurotic level
of organization that typifies the forbidden – although Klein's
concept has more to do with pain over the infant's fantasies of
having attacked and destroyed the good breast. On the whole
I have been more influenced by Bion and Lacan in trying to
formulate my own hypotheses ... This reminds me of a time
when I had a chance of sitting beside Bion at an official
dinner. He had been invited to spend a few days with our
Society. During the dinner I told him that in many ways his
theories of thinking were very close to Lacan's. He said, "Yes
I've been told that before. It worries me terribly." I said: "But
Dr. Bion, even if your theories have something in common,
your personalities are totally different." He asked me to
explain further, and I said, "Your concepts are as complex as
those of Lacan, but Lacan talks in an abstruse way which
masks the clarity of his thought as he plays around with words
and idea, whereas you try to get your thought across. You give
yours in a generous way, and this is a different personal
approach." He said "Thank you for telling me this."

*Do I gather that Lacan was marvelously engaging, but somehow
communicated a sense of fundamental distrust or a wish to confuse?*

You never really knew ... especially when he behaved particularly
badly towards some of his closest disciples. He would push them
to the limit in certain cases. I once heard him announce in a group:
"I've only ever been followed by fools." Yet he had some very
brilliant followers, but would make provocative statements of this
kind, perhaps testing the limits of their attachment to him. Many
eventually broke away from him – some fine thinkers among them.

Nevertheless he was a fountainhead of inspiration, as was Bion. Both were inspired – and inspiring – thinkers.

In line with these reflections, in Theaters of the Mind *you talk about Freud's central notion of the human value of arbeit ...*

... Arbeit ... Durcharbeitung ... psychical elaboration ...

... where you discuss the two modes of work, or labor, that characterize the psychoanalytic profession: namely, clinical and theoretical elaboration. In those pages you suggest that "many fine clinicians who think deeply about their patients have no particular desire to 'write psychoanalysis.'" And yet you obviously do. For Joyce McDougall, what are the functions of "writing psychoanalysis"?

Perhaps for me it's a way of trying to put order into the chaos of the human psyche; I was always tempted to write at moments when I was the least clear about what was happening in the psychoanalytic voyage with a patient. I take notes when I'm puzzled, not when I'm happy about my work and feel I understand what is happening in an analytic process. There's nothing to write about then. Of course, you never really know what is original about your own thought until other people play it back to you. "Writing psychoanalysis" has many functions for those of us who enjoy doing this. Many analysts have no particular interest or pleasure in this kind of writing; they'd rather spend their weekends doing painting or handicrafts or music. As far as I'm concerned my writing takes me out of the analytic situation and brings me an intellectual pleasure which is quite different from the pleasure I find in my daily work (which is not basically intellectual). Others who feel impelled to write do so for other reasons ... some want to teach and write remarkable textbooks; teaching has never been one of my aims. Behind everything I've written there's always a polemic dimension.

I was usually motivated to write when traditional, time-honored theories did not fit with what I was observing in my clinical practice and were causing some confusion in my mind. And when there was no concordance between the theories I'd been taught and my own clinical experience, I would begin to question and say, "this is not the whole story. I've something else to say." That applies to everything I've written – even *Dialogue with Sammy*, because I couldn't agree with all that I was being told about psychosis. I learned a lot about the mother–child relationship and its contribution to psychotic thought because Sammy's mother came into therapy with me after Sammy had gone. When I wrote *Theaters of the Mind*, I particularly didn't agree with the attitude taken towards sexual deviations: I saw these as creative attempts to save something out of the catastrophic collapse of any possibility of having love or sexual relations because of childhood trauma or the traumatizing effect of the biparental unconscious. In *Theaters of the Body* I questioned established psychosomatic theory. And so on. Then, continuing on my polemic way, in *The Many Faces of Eros* I also examine the narrowness of Freud's thinking in reducing female sexuality to penis envy, and to the idea that all a woman wants is a male child. When theories that were sacrosanct didn't fit with my analytic perception of my work I was motivated to write – first of all to get my own ideas clear. Then, perhaps, with a wish to take issue publicly with dogmatic or religious adherence to theory.

In one of your loveliest and most detailed case histories, you explore the life and struggles of a novelist, a woman you name Benedicte. In the context of the case, you seem to suggest that the major function of your writing is always in the service of theoretical understanding. At the same time, however, you are such a fine writer that I couldn't help but think of Freud, of his own fascination with creative writers, and of the exceedingly high esteem in which his own case histories are held – not only as clinical documents, but as literary creations. When I asked you earlier about the functions of your writing, you said nothing about an aesthetic function, or of the aesthetic pleasure that informs your creativity ...

No, that's true. Well, I feel that a great deal of my inspiration to write does come from my patients – of course there are very few analysands whose work one can quote. In forty years I've probably not quoted more that about fifteen, and I never quote them without asking permission, nowadays, to use small fragments of the analysis to illustrate concepts and ideas that have come from our work together. But again I can only ask this permission from analysands who have already terminated, or are near termination. Sometimes I am referring to work that was accomplished two or more years ago. Of course, it's an eternal cycle between clinical experience and theoretical concepts which are then nullified or confirmed by further clinical experience ... and this in turn widens one's conceptual understanding.

But what about the literary creation, what about its aesthetics? There is an aesthetic quality to your work ...

Perhaps there is. I'm less aware of that. I try to re-create the atmosphere of the sessions or the particular part of the analytic adventure that we have shared. I try really to convey the whole movement between the transference and the countertransference, and the way in which my analysand's words, images and thoughts fertilize my own. The analytic voyage is in itself a creative endeavor, of course. I suppose it has a certain aesthetic quality of its own too, that grows out of the attempt to transmit the experience.

I'm thinking now of Bollas, and his ideas on creativity, pleasure, and the transformational object ...

I take great pleasure in my work and in trying to solve the problems that it places before me ... There's also a further pleasure in that we never, ever reach any final understanding. There's always more unknown territory to investigate – it's an endless process of unfolding and exploring the infinity of the human psyche.

A mutual friend of ours has remarked that the grace with which you treat your patients is somehow reflected in your writing style. There's an interesting equation here between aesthetics and ethics, or between an evidenced literary sensibility and a fundamental respect for what she called the "suspension of judgment" that defines your position, and ideally that of any analyst. Is our friend on to something, where the equation between aesthetics and ethics is concerned?

Well, I do believe that one strives eternally to be non-judgmental, and of course I take the standpoint that all symptoms are creations ... in the attempt to survive psychically, to maintain some kind of harmony in the face of conflict and fluctuating circumstances. And if I treat symptoms with great respect I must add that I'm very grateful to my analysands too for all the things they teach me ... for the new worlds they open up for me. It's a mutual process of understanding and deepening, which does have an ethical quality.

Do you see a bridge, however, between an aesthetic "grace" and a quality of ethical gracefulness?

No doubt it's graceful to have an ethical respect for the human psyche of those who have come for help and generously offer all their deepest thoughts, feelings, experiences and visions. These also I treat with respect – perhaps that has a gracious aspect to it. I suppose it's an ethical standpoint too. As Montaigne said: "all that is human is also part of me."

You mention Montaigne. In thinking about the comment of Devos that you cite at the beginning of Theaters of the Mind, *it strikes me that the French, going as far back as Montaigne, have always been particularly sensitive to issues of multiplicity. I'm wondering, what is it that connects, in your view, the sensibilities of a sixteenth-century moral philosopher with a contemporary comedian?*

I see an intimate connection with the allegiance to the humanist spirit and their attempt to identify with it. This makes me think of my meeting with the Dalai Lama a couple of years ago. I was invited as a psychoanalyst, with six other people in six other disciplines, to meet the Dalai Lama. He wanted to meet occidental thinkers in different fields – a philospher, a near-death expert, a cognitive scientist, a brain surgeon, a psychoanalyst. We were invited to a small town in the Himalayas for eight days on what he called a mind–life seminar, which had as its overall theme, "Sleeping, Dreaming and Dying." When I asked why the Dalai Lama would have invited me, the organizer replied: "You have the reputation of being a humanist open to everybody's religous beliefs. Your work has attracted attention and people have brought this to the notice of the Dalai Lama." I accepted of course. And now the conference proceedings, by the way, are soon to be published, in a book by the same title.

Each participant had one whole morning in which to talk about sleeping, dreaming and dying from the point of view of their own particular discipline. So in three hours I tried to convey the whole of Freudian theory on sleeping, dreaming and dying. I read what I could on Tibetan philosophy before setting out for Dharamsala, and discovered that the Tibetans are psychosomaticists in their soul; when there is any physical ailment their first question is "What's going wrong in the person's mind?" Amazing! Anyway, the talk I had prepared didn't work out the way I had imaged because, first of all the Dalai Lama wanted to understand the importance of psychoanalysis in the Western world. So I found myself talking about Freud's influence on the occidental culture: the impact of his thinking in the

world of education ... social systems ... art and literature, that
went far beyond the medicine of the mind or the medicine of
the body. This was very interesting to the Dalai Lama, who then
said: "but what is the essential quest of the psychoanalyst? What
are you looking for?" And I said: "Well, the psychoanalytic
experience is directed to discovering the most intimate and
deepest truth about oneself." He replied that this was also the
aim of meditation. So we agreed that there was a basic similarity
about the psychoanalytic process and the processes of meditation ... I don't know how we got on to this topic ... anyway the
body–mind unit was something that the Dalai Lama was very
conversant with. He also wanted to know how we used dreams,
and I tried to illustrate this by quoting a dream of a patient and
also one of my own – and what it taught us both about ourselves. Actually that's quoted in the *Eros* book.

I never got around to trying to explain Freud's theory of the
death instinct. There are many words that don't exist in Tibetan:
ego, id and superego ... conscious, preconscious and unconscious
... forget it, there are no such words. We did find a Tibetan word
for the unconscious – *alia* – which the Dalai Lama described as a
deep current that links all humanity together (a little like the Jungian unconscious). I said yes, your holiness ... let's call it *alia*. I did
discover that there were no bad mothers, all motherhood is good
... there the Tibetan philosopher is somewhat Freudian ... Then
again there was no word for affect in spite of the efforts of the two
translators, a Tibetan Lama who had a degree in philosophy from
Cambridge University and Dr. Wallace, an American, but who
after many years in Tibet speaks perfect Tibetan, and has
published books on comparative religions. Both translators were
constantly trying to communicate to the Dalai Lama what we were
trying to transmit. There were many other words, I learned, that
had no equivalent in Tibetan, such as our terms for guilt. There
must be a word in Tibetan for guilt. But the translators said there
isn't ...

Where there is no word, there is arguably no such experience ...

Or it's put in some other way. So these were deep cultural
differences that looked like linguistic differences.

*On the matter of cultural and linguistic differences: if Joyce
McDougall had stayed in England, and hadn't been exposed to the
nuances and rhythms of French, as well as to the particular preoccu-*

pations of the French, would she be writing the way she writes today?

I probably would have written in the same style ... with the same ethics or aesthetics ... but no doubt I would have had different polemics.

Do you think the concern with sexuality would have been as marked as it is in your writing?

Oh, I think so, yes. Sexuality is somewhat universal ... I don't think I'm more "concerned with sexuality" than other human beings. But I do refer to the search for solutions to human-kind's erotic and sexual impulses as an eternal quest. Never-theless it's easier to talk about sexually charged topics, when guilt-laden, in a foreign language, because they don't have the same impact as in one's own tongue. The fact of speaking in a foreign tongue may also cover up conflicts attached to very primary emotional experiences, though these too include libid-inal impulses.

Does needing to meet on the common ground of a language other than the mother tongue of patient or analyst jeopardize or com-promise an analysis?

No, although it's simpler if the analysis is done with two people who speak the same mother tongue. But this is a world problem for analysts. Let's take leading analysts in London whose mother tongue was not English ... Anna Freud, Melanie Klein, Rosenfeld, Segal, and many others ...

Yes. Bollas told me of his three analysts, none spoke English as their mother tongue. How was it for you in France? I'm not clear as to what your degree of proficiency was in French when you began your second analysis ...

Oh, my French was terrible ...

Then what about your own experience of analysis?

Well, first I had two years of analysis in England; then Dr. Schlumberger, my French analyst, spoke excellent English. But many years later I went back for further analysis with Dr.

Renard who only spoke French, and although by then I spoke French fluently, that's where I realized how easy it was to say certain things in French that were more difficult in English ...

I guess what I'd like to explore with you is the ways in which both languages, French and English, mark your experience of the world ...

Well, to the extent that both my parents were English-speaking this does leave its imprint on my mother tongue, but after so many years of living and working in France this feeling of speaking a foreign language has been worn down. My husband and I are often unaware of whether we're speaking in English or French, or whether we have been listening to a French or English television show. And I dream in both languages. But of course there are sociocultural differences between one country and another that can't be ignored. Consider, also, that my patients come from many different sociocultural and religious backgrounds. As far as the work goes, the basic search for one's personal truth is not particularly determined by sociocultural factors. On the other hand these differences have a considerable impact on theory and research. It's probably no accident that in the "new world," the idea of an "autonomous" ego and so on was developed. It's no accident that in France there's such emphasis on language. These national differences affect the metaphors and the theories that will be developed.

You mention the French emphasis on language. Does any awareness of the clinical distinction you make between voice and word inhere in your own creative process? Have you reflected on that at all?

Oh, I've thought a lot about it: "in the beginning was the word." But no, in the beginning was the voice ... the way the mother is feeling, all her emotional states are transmitted to her baby through her voice, her skin and her smell ... I'm thinking in terms of an infraverbal language ... While an infant is born into a speaking environment, socioculturally determined and so forth, at the same time there's another language being transmitted. A language absorbed by the child as a body language ...

If you were to reflect on your own writing, and on your own creative process, is it possible for you to provide an overview, as it were, of

*how the masculine/feminine tensions inherent in the process unfold in
your own work?*

I suppose I could. When we ask our analysands to say everything that comes into their minds ... to think, feel, imagine, and
say anything and everything ... this is the maternal function. I
see the paternal function as a setting of limits: the session ends
when the analyst says it ends and there's a fee to be paid; then
there are our affiliations to institutions and so on ... all of which
represent something like a paternal order ... So if I attempt to
answer your question, I guess the processes of introjective
identification and the gestation of ideas feel like a maternal preoccupation, whereas putting them forth onto paper and reorgan-
izing my ideas and intuitions into a form that is communicable
to a public, I could see as a paternal function. But with regard
to writing, we all use both the masculine and feminine aspects of
our selves. I have learned from my analysands who suffer from
creative blockage that such impediments may stem from many
sources, including the integration or non-integration of one's
masculine and feminine dimensions. Let's say a man feels he has
a creative womb in which he nurtures a "child" – his painting,
play, musical production or intellectual research – should he feel
that he must reject this feminine identification, he risks becoming inhibited. A woman who feels, when she is creating, that
creation is a masculine activity ... like having a penis in her head
... may become conflicted about this, and that too can be a
cause of inhibition ...

I think my own analyses helped me sort out the factors that
prevented me from writing earlier on. Then Sammy also helped
me a lot through his psychotic thoughts, in that they freed up
my own ways of thinking. It's very important to be able to
"think crazy." The first paper I wrote, after the Sammy book,
was on female homosexuality because I had three lesbian
patients in analysis. And that forced me to identify with how
they felt, and question why their sexual orientation was different
from mine – and I realized that I had to be aware of not trying
to force them to think or feel heterosexually. In fact in psychoanalytic practice we're identifying all the time with the masculine
and feminine parts of our patients through our understanding of
our own masculine and feminine identifications. But this concept
is not original with me. I think Bollas writes something similar
... and Groddeck was very clear about the human bisexual sub-
st·atum. My contention is that we use our identifications with

both parents – and both sexualities – to create anything, not only babies. But I've observed a difference there between men and women: when women are blocked in their creativity, they tend to say: "I feel completely sterile." When men are blocked, they say: "I feel utterly castrated." This difference of metaphor is probably important.

As a writer of case histories where the sexual dimension is invariably and markedly privileged, do you find the differences between your own conception – I use the word intentionally – onto the page of a woman's story as opposed to that of a man?

Well, I am always aware that I am writing about a man and his ways of being and of knowing, or a woman and her ways of being and knowing. But the fact that you stress the sexual dimension in the case illustrations is because it was important to the analysands I am quoting. Of course woman's sexuality is markedly different from that of men. It might typify my writing better if I were to use the term "libido," which then could also include the narcissistic problems that so often take precedence over sexual problems; here again there is also a difference between men and women. But to get back to your question: there is a feminine way of thinking, feeling, expressing and being in conflict, whether homosexual or heterosexual ... and the same may be said of masculine ways of feeling, thinking and expressing oneself.

But does writing a case history of a man as opposed to a woman's engage you differently?

I don't think so. I struggle to identify with both and I am happy to be in the roles that either male or female analysand might need to give me. I can say to a male patient, "It seems you want to take my penis for yourself." This presents no problem to me as it should not present one for a male analyst to say "You want to put your baby into my womb." We are there to accept every projection, as father, as mother, as brother or sister, and when we do this we're already identifying with what the patient is projecting onto us – trying to introject and feel it. I suppose these notions apply also to my writing ...

I can say, however, that at the beginning of my analytic practice I was afraid I might not understand my male analysands as well as my female ones. Later this no longer seemed to be the case. There are many things I don't understand about some of my female patients; and there are some male analysands that I understood very clearly from the beginning. But whatever the sex of the patient, neurotic conflicts are easier to understand than the acting-out neuroses, or deeply buried, addictive and character patterns, or silent psychosomatic processes.

Freud's own cases have often been compared to wondrously engaging detective stories. In a similar way your own histories are often suspensefully spread out over several chapters of any of your books, threaded with everything from theoretical speculations to stage directions, before all the pieces to the puzzle that is a human life come together. What I'd like to question – even provocatively – is the final product. The cases you write up always seem to come together perfectly. The one exception I can think of – in presently recalling only two of your books, Theaters of the Mind *and* Eros *– was of a woman whose life ended in suicide, who only met her tragic end after she'd abandoned her analysis. While a history necessarily condenses many years of work in the space of only a few chapters, yours nevertheless come together so perfectly that I've often wondered if you ever experience, and perhaps occasionally indulge, a literary "temptation" to resolve a lifestory on the page?*

Perhaps. As I only ever write about one tiny dimension of the analysand – from whom I might quote an even smaller fragment of the analytic voyage – that tiny dimension usually has some kind of conceptual conclusion in my mind, even though there are always many unanswered questions. Fragments of a case history are only intended to illustrate a concept, itself derived from clinical work. I happen to think that a fragment of a case history better illustrates a given theory than chapters of theoretical explanation ...

In fact, an analysis could go on forever. You never reach the end of the mysteries of the human psyche and there are always many unresolved issues and conflicts in every analysis. I think it was Roy Schaefer who said that the story of an analysis is a story written by two people. I would add that our analysands frequently come into analysis with an unbearable lifestory, the "family romance" Freud called it, and they leave with another lifestory which is more acceptable, more liveable, but it's by no means the end ... The analytic process goes on, after patients terminate their formal analytic adventure, sometimes for years to come – particularly for those patients who enter the mental health professions.

What is it like for you in the course of the infinite process of an analysis, to be in the throes of "not knowing"? I marvel, when I read your work, at what I sense to be the workings of your mind and at how much you seem to intuit and know about your patients. Rarely, in fact, do I get an image of a Joyce McDougall that's groping, or assailed by the anguish of not knowing ...

Oh dear. how unfortunate. Yet I'm always emphasizing the things I don't understand, the work with difficult cases in which I'm continually trying to achieve a little clarity about difficult and un-understandable aspects of the human psyche. As I've already suggested, the actual cases are only little pieces of a very long analysis that have been chosen to illustrate a theoretical point of view, so of course they tend to give the impression that one knows what one is talking about ... But one is constantly in the throes of not knowing. Winnicott talked pertinently about the need to be in a state of non-integration, like the infant ... and the need to support a state of not knowing. Bion too emphasizes this aspect of psychoanalytic listening when he states that we must be devoid of "desire and memory" as we listen to each individual analysand. I myself point out frequently that the essence of the psychoanalytic process is largely infraverbal, more important than what is being communicated verbally by both partners to the analytic voyage. There was a world congress in Buenos Aires some four years ago, on the theme of psychic change, and I was asked to speak on one of the panels. I said in my paper that we never ever know, nor ever will know, what is the actual cause of psychic change. So many things happen in the analytic relationship that are never put into words ... Our interpretations may have some effect on the changes that occur, but I think it's relatively minor.

What function or role does interpretation have for you? Many schools argue that where the pathology is distinctly preverbal or pre-Oedipal, interpretation is not instrumental to the work of psychic change. From your books, it seems instead to be a cardinal aspect of your work.

With certain patients, yes. Although I too still maintain that interpretations are not the cardinal factor in psychic change. Or rather I should say it all depends on the analysand. The notable thing about any patient is his or her singularity: for some, interpretations are important; they make use of them and eventually provide many others; after all, as you know, it's the patient who does most of the work. But for others interpretations mean nothing – they resent them or use them back to front: when you've said black, they use it as though it were white. Bion talked about that, particularly with borderline and psychotic patients. He called it "reversed perspective." I find this frequently with people who have had very troubled childhood experiences ... sexual and other kinds of abuse. They tend to turn around everything, accusing you for what you said or didn't say to the point that one has difficulty in understanding the drive to misinterpret everything. The need is frequently to keep on attacking the parental figures that we stand for, the worst aspects of them, and to see if we can survive their anger. These distressed children have something important to say in which the saying is more important than any interpretation.

Are there patients with whom, or indeed long phases of any given analysis where, you won't interpret?

There are often long phases during which I say practically nothing because the patient is associating and analysing without my help. In other cases the patient does not want to hear anything from me. One of my analysands with whom I had learned to restrict my remarks to about once every six months, on one occasion said: "I can't bear your interruptions ... I mean your interpretations." Beautifully put – I was interrupting his thinking. And this is where the comparison with meditation comes in – all these analysands ask for is a containing space and a person to accompany them throughout their search for their own truth. In many analyses I've conducted, I've hardly ever said anything. And considerable psychic change takes place. So often, a person wants only to hear one's voice and is totally unconcerned with the meaning of one's words. One of my patients, quoted in *Plea for a Measure of Abnormality*, said: "It isn't what you say that matters to me – it's like when I listen to a song ... I'm only interested in the music" ...

That's quite lovely. Already in Theaters of the Mind, *and most recently in* The Many Faces of Eros, *you argue that symptoms are the infant's creative effort at self-cure. Indeed, you go on to address the metapsychological problems posed by such a contention: first and foremost, the implication that such a position necessarily overrides Freud's contention, that of the repetition compulsion being in the*

*service of the death drives. I was wondering if you could say more
about this paradox, and of how you came to equate symptom formation with the sustaining of ego-identity?*

In the final section of the *Eros* book – "Psychoanalysis on the
couch"– I suggest we could attribute to our work the aim of
protecting psychic survival, and that symptoms, even though
endlessly repeated, are nevertheless on the side of life. They're
the best solution that the infant or child was able to find in face
of early psychic conflict. The symptom has a basic life-giving,
life-preserving, psychic-preserving quality. Freud, in any case,
developed the idea that the death impulses grew out from the
libidinal impulses; but he felt that in many people the death
drives were deeper than the life forces. He agreed that aggression, of course, was a fundamental part of humankind – he had
no illusions about humanity. But there is some confusion in his
concept of the death instinct, and he saw this perpetual replay-
ing of the same old symptomatic solutions as on the side of
death. This is where I took issue, and proposed that they are on
the side of life. Freud's theory of a death drive has attracted a
lot of criticism, and was never very popular ... though I find it
most interesting. Laplanche, who is one of France's leading
psychoanalytic theorists, says we can get by without this theory
– we don't need it for metapsychological understanding. But a
theory is only important to the extent in which it can help you
in your work and in thinking about your work. When Freud
described the death instinct as a wish to destroy oneself, and
eventually other people, this was not very reassuring. People
readily accept that they're on the side of pleasure and life but
they don't want to hear that there's an equally strong drive in
them to be self-destructive and to strive against what is pleasurable, valuable and aesthetic. I feel convinced that there is a
tremendous drive toward destructiveness in the human being
which shows up in ever so many ways – self-destruction and/or
violently felt aggression to others. We can call this, if you like, a
"death instinct" ...

*Certain contemporary schools of thought – Kohut's most notably –
question the Freudian idea of a patient's libidinal investment in a
symptom, arguing that the patient has "no choice" in the articulation of his or her suffering. The symptom is seen as a disorder of
the self which cannot be any other way. You seem to take issue with
such a view when you write: "Thus our analysands, whose symp-*

tomatology brings mental pain and a restriction on their liberty to live and love, fight implacably to keep their symptoms even while asking the analyst to remove them." Can you address these polarized positions in greater detail, and how they might structure a clinician's approach to treatment?

I take issue with many of Kohut's formulations, though I think his metaphors ... such as "self-objects" and "mirroring" ... are very telling ... But if he holds that the patient has "no choice" of being any other way ... Well this is the impression that every human being has – there's no awareness of choice, because the choices were made so early, sometimes almost from birth onwards. Babies are fantastic pleasure seekers, discovering very quickly what will bring a smile or a cuddle and what is not appreciated by the mother, that will leave the infant out in the cold. They're already beginning to develop their ways of being. And later on – when people talk about homosexual or heterosexual object choice – again there's no awareness of choice. But choices are being made throughout infancy, so I don't know to what extent I can agree with Kohut. The choices are there, but they were made before there were any words for them, or before a capacity for verbal thinking was very developed. But this is the classical Freudian theory of causality – that the psychic structure of the individual originates from the earliest years ...

Along these very lines, you often talk about responsibility. Can you comment on what you mean by patients "authoring and enacting" the unconscious scripts of their lives? How is an element of responsibility retained when a life, consciously suffered, is unconsciously driven?

One of the major aims of the psychoanalytic adventure is to arrive at possessing one's character traits, symptoms and sexual patterns as one's own internal creations ... which most people tend not to want to do. They say: "Well that's just the way it is" ... or, "it's not my fault, that's what they did to me." I guess we're always looking for who's to blame, trying to get our internal persecutors out onto the world's stage – but it's what we do with the traumatic events that have occurred in our lives that counts. As analysts we are more interested in psychic reality than external events and realities.

Are you suggesting, then, that there is an element of choice in symptom even prior to one's being conscious of the symptom's determinants?

Yes, we have to assume that we have done this to ourselves, that we have found this kind of equilibrium even though it's painful. And it's very difficult to get patients to accept that they are the author of everything they carry inside them. Although none of us are responsible for the events of our past, or the unconscious problems of our parents, we are all totally responsible for our inner psychic world. We have organized it and must accept that we own it and that we alone are in charge of it.

Just a few more questions before we finish up ... In The Many Faces of Eros, *you privilege an element of political concern – for example, in your discussion of what you term "neosexualities." Could you address this focus and intent of the book?*

Well, I hope it will create greater tolerance in those who read it – tolerance towards those who are different, who have different options ... different sexualities ... different psychoanalytic theories ... or different ways of seeing the world around us. There are many roads to truth. I would also hope that anybody reading the book might attain greater tolerance towards their own inner world: to their right to have conflicts and problems, even their right not to lose their symptoms ... or their right not to consider what other people might call a symptom, as such, particularly if their way of being is not causing pain and suffering to others in their community.

I was reminded, in this context, of a comment of a patient of mine, a young gay man whose powerful ambivalences also invest his sexual life. He told me of a conversation with a senior colleague, a man known to inspire all sorts of submissive transferences, in which the latter reportedly boasted that he had cured two men of their homosexuality ...

Is this an analyst talking? He thinks it's a cure to change somebody's sexual orientation? If that's what patients deeply want for themselves, then they may feel happy to have found what they were looking for ... but this applies to so few gay and lesbian patients. Very rarely do they want to be "cured" of their sexuality – as rarely as a heterosexual would wish to be changed into a homosexual. Isn't the therapist saying, then, "I want everyone to be like me!" – so as to "cure" them of their own way of being? I guess such therapists have failed to analyse their own underlying homosexual dimensions.

*What about this normopathic strain that invests so much of our
profession?*

I think it's breaking down ... no doubt the gay liberation movement
has helped to widen people's judgments about sexual orientations,
enabling more people to say: "Well, each person has his or her
kind of sexuality, so why should I want them to follow my sexual
pattern?" And yet there are still may analysts who hold that the
homosexualities, or those inventions I call neosexualities, are all
pathological. Well, are they? As long as two consenting adults are
happy with whatever they're doing, I don't see why an analyst
would want to change this. Unless they have some idea of making
everybody like themselves, or have set ideas of what they think is
"normal sexuality." What's normal about it, anyway?

*Can you extend your reflections on perversion to address the politi-
cal contentiousness between various psychoanalytic schools of
thought? You close* Eros *with a call to order, as if invoking an
ethical basis that ought to be common to the efforts of anyone
involved in the practice of psychoanalysis ...*

I think our greatest perversion is to believe we hold the key to
the truth. And I still hold to this idea ... Any analytic school
who thinks this way has turned its doctrine into a religion ... I
don't want to belong to anybody's religion ... when we make our
particular psychoanalytic theories into the tenets of a faith, then
we're restricting our whole capacity for thinking and developing.
One's school of psychoanalytic thought must not become a
Procrustean bed!

*Why do you think the hold of such psychoanalytic groups ... sects,
as you call them ... is so strong?*

I often wonder too. What's their insecurity? Perhaps it's partly
determined by the transmission of a psychoanalytic education
which is largely based on transference: the attachment to one's
analyst, as well as to supervisors and teachers, is permeated with
strong transference affects. This may result in the idealization of
thinkers and theories as well as leading to the opposite – the
wish to denigrate them. But I guess this is part and parcel of the
history of psychoanalysis and something we must strive to
understand.

WORKS CITED

Freud, S. (1901). *The Psychopathology of Everyday Life*, in J. Strachey, ed. *The Standard Edition of the Complete Psychological Works of Sigmund Freud*, 24 vols. London: Hogarth, 1953–73, S.E. vol. 6.

Varela, Francisco J. (ed.) *Sleeping, Dreaming and Dying: An Exploration of Consciousness with the Dalai Lama* (1997). Boston: Wisdom Publications.

JOYCE McDOUGALL: Selected Bibliography

The Many Faces of Eros: A Psychoanalytic Exploration of Human Sexuality (1995). London: Free Association Books; New York: W.W. Norton.

Theaters of the Body (1989). London: Free Association Books; New York: W.W. Norton.

Theaters of the Mind: Illusion and Truth on the Psychoanalytic stage (1985). London: Free Association Books; New York: Basic Books (revised edition, Brunner/Mazel, New York, 1990.

Plea for a Measure of Abnormality (1978). London: Free Association Books; Madison: International Universities Press (revised edition, Brunner/Mazel, New York, 1992).

Dialogue with Sammy (1969 with Serge Lebovici). London: The Hogarth Press; (revised edition, Free Association Books, London, 1989).

MICHAEL EIGEN

Something about Michael Eigen makes for a stream of oxymorons. Maybe it has to do with what he calls the *distinction/union structure* that character-izes human thought and experience, something he talks about at length in these pages. "In the beginning there was both separation and union, or distinction and union ... ," he says at one point, explaining his own take on the Creation myth. Maybe that's why, when I think of him, phrases come to mind like "eased awkwardness," or "befuddled clarity." Phrases that describe his bodily expressions as well as the arching breaths and insights of his words and thought. Earthbound and visionary, Eigen goes against the grain, struggling to articulate the spiritual gropings of today's patients, while also tugging at the blinders of those who insist that Freud, on the matter of the "oceanic feeling," did indeed speak the last word.

When I think back at my first encounter with Mike years ago, my memories are of a shy, self-effacing man, dressed totally in black, perhaps even wearing dark sunglasses, talking about Bion and death at a Modern Freudian training institute. Had he come with a guitar, he might easily have been mistaken for Roy Orbison. Already then, I sensed, this man's comfort zone was on the fringes: of psychoanalysis and mysticism, perhaps, but more importantly, on the fringes of an embracing, radical "otherness." And indeed, as you'll note in these pages, Eigen does walk, or jog, or step, or dance, to the beat of a different drummer; what you won't find him doing, though, is marching. It's simply too rigid a posture, for a man who knows that there are as many drummers as there are patients, and as many beats as there are lives and fears, tears and trembling hopes.

A funny thing about this interview is that Mike cheerfully swears he never wore black, let alone appearing publicly as my feeble memory, or elaborate fantasy, would have him. Even the sunglasses are the result of my dreamwork! But so be it. One thing he did do, however, in the course of our talk, will forever remain imprinted on my mind. You see, Mike squints a lot; in fact, throughout the entire five-hour interview, only once did he fully open his eyes. We were about halfway through our work, when I asked him how he imagined an infant's experience of the mother's face. Then, all of a sudden, his eyes opened. First widely, slowly, then, almost wildly, as they both wandered up and far to the right, as if following a

conctul words to the selfintergs,
of fantncnes of
how one will
like to he...

94   FREELY ASSOCIATED

penlight an ophthalmologist might wield. Then, as he began to answer, "Well, there is the eye-to-eye contact, where the eyes are shining or dull or a shade in-between ...," his eyes refocused, and settled, and met my eyes for the duration of his answer. Or maybe, I should say, of his meditation. A word, we should remember, that like "medicine" comes from the Latin *mederi,* "to heal."

The interview which follows was conducted over the course of two days, on December 3–4, 1994, in Mike's home in Brooklyn, during Hanukkah, the Jewish Season of Lights. The topics discussed prefigure the theme of his two latest books, *Psychic Deadness* and *Reshaping the Self,* not yet published at the time.

AM: *As a starting point, I was wondering if you could comment and elaborate on a statement you once made, "Freud is right to think of psychoanalysis as wounding the Western ego, although it does not create the wound so much as grow out of it." What is this wound and how do you conceptualize the Western ego?*

ME: I don't know. In terms of the wound, of psychoanalysis wounding Western narcissism, Freud had in mind the three great revolutions which kept decentering the human being, so that the human being was no longer the center of existence, nor the ego the center of human existence. In a way Freud's psychoanalysis presents a series of wounds, a series of traumas, a series of woundings, from birth trauma to abandonment anxiety, annihilation anxiety, castration anxiety ... There's a catalog of anxieties, a catalog of catastrophic states that the infant and child go through, that the human being goes through. It's sort of an anthology of catastrophes. In Freud's informal presentations he depicts these as humiliations, humiliations that the ego goes through, humiliations to self-esteem ... blows, blows to the ego ... and he means "blows" literally, not just metaphorically: like a stab to the heart or a blow to the face, the way a poet might mean it. So that his picture of the human being is of the human being going from one wound to the other, and of how the personality congeals, grows, displaces itself around wounds.

When I was in the Nevada desert, a guide told me that a cactus would grow straight forever, would grow forever straight if it didn't get wounded, and that the branches of the cactus grow out at the place where it's traumatized, at the place where it's wounded. Freud depicts the personality in the same way, displacing itself, or deforming itself, around the point of impact, of wounding impact. Hit the psyche, and it displaces the self like ripples or waves, it deforms itself around the points of wounding. And Freud describes those woundings in so many different ways, in terms of different developmental phases. But the wounding Freud talks about has always to do with displacements: with how the self-importance, or the self-centeredness, of the human being, the amazing arrogance of the ego, keeps getting wounded by re-centering itself in a larger existence. Psychoanalysis is part of this revolutionary decentering process, another in a long history of ways of placing or replacing the self in a larger context, while breaking the relation to being a big fish in a small pond.

If we somehow conceive of re-centering or decentering the self, there still persists the idea of a "center." Do you have an operative idea of a center when you talk about decentering or re-centering?

The first nub, of course, is the seed. There's just the seed of a self ... But I nevertheless do feel a sense of the value of the idea, in spite of deconstructionism. In certain exercises, for example, I feel more centered. But what that center is, or how to describe it, I wouldn't know. It's not an idea I have an investment in. I wouldn't fight a holy war for one picture of it over another.

I'd like to address what I see as a confusion that surrounds a set of concepts that is invariably central to psychoanalytic theorizing. How do you understand the terms ego, self *and* subject, *all three of which appear prominently throughout your writings?*

I have never thought these things through, basically. I've thought about them at different points of my life, or through different theoretical systems: for example, what the subject is for Lacan, what the self or ego is for Jung or for self psychology or for ego psychology, or for the British school or Sullivan. What the self or ego is, or what the subject is, shifts in meaning. It is partly a matter of context: what seems to be subject in one context can be object in another. It could be like a Chinese box, or a shell game ... For Freud the ego is a kind of "I" subject, but it's also a system of functions, it's also the love object of the id. So in a sense it's subject in one context, the system of autonomous functions in another context, a personal "I" in another context, and an object in yet another. So that even in Freud's work, the meaning of ego keeps shifting according to how it's used. I wouldn't want to go to bat for pinning down a single meaning, because it's really dependent on context.

Your own use of the term self *is very elastic and multi-faceted. You don't hesitate, for example, to resort to the plural notion of "selves"; you speak of a "body self" and a "mental self"; frequently, of the "growth" of self, and the "gift" of self. Sometimes the word* self *is preceded by the article "the", sometimes not. Can you clarify and expound on your own usage and understanding of such terms, both theoretically and clinically?*

Maybe I've used the word *self* at different times, at different points in my life, for different growth purposes. So maybe the term has meant different things to me at different crises, at different junctures. Sometimes I think I've held onto the word "self" as an organizing principle, to make me feel more whole. At other times I use the word to give a context or horizon, a vantage point outside of the smaller ego. Sometimes I've used the word "self" because it refers to a feeling of own-ness: a kind of feeling of my own, something very personal. But I don't know that I would be intellectually equiped – to pin down the many meanings of the word. My use of the word *self*, at this time in my life, isn't quite the same as it was when I was twenty. I think our capacities generally involve some mixture of how we experience ourselves: on the one hand there's a personal, warm and immediate experience; on the other hand, there's an awareness of being given to ourselves as pretty anonymous, as pretty impersonal. What we do, then, with what's personal at one moment and what freaks us out as anonymous, or as standing against us from within ourselves in another moment, can vary. I don't know whether I can add anything to the subject in terms of intellectual clarity. It's a matter, I think, of informal use and what mileage one gets from a term like *self* at a given point in one's life.

Would you feel comfortable providing some anecdotal sense of the kind of crises you mentioned, that may have distinguished a shift in your own personal understanding of what "self" might have meant at any given time?

I can think back at when I was in my twenties, on a bus, being in extreme agony. I just suddenly lost consciousness and dipped into this sense of agony, and stayed with an agony that seemed to be located in my chest. It was a terrible psychological pain, not a physical pain so much as a horrendous emotional pain, that I imagined and felt in my chest area. I went further and further into it, and I doubled over on the bus, and then all of a sudden, quite surprised – not having any mental frame of reference for what was happening – the pain opened up and became radiant light. Where before there was just agony and horrendous pain, without my knowing what had happened, suddenly there was bliss ... It turned into a terrific light, that left me wishing it would never end. Of course, the pain didn't go away, but the bliss has never left me either.

In your "Afterword" to The Electrified Tightrope, *you write: "There is much pressure not to hear oneself (or selves)." Clearly, the idea of the self's potential multiplicity is present in your thinking and experience. First put forth, arguably, by one of your early teachers, Marie Coleman Nelson, it's an idea that's been taken up recently by the likes of Stephen Mitchell, Jane Flax, even Christopher Bollas. How is the concept present in your thinking and, more importantly, how does the idea of multiple selves bear on your practice of psychoanalysis?*

I guess I came into contact with the idea first through literature rather than through psychology. In psychology, my first contact with it was through an early book by Erich Fromm, *The Forgotten Language*, and through Jung's writings, when I was still a teenager. How it finally translated for me personally was when I came to be amazed by, or thrown by, or utterly flabbergasted by, the changes of state that one can go through in a single day: the amazing changes of state of which the psalmist writes, how we go to bed crying and wake up laughing ... How that happens is astonishing, is amazing. Freud wrote about how the very fact that we dream is a signal that it might be possible to cure psychosis. Because if we can dream, if we are plastic enough, elastic enough, to go through such amazing changes of consciousness from normal waking to dreaming states and back again, then why shouldn't it be possible to cure psychosis? The idea of multiple selves, that we are all these things, the actual concrete, immediate experience of change of state, is problematic: what does one do with that? Is one different people when going through these different states? William Blake talks about states, all states, every state being eternal: how all states, once experienced, are forever ... Or we have to try to picture a unified personality identifying with different states, going through different states. Jung depicted an archipelago of selves.

But I don't think either vision is necessarily comprehensive. I think the crucial thing, now, is the debate about multiple personalities or dissociated personalities. I think it's really quite useful, quite wonderful, because it brings the problem out. Perhaps it makes the problem of multiplicity sound strange or unusual, but I don't think it is very strange or unusual at all ... What do we do with the amazing plasticity and range of states that we actually go through in a day? From feeling more in one's body, more out of one's body, more mystical, more realistic ... in love ...

Isaac Bashevis Singer somewhere writes about how all human beings, how even an idiot, is a millionaire in emotions ... It's a fantastic gift, a gift and liability we're given, to have this extravagant experiential capacity. And it's not at all clear that we know what to do with it as yet. One of the amazing things about going through all these states, for me, is the fact that I'm going through them at all, that I can feel so differently in so many different contexts. It's not a different self that's going through them; it's sort of, how can I be all that? But it's still me being "it"; it's not a different self, or a multiple self necessarily. It's me. It's me being other to myself too. But how is that? How can I be other to myself? How is that possible? It's mind-boggling. The kind of beings we are is really mind-boggling. That we are somehow other to ourselves; that it's "not me"; hey, it's not me!

Then what's the difference between Michael Eigen saying this to me now, and what you've explored and experienced clinically with so-called multiple personalities or in dissociative states?

I think one of the big differences, is that I'm more used to it. Someone else, a patient, may not be able to make the links, may not be able to stomach the multiplicity, or take it in and digest it in some psychic way ... A patient might not be able to say: "Hey, that's me ... Oh! hey that's not me!" There's not always a place big enough, in a patient's psyche, a house big enough, to make space for these different rooms ... Someone comes upon another room in the house, and imagines being completely in entirely different territory. They might not realize: "Hey, I've just moved from here to there ... that the link between ..."

What provides that link?

That's what we're working on, at the cutting edge of psychoanalytic praxis. Winnicott's whole career was a testament to the fact *deadness as a result -/ an example, shock* [handwritten annotation]

that depersonalization, not feeling real to oneself, is the central clinical problem. I believe the link, then, lies in those conditions that make it possible to feel real to oneself.

Depersonalization, or what you refer to in your present writings as psychic deadness ...

The sense of a life not having meaning is a phenomenon that's struck me. Nowadays, more and more people come in and actually say that they don't feel alive. It's experienced by many of them as a very painful situation. Now that's a good prognostic sign, because if they were not experiencing this as painful, the situation would be even worse ... Somehow, these people know what it's like to be alive, if the absence of vitality so troubles them. It's becoming more and more common to get people in practice who feel dead and who want to come back ...

What are the factors behind this pervasive sense of psychic deadness?

The most obvious, I would imagine, is the general degree of over-stimulation. A patient comes to mind who had a massive dose of over-stimulation all at once. He pins down his dying to a time when he was about eighteen, to an evening when he, his mother and his father were sitting having dinner. The father went into an unusually pitched rage at him and walked out of the restaurant screaming. The boy felt himself collapse at that moment, and die out, and he's been dead ever since. It was a massive shock that he felt, and it made me think that in some way or other so many people are numbed out or shocked or put in a state of shock by a kind of massive implosion, or massive impact ... almost like a scream, or someone screaming at them ... it's almost as if there were a silent scream that is deafening people, who can no longer hear themselves, and are thrown out of balance ...

You mentioned wanting to substitute the idea of "multiple states of being" for "multiple selves." That very distinction is, to a large extent, at the crux of the postmodern debate on the self. James Glass, for instance, in a book entitled Shattered Selves, *is highly critical of the seductiveness of the postmodern exaltation of multiplicity. Conversely, Jane Flax talks about "fluid subjectivities" as a defining characteristic of this postmodern epoch, and seems to be suggesting something along the lines of what you're talking about: a condition where these fluid states do not necessarily involve fragmentation. What is your under-*

standing of postmodernism and its distinguishing features? How has psychoanalysis and your own practice been influenced by a supposed postmodern turn?

I've liked parts of what I've read of Derrida; I've heard him talk a few times. Still, I can't always figure him out, because a lot of the results of his work seem to reflect what we as therapists were already doing clinically. I'm sure I haven't grasped the depths of his writings, but I haven't learned anything new yet. What I like is the analysis. I like the poetry of the analysis in the people I've read. I've been entranced by some of the poetry of the prose, which is breathtaking. But clinically postmodernism hasn't added all that much for me. What it's confirmed, though, is that one can transcend almost any clinical situation, and look for another way to handle it: so that whatever lock, whatever impasse is created by the patient and therapist together, one knows in one's being, as well as theoretically, that one can always be doing and being something else. One gets to know that it's always possible to pick another loose end to organize oneself around, to costume oneself in; it's always possible to pour oneself into another mold, and come at a situation from another way so that one always recognizes and utilizes the plasticity of the materials at hand. One doesn't have to be resigned to being boxed in. There is, I suppose, a certain transcendental element in how free one is or can be with any particular patient ... so that one can imagine becoming someone else, can become another self, or another part of the self, or enter into another state that might yield a different effect on the clinical situation.

There's a section in The Psychotic Core *entitled "The Point of No Return." There you write: "Many patients complain of an endless sense of aloneness. They do not find a social milieu in which they can feel they really belong. The usual categories of connection such as family, race, nation, work, various subgroups and friends do not work for them ... For an increasing number, nothing can truly palliate the nagging sense of being different and not quite connecting. In some basic sense, one is not understood and does not understand oneself. One has nowhere to go. One is on one's own." Looking at this, I couldn't help but think of it in cultural and historical terms. Is this aloneness somehow different, say, from the angst of the heyday of existentialism?*

I don't know whether it is or isn't. I think it's like a blind man having each hand on a different part of the elephant, or like the same echo at a different point of time, the same wave at a different point in space. When I wrote that, the person in particular, and the people in general, that I had in mind were totally disconnected. They had no place, were off the map, completely had no hope. They had no hope of ever making a connection they would regard as being on the map. And yet it really was miraculous that some of the people I was thinking about at the time did manage to become part of the tapestry of life, without compromising in some essential way the alone self that had been hopeless, that had earlier been hopeless to connect up. Now, how that did happen is rather baffling: persistence, staying with it, staying with the aloneness, making room for the aloneness.

I think that in that passage I was being a therapist to the alone self. I was trying to establish a context for it, for that alone self to be, to be validated and valorized. I remember certain people I've met in my life, like Winnicott, Allen Ginsburg, or the rebbe Menachem Schneerson. When I was with them, I felt it was okay to be the sort of person I am. With them it was okay for me to be somehow off the map, beyond the map; it was okay for there to be in life such a person as I was. In that passage, then, I was trying to encode, for whomever it would reach, something like a message in a bottle. Floating on the sea it might then reach some people, who would hear the message that it's okay for them to be the sort of alone person they are. And by some miracle, by making room for such a message, some of these people, through the course of years, have tentacled out, have tapestried out. They've found themselves situated in a larger tapestry that makes room for the sorts of being they were and are, whereas earlier there didn't seem to be any place for them. Now, how did that happen? How was room made for them, a space for life to begin?... It's miraculous, making room for the multiple selves ... Again, I'm not so sure I like the term "multiple selves" ... I suppose it's comforting, in a way. And I don't know that "multiple states" is much better. But the idea of making room for this alterity, or multiplicity, or self/non-self, self/otherness that one is, is one of the functions of therapy.

Is this what you mean perhaps when you write about a "friendship of self"?

Make friends, yes. And it's okay to be your own enemy, to be adversarial and antagonistic too. It's okay to be your own worst *[handwritten annotations: "NB)" "1 advocates vacillating ambiguity"]*

enemy. It's inevitable. I think the idea of normality can be horrendous, because one carries around this picture that normal people aren't insomniacs, or normal people aren't so hyper-nervous, or they don't obsess, etcetera ... So you have this picture of what normal people are, but then ... where are all these people? If you find them, they're probably driving someone else crazy. What's normal is that there is a background radiation of the universe with different, molecular densities that different worlds issue from, and we are part of that universe.

Within a historical moment that either privileges or generates an excess of psychic disconnection and dislocation, and makes of geographic dislocation a basic experience, can psychoanalysis somehow confront the economic and social structures that generate this surplus of social fragmentation?

I'm more Buddhist there. I don't know that it's my job to, or that I can. To think about doing that, on a small level, analysts should be less frightened of speaking out publicly about public issues. For example, it is becoming more commonplace to see how so much of political discourse hinges on winning lies, so that a one-up/one-down structure, or an adversarial structure, is becoming increasingly prevalent. Take, for example, the Clarence Thomas/Anita Hill hearings of some years ago, where from one vantage point you could see so many different political maneuverings to gain the upper hand. It was less important to determine the truth than it was to see which lie would win, or which spin would win; or how best to appear as the more aggressive, the clearest, the one who could knock the other person more efficiently. The premium was not so much on truth as on who could present the clearest, most aggressive and effective image. The choice being offered was rather sickening ... Within the same arena, one of the things I like about Clinton is that whatever is wrong with him, or whatever the problems with him, he at least makes vacillation, or oscillation or indecision, part of the public milieu. Part, and only a small part, of the reasons he's come into so much trouble is not because of what he's done or not done, but how he's appeared. He hasn't been able to cosmeticize his vacillation or oscillation, or his unsurety, in the public domain, and he hasn't been able to present an effective one-sided, me-against-you, adversarial, axe-man approach. He hasn't been able to develop a winning-enough lie to stand by, with which to knock others down. Personally, and without any delusions about my effectiveness, I like to feel that if I make a public appearance, that I'm a spokesman for ambiguity, or a spokesman for oscillation.

In the epilogue to The Psychotic Core *you specifically address the deforming effects of television and what you call "the collective brainwashing inherent in the maneuvers of contemporary political campaigning." For you who have written so extensively about psychosis, to what extent do these phenomena play a part in its genesis?*

I don't know if the media plays a role in promoting psychosis, though it certainly can. I think psychosis and the media are different branches of a deeper, more pervasive tendency toward madness in the human in general. I think madness pervades so many human dimensions, that it is not so uncommon at all. What's uncommon is unmadness. It would be rather unusual to find something happening that isn't quite crazy. But the fact that human beings have invested so much in one-upmanship and territoriality and economic riches ... me-against-you, me-above-you ... this has a madness to it. It's kind of crazy in a way ... but I suppose not doing it would be mad too. I think that our tendency to live a dream, to live according to a fantasy ... a fantasy of what one would like to be like, and of what life is like, that tendency is rather widespread, and madness is not a rare thing at all.

The polarized debate of the "singular" versus the "multiple" self seems to fit within a dialectical structure that is elemental to your thinking. You've written: "For practical purposes, I posited a distinction/union *structure that characterizes the self at all of its developmental levels." I was wondering if you can elaborate on this idea, even in terms of its acknowledged antecedents in the work of Federn, Mahler, Winnicott, Grotstein ...*

Since I now have to use words, and not just grunts, let me say that it's along the lines of what Winnicott has in mind, when he portrays the psyche as being essentially paradoxical on all levels of development. To use words like distinction/union, to become united with this double capacity, runs through the human psyche at all levels: cognitive, emotional, relational, and social. And we don't really know how to conceptualize this capacity except to point to it, and say something seems to be there ... "I am," but I am in a context, in an intersubjective context ... I'm you, you're me ... but I'm not you and you're not me ... It's a matter of what one can come up with, what one creates with that dichotomy ... In this sense, I think psychoanalysis today is a kind of poetry. Nowadays, I think of psychoanalysis as an aesthetic, as a form of poetry ... You have all these psychoanalytic singers and poets trying to express their aesthetic experience: of a session, of the emotional content of a session, or of the impact a patient generates in session ... It's all portrayed as a cultural microcosm. We have all these wonderful and moving psychoanalytic singers opening up worlds of experience, and it's a matter of whether someone moves you along at a certain point, promotes your own growth towards openness.

*When you talk about this "distinction/union structure that character-
izes the self at all its developmental levels," I get the impression that
you're not talking simply or only about the Freudian developmental
schema, of oral, anal, phallic, genital stages. I get a sense that you
have implied a different, or at least a complementary, idea of what it
means for the human being to develop. Coud you illustrate that idea?*

Well, it originally grew out of my early work with regression, with so-called "primitive" patients. I was very influenced early on by the British school, where there were a number of people working who seemed to see a positive, regenerative value in what used to be called regression ... I remember noting at the time how different theories seemed to suggest that one could regress as far back as to a symbiotic state, or to an autistic state; but if that were true, then regression would be extremely dangerous, and the farther back one went, the more isolated or the more fused or the more self-less, in a negative sense, one might become. So, instead of regression being regenerative, it would have to be destructive, and the best thing to do would be to build up defenses against regression. Nevertheless, my clinical finding was that so-called regression or opening up of the self or letting down the boundaries, could be extremely fruitful ... This seemed more wholesome, in common sense, and healthful to presuppose ... My myth, my story was: "In the beginning there was both separation and union, or distinction and union ...," so that one doesn't have to be frightened of going all the way ... that, as far as one can go, whatever world one enters into, you'll be both self and other in various forms of relationship and non-relationship, and that one doesn't have to make a decision, doesn't have to decide whether to be simply alone or simply with others. It's more fun, and less frightening, to be and allow for all of these possibilities: to just glide along, or be able to flow from one state to another. Or to be in mixed states at different times, without prejudging: "Oh my God, I shouldn't be this now," or "I can only be this now!"

I was wondering whether your emphasis on psychic structure and polarities of experience was somehow influenced by the work of Lévi-Strauss. I haven't seen him mentioned in your writings, but I'm reminded of a book of his called Totemism ...

Well, I never got as immersed in Lévi-Strauss as I did, say, in Bion or Winnicott or Lacan. It's just a matter of luck, a throw of the dice, what authors I got immersed in at an earlier age, and he wasn't one of them. But when I did read him later, I found his work fascinating. The connection, for instance, in my mind and lots of other people's minds, between structure and process, is truly baffling. Years ago, I think it was Gene Gendlin, in a book called *Experiencing and the Creation of Meaning*, who saw an enormous difference between process and structure. I don't understand how he derived the idea of structure as something more solid and fixed, and process as something more fluid and moving ... *(thinking out loud)* Gestalt psychology, I think, suggests that bones, for example, are the results of slower, more fixed processes ... but it's not like bones are process-free ... they're made up of slower, relatively stabler patternings ... The bones of the system on which the flesh and nerves all hang, that's all process too ... I don't understand the difference between structure and process. I've never felt the need to posit a difference. Just talking about structure is a very creative thing because one picks how one's going to slice it, you know ... One is always selecting the processes that one's going to talk about, and in what form ...

In elaborating this idea of the structure/process, you hint at what could be called an originary matrix of being, at what you call the "living experience of union and distinction out of which the self arises." Your own contribution in this sense is unique, in that there seems to be a "maternal" dimension of the infant's originary experience that somehow goes beyond object relations and even predates the relational embodiments and personhoods of mother and child. Again, we're stuck with words: but you seem to suggest a living experience of this union/distinction structure that actually predates the self, as well as the personhood of mother and/or child ...

I think that's right ... Something that both mother and infant get situated within, though I'm not sure what to say about it. The age-old folklore that we're children of God before we're children of our parents probably hasn't been tapped as well as it might in psychoanalytic thinking, where we're always children of our parents first ... It actually may take quite some time for an infant to de-infinitize ... where the infant may go through different states, now more finite, now more up against the solid, real facts of things, and at other times be more and more in an infinite field or infinite horizon ... To actually come into the realization that I have to be where my body is, that my body is this bounded packet, really takes quite some time and quite some sophistication. Some people feel that schizophrenics resist this development, or that certain sorts of schizophrenics resist packeting themselves that way, or have an inability to tolerate the physical limitations of embodiment. It can't be taken for granted that the sense of infinity or of the emotionally infinite doesn't somehow antedate the experience of the mother or even of the infant.

You seem to be reclaiming for psychoanalysis an actual, experiential dimension of mystery, of the infinite, of the immaterial: words that have always suffered the weight of Freud's "oceanic feeling" ...

Well, I've felt the oceanic feeling. The term itself has unfortunately watered down psychoanalytic discussions of mysticism because mystics themselves, while enjoying oceanic feelings, sometimes were often brought upshore and left terrified by the onset of a numinous awakening. They were overturned, and shaken to their core. The prophets, whenever God or an angel appears, get the dickens scared out of them, they get scared stiff, and it's terror, terror ... So God has to say, "grab your balls and stand up like a man, let's get down to work," because there's such a terrifying impact of the uncontainable, and it's not all peaches and cream and oceanic bliss ... That's the way it is with mystical experiences, or encounters with the divine. They can be too much for the human equipment at a certain time. Flannery O'Connor, in her short stories, depicts this over and over, where even religious, fundamentalist Protestants are broken by the discovery that what they were preaching actually has reality, and so they become shattered by the actual experience of what they had only been rehearsing. Over and over, her characters are shaken by a divine or demonic happening that makes real what before were only words. It's like the experience of a child, who is intensely wishing or praying for something. In the absence of the desired object, that kind of wishing can make for an altered state. Even as a child, one gets a sense of being different than one imagined one could be, and that sense can grow. It can even have a biography: the sense of the infinite can have a biography.

All your writing is imbued with a deeply charged sense of religiosity, of mystery and wonder. There is throughtout the evident sensibility of a mystic. You speak of Bion as a mystic; you often cite Buber's I and Thou, and speak of the co-union or communion, not only of self and other, but of self and God ... You've written on evil and often mentioned the devil ... You talk comfortably of both prayer and Buddha. In your epilogue to The Electrified Tightrope, *you astonish a reader with ideas like: "From the depths of one's being it is as easy to get to God as libido. For Freud libido seeks an ideal imago in traditional terms, ultimately God. The unconscious does not do away with God so much as provide a privileged point of contact with the unknowable." Later, you mention your father's death, and your subsequent immersion into the roots of Jewish mysticism. You then continue: "I used aspects of Oriental and Roman Catholic teachings to organize my mystical propensities. The paradoxical, dialectical, dialogical way of listening/ speaking that marks clinical practice mitigated against religious orthodoxy, but my encounter with Judaism made me a richer and better person. The flow between divinity and libido is so much freer now." This kind of language, this kind of revelation, if you will, in both senses of the word, is courageous on the part of an analyst. Beyond the oceanic feeling, I'd like to invite some free-flowing reflections of yours on psychoanalysis and religion, from both your clinical experience and your own life history.*

Well, at the risk of sounding utterly trite and trivial, so be it. From the first session I've ever had with anyone, I've always felt a sacred element in psychoanalytic psychotherpeutic work, and I've never quite understood the animosity so many analysts have had against the seemingly oceanic feeling. I'm astonished, for example, that as terrific a worker as André Green tried to argue it with me ... I was astonished that, in his reading of Bion, Green played down or totally parenthesized, nullified, actually, Bion's use and reference to faith. He emphasized almost exclusively what Bion called k, or knowledge, or the scientific approach to knowledge, and was convinced that Bion too thought as he did. But as Bion's work evolved, he more and more transcended the primacy of k, or the lust for knowledge, or the search for and use of knowledge, within a faith context, and as a matter of fact, he proceeded to almost

define the psychoanalytic attitude as an act of faith. And he uses
those words ...

Now I think Green is a terrific analyst and thinker, but this
blanket statement, with regards to an enormously important part,
the climactic part of Bion's work, is astonishing. I take that
incident to be a paradigmatic example of how, even with the most
imaginative and generative people in the field, there seems to be a
strong animosity against the faith freaks. Why faith is played
down, though, is puzzling. Maybe there's the threat of fanaticism,
or of losing scientific ground; but I think one can be a fanatic in
the other direction as well. One can deplete experience in different
ways. One can be too realistic, one can be too fantastic, one can
be too scientistic, one can be overly fanatical and zealous ...
Rather than have a war between all these different dimensions of
experience, it's much more fruitful to keep open the possibility
that each has a voice, that each has a say in the play of voices, and
to see what happens ... But whatever faith is, Bion associates it
with opening, with the propensity to become open. To go in the
other direction, towards k, would be a premature exclusion of one
voice in favor of another, as opposed to a plurality and balance of
voices.

Jung has his funny things too. I can certainly imagine a Jungian
saying I'm wrong, but in my reading of Jung, there's so much that
is devastating if one takes it to heart. For example, his attitude
toward dependency can be shocking at times. He puts down certain neurotics as mother's boys and addresses them with a certain
contempt. There's a contempt for dependency and weakness that
runs through his writings, which is kind of odd, because he seems
to really have generated a lot of positive transference, and then
from that position seems to have a contempt for weakness. So
there's a kind of double bind that I imagine Jung put a lot of
patients in: "You must worship me, but if you do I have contempt
for you." It's a funny thing. Now Jung, of course, feels he pulled
himself up by his own bootstraps. As a neurotic or psychotic
adolescent, he felt he'd strengthened himself and deliberately con-
quered his weakness, transcended his weakness, by hard work and
creative endeavor. And so he developed a certain mistrust of
people who couldn't do that. He may have made his living off of
people who couldn't do that, but he nevertheless seemed to look
down at affliction and adversity. So while Jung had a certain depth
that few people reached in psychological writings before him, there
was an attitudinal problem I recognized. So I tended to gravitate
toward the British school partly because, for the first time in

British school valued dependency

psychiatric writings, and in a consistent way, there didn't seem to be a contempt for weakness or a contempt for dependency. It seemed like dependency was now getting its due or valorized as being a legitimate part of life, that ought not to be precociously short-circuited or treated abruptly ... or dealt with by just tugging at your bootstraps and acting bigger or stronger again. The emphasis in the British school is on staying with the dependent streak until the growth process can come about. It was that different attitude toward human weakness that appealed to me, I think. In practice, the British school also did a lot of goosing into independence, pretty much as Jung did in his own way; so the dependency business does get rather scary with the tendency, even in the British school, to perpetuate it. Nevertheless, there is an attitudinal shift, away from Jung's contempt for weakness, that is evidenced at least in Winnicott's writings.

faith

You've written about faith as you see it in the work of Bion, Winnicott and Lacan. What is faith for Michael Eigen?

Differenct things at different times. I guess there's spiritual faith and there's natural faith. I place a great deal of weight on natural faith. I've nothing against spiritual or mystical faith ... but there's an awful lot of faith that springs simply from sensory experience, from how good it feels to be able to walk down a street and move one's limbs and not be in prison ... It brings up a feeling inside that, while it might be stretching things to call "faith," I really do have to call it that ... It makes one feel good to be alive, it makes one feel that life is good ... The body seems to have this faith ... Very often I've been astonished by how a dying animal seems to not know it's dying, by how it acts in the face of death, and seems to live, to be moving or trying to move or live to the last ounce ... It just keeps going to the end ... Or even when it stops moving and gets into a dying position, it doesn't seem to be angry or yelling about its imminent end. Somehow there seems to be an acquiescence, a simple ebbing of energy in the direction of death. It's a kind of body faith, a faith the body has. I suppose one could talk about an affective faith or an emotional faith: the "ouch!" and "yum!" of things ... "Ouch! That hurt!" ... or "Yum! That was worth it!" So it's more than pleasure and pain, I think. When one talks about a pleasure principle or a pain principle, one's de-animated it, because it's not simply bad or good, it's heavenly, it's heavenly ... It's wonderful!...

it feels yummy all through ... You know, one would have to be totally mad not to have a secular or ironical self and see the limits of things, but I rather like siding with this feeling of "good to the last drop" in psychoanalysis ... like a bug that never stops moving ... There's just a sense of never giving up ... never giving up on a case ... not giving up on anyone ... Who knows better? ...

All this begs another question. What does Michael Eigen mean by God?

God only knows! I think I have to be honest to say I mean a biblical God, the God of Abraham, Isaac and Jacob ... But having said that I can step back and say: "Hey, well, what I mean by God could be anything, because I don't know ..." In a sense God is a total unknown, and yet in others the very notion ties the so-called biblical, personal God closer to me than I am to myself ... And then there are times one can just lift up one's hands and say, "Wow, all this out of nothingness" ... which feels wonderful ... to blank oneself out and be totally open to whatever currents pulse this way or that ... whether you're into body, or emotions ... Taoist or Buddhist, whatever, it feels good. You know, in the Kabala, God has ... is ... goes beyond names ... the *Ein Sof*, the infinite of infinites, the great unknown, the "I-itself"... By the time God gets named! ...

I had a patient once who, in the midst of a fierce negative transference, blurted out loud "I am that I am," without any apparent sense of the phrase's biblical echo. The woman was stating her difference and uniqueness in a rather commonsensical sort of way, but the sheer power of her words was unmistakable.

That's wonderful. I think Ben, in my book *Coming through the Whirlwind*, does something like that at one point. It's what we're doing all the time: we're "am"-ing ... and we're "am"-ing each other too ... we're enabling each other *to am*.

In getting back to that early "am," you seem to have supplanted the centrality, for psychoanalysis, of both the real and the metaphorical breast in the early life of the infant, with what you imagine to be the infant's formative relationship to the face. The face almost becomes as important, if not more important, than the breast. In a way, the face takes on a mythic quality in your work ...

Well, that comes again from a Winnicottian sense of paradox, from the idea that we shouldn't ever favor only one element of a dichotomy. Why should psychoanalysis have opted for a primacy of the tactile and diminished the visual? Why oughtn't both grow about together in a mutually constitutive way, feeding what everyone calls mind, or self, or being ... Bion can be quite funny sometimes when he talks about *common* sense, or getting the senses to work together ... which can't always be taken for granted, you know ... In an autistic state, for example, a child can be pulled one way by one sense and another way by another sense ... We oughtn't to need, in theory or in practice, or even in our personal lives, to compromise the multiplicity of the senses, and the different information they provide. But there's more! The different senses don't just give information. They give different worlds, or different qualities of worlds, or different textures to live in, not just information to process, but different tastes, different ways the world tastes through touch, or through the other sensory organs. Or there can be harmony, at various times, between distance senses and closeness senses, a paradoxical interplay again between near and far. It seems quite limiting to say we are primarily near-creatures or that we're primarily far-creatures, or touch-oriented, or vision-oriented ... In other words, and this seems obvious, as Freud already noted and Derrida points out in "Freud and the Scene of Writing," there is a primacy of multiplicity.

This is the first answer where you've privileged a theoretical reply as opposed to an experiential one. Since so much of psychoanalytic theorizing about the breast involves the writer's fantasies of what the infant experiences or "phantasizes" at the breast, what does Michael Eigen imagine the infant's experience of the face to be? What does the face do to and for an infant?

Well, there is the eye-to-eye contact, where the eyes are shining or dull or a shade in-between ... The eye-to-eye contact, together with the skin-to-skin contact, generates, so to speak, different sets of feelings, currents and subcurrents of feelings. From eye-to-eye and skin-to-skin, there are currents and subcurrents, some antagonistic, some harmonious. But part of the fate of eye-to-eye contact or face-to-face contact is to enclose worlds, worlds of experience. The face does shine, you know! So I can get a double faith ... I can get a faith from the breast and faith from the face. Normally, now that's not the case; normally, they very often tear each other apart, with fights for the upper over the lower; fights for the lower over the upper ... Normally, there's probably a state of war between capacities; but optimally, that may not be necessary.

A few more things about the early developmental stages. Is there an echo of Lacan's mirror stage in any of this?

I love Lacan, but I twisted him out of shape for my papers, for my writings on faith ... because face for him, Lacanians insist, really has to do with seduction. The face for Lacan is part of a seductive enterprise, as it also might be for Sartre. On the other hand, for Winnicott the face can be the center of an experiential movement that goes beyond seduction, that connects up with Levinas' sense of the face as infinite. It strikes me both viewpoints are right, and there is much to say about each. We *do* seduce each other through our looks, as well as through much else. One can't localize seduction. Seduction is everywhere. Nor can one localize faith ... You can have breast faith and face faith. One could have breast faith and not have face faith; and one could have a face faith and not have breast faith. There is faith sliding into Klein's or Lacan's early paranoid, aggressive play of desires, a seductive, demanding faith, enticing-ruling, being enticed by / ruled by the desire of the Other. Levinas writes about the face as it evokes the infinite, or as part of the experience of the infinite, of infinity, of opening infinity. How could one decide between Lacan and Levinas? Why should one have to?

I have a few more questions on issues concerning postmodernism ...

Those are funny terms, aren't they? Postmodernism ... modernism ... I sort of picture dinosaurs walking around ... It's funny ... bit names ...

There's another passage from The Psychotic Core *where you evidence a clear awareness of what might be termed a postmodern sensibility: "Writers today emphasize how present-oriented, episodic, and fragmented our experience is. We no longer simply gain identity from well-defined social roles and institutions." Similarly, in* If on a Winter's Night a Traveler, *Italo Calvino writes: "... Long novels written today are perhaps a contradiction: the dimension of time has been shattered, we cannot live or think except in fragments of time, each of which goes off along its own trajectory and immediately disappears. We can rediscover the continuity of time only in the novels of that period when time no longer seemed stopped and did not yet seem to have exploded..." If what Calvino says is true in some way, if time and space have been compressed, or if our experience of time and space is different than it might have been twenty or a hundred years ago, how does that experience now unfold in the analytic situation?*

I'm intimidated by questions like that because they're so broad ... though I love descriptions like the one you read because they're so fun! From early on in my writings, I've been drawn to particular portrayals of time worlds for people, and of time worlds in analysis. In an early paper called "The Recoil on Having Another Person," I write about the importance of time experience in the constitution of self. It's about how temporal meanings of the Other, dimensions of time in the experience of the Other, relate to approach–avoidance patterns, to two people being drawn to each other or repelled by each other. The exploration of the concept of time has a long history, in philosophy, literature, and in human experience ... Condensing time, or exploding time ... Erik Erikson or Alfred North Whitehead portray a kind of emotional time, or an affective time, or time in terms of pulsations ... how long, for example, it takes for an experience to develop and be seen through.

By implication, I think of John Dewey's work, *Art as Experience*, where he talks about how an experience has its own particular build-up time, development time, shifts around, comes to a climax and denouement. The question, perhaps, is how is it possible to help people allow this process to happen, and not short-circuit seeing an experience through ... or how can we enable them to sustain the tensions necessary to fully go through and not thwart an experience?... Even the question is hard to organize, because time is such an intimate part, in analytic work, of allowing time to be, of allowing an experience to be.

Has there been, in your clinical work, an experience of time shattered or subverted that was fully shared with a patient?

In general, the so-called borderline personality presents the problem of not giving time a chance, of not giving the analyst or analysis a chance. It's all tooth and nail ... Time gets eaten up, gets eaten away, gobbled up by the patient in analysis. Let's relax into giving time a chance to develop its own flow, and allow that there should be a "later"... or a "then," or enough room or enough of a gap, so that some kind of approach, of movement from here to

therapy as a psychic gymnasium – help
114   FREELY ASSOCIATED
people to experience to stay in time

there is possible. So that analysis can be possible, and develop over
time. So that development, over time, can take place. In this sense,
you might want to help a person view therapy as a kind of psychic
gymnasium, to help build up tolerance, at certain times, for just
seeing a moment through ... for the patient to know, "Ah, look,
something was just about to happen between us, but it got short-
circuited. Where did that moment go? It looked to me like you
were about to feel afraid or angry, and suddenly it's gone!"... or
maybe, "You suddenly felt relaxed here ... you relaxed here
because I wasn't bugging you about anything. All of a sudden ...
Where did it go?" Therapy as a strategy to outflank the thing that
kills off or short-circuits the possibility of experience, of letting a
moment grow ...

What about space?

I love space. But I've come to have the odd view that there's a
primacy of time in analytic experience. I know that most of the
literature is concerned with analytic space and preserving the
integrity of analytic space. But I think there comes a moment ... a
time ... when space dissolves, but time keeps going ... a kind of
timeless time, where the person becomes, gets dropped into, gets
immersed or in touch, with some unfolding of affective nuance, of
affective resonance. And space, for that time, seems to dissolve,
while a kind of pulse time ... a kind of psychical artery time keeps
on going. It's as though one discovers time by losing space at a
certain point ... a kind of timeless time ...

The inverse phenomenon of the spaceless space where time dissolves?

I've experienced many patients overly obsessed with space, who
have no playful space whatsoever. What they have, actually, is not
so much a playground as a coliseum, where there's a battle for
survival going on: a territorial battle over who's going to survive in
space. These patients inhabit a corrupted space, a violent TV-like
space, where the emphasis is on who's blowing away whom; where
the violence makes for one explosion after another. So the session
itself becomes a kind of explosive or violent space. It becomes an
annihilating space, a space that eats up, where the obsession with
space again blows away the possibility for time to develop.
    It's a void space, in a way, or a big-bang space, or a black-hole
space that seems to foreclose the possibility of letting something
unfold. Just as something's unfolding, a violent enactment blows it

away, so that the experience doesn't get a chance, in and of itself, to come to a conclusion. You never get a chance to find out what the experience could be because the sort of space it occupies nullifies it. It nullifies the experience, blows it away before it has a chance to complete itself. Clinically, then, the problem is one where negative space eats away at the possibility of letting an experience be. It's a very violent, Pac-Man, black-hole kind of space that explodes the possibility of giving people a time to complete any particular trajectory of experience.

Would that scenario preclude or diminish an essential capacity like introjection?

I think that's certainly true. But the problem is even more pervasive, because it precludes the possibility of completing a perception. On a sensory level or a perceptual level, you can't even perceive or see what the world would look like without something blowing the experience away before it has a chance to build. So, it wouldn't be a matter of just precluding introjection or projection. It's a matter of stopping actual innate capacities from having a chance to operate.

Regarding those "native capacities," one of the writers you address extensively in The Psychotic Core *is Federn. You talk about his concept of "I-feeling," and his radical contention that mental ego-feeling (and not the ego-feeling related to the body) is the first to be experienced by the child. This seems to have provided a spring-board for your own ideas. I was wondering if you could comment on this, and on how our sense of the psyche gets spatialized within us?*

Wow! I seized on the Federn business because it was pretty unique. I mean, no psychoanalyst before him had theorized in that way. For the general psychoanalyst, the ego is first and foremost the so-called "body ego," and it was kind of stunning to see that, for Federn, the psyche is first a mental ego. How he did he get to that? Probably because he read Husserl. He was a student not only of Freud but of Husserl; so that a Husserlian-kind of phenomenology of consciousness informed his work. As a result, even while he was a staunch Freudian and remained in Freud's camp throughout his career, Federn wasn't able to begin his account of the ego's origins as a body ego. Now, that's an amazing position for an analyst to take!

Idea of getting the mind into the body — very interesting

It also occurs to me, in working with psychotics, and if we think of how psychotics describe their own experience, that Federn's descriptions fit certain sorts of psychosis: with regards to how the body ego can fade away, while an I-feeling still remains. Of course, this I-feeling can be lost too, in more dire states of depersonalization; or the I-feeling itself can persist, but feel unreal. One could also have the I-feeling without any quality of its being warm or immediate or real ... or a sense of painful estrangement from the I-feeling, that the "I" is going on but I can't experience it. One can have even further I-losses ... But Federn, in any case, has this range of experience of working-through with psychotics, where he can have the body feeling unreal, or the "I" going on after the body drops out ... And there's a long tradition in esoteric religious thinking that also fits Federn's descriptions. One sees this, for example, in the esoteric Gnostic tradition, where you have ideas of one existing prior to the materialization of the body.

In a way, the Freudian enterprise implicitly has to do with getting the mind into the body. Freud's whole oral, anal, phallic thing is about ways the mind is incarnating, or a way the spirit incarnates. It's about phases of incarnation, or a development of incarnation. Whereas Federn's question, in working with psychosis, is: "Well, what if I don't incarnate? What happens then?" It's not like R.D. Laing's question, which is more: "How did I get out of the body?" For Federn, the question is: "How do I get into it?" What happens if I don't want to get into it, or if the body isn't sufficiently inviting for me to want to be a part of it? Or if the body subjects me to too much horror?

You know, in the Gnostic myths, the soul has to be enticed or seduced or fooled or tricked into going from the dry domain into the wet ... Contrary to so much analytic thinking, the first fall isn't from womb to birth. The great catastrophe isn't in going through the womb to getting born. The great catastrophe is going from heaven° into the womb. I think that's a worthwhile distinction to remember, especially as experimental psychology is now finally catching up with Gnosticism. We now know that the womb is not such a very perfect place at all. The fetus has traumas in the womb too, and maybe so does the embryo ... Can you imagine what it must feel like, if there are things like feelings at so early a stage, to go through such momentous upheavals or growths, one after another? It's more titanic and cataclysmic than the unfolding of geological ages on the earth, with its cyclones and earthquakes and climatic changes and ice ages! I mean, what the embryo undergoes in a short period of

[handwritten: Idea that we are born with a bigger more mystical "I" - that then shrinks into the smaller "I"]

time is monumental ... And should anyone be there experiencing it, God knows what sort of experience it must be!

About Federn's notion you write: "Primordial I-feeling drenches the entire cosmos ... Original I-feeling is infinite." Through your reading of Federn, there's a mystical quality in his work that seems just as radical as his argument for the primacy of a mental ego. I'm wondering if this was something that you were aware of or sensed an affinity to ...

Well, I have my own tongue-in-cheek love of that kind of thing, because in the way Federn presents his ideas, the question becomes: "How do we all, who begin life as mystics, become anti-mystical?" How do we develop anti-mystical properties as our ego contracts into our body and into the spatial world filled with the objects that we know and love and hate. The so-called "I" – whatever that is – begins as a bigger I, as a bigger, more cosmic I, and then contracts through coming up against the hard facts of life. It develops a contraction, and we then develop a smaller, more realistic "I" that maps out the spatial realities we have to deal with. The problem then becomes: what happens to the big "I"? What happens to the cosmic "I"? Does it get funneled through the smaller "I"? Does the smaller "I" draw nourishment from the bigger "I"? Are they at war with each other? Do they battle for supremacy? Is one psychotic when one meets the cosmic "I" and delusional when one gets to the smaller "I"? If a development statement such as Federn's has anything to it at all, what kind of relationship can be worked out between larger and smaller "I" states? How do we get along? Can we make a playground big enough to accommodate the bigger and smaller states?

Again in The Psychotic Core, *in writing about Federn, you state: "The subject often encounters pain when he acts on his sense of boundlessness. He meets the resistance of spatial realities and other I centers." It's the notion of I centers I'd like to explore. Is this somehow an early prefiguration of the idea of a multiple self, or what you call multiple self states?*

Well, I think of the joke about the guru who convinces his disciple that he's God. Years later the guru meets the disciple, and finds him limping along, all crippled and bandaged up. So the guru asks: "What happened?" And the disciple says "Well, this guy riding his elephant was in my way, and I kept thinking and telling him 'I am God, I am God' ... and he ran right over me." And the guru says:

"Schmuck, he's God too!" An entire range of phenomenological and existential and philosophical literatures have explored different phases, or different aspects, of what it means to be a being who sees himself through the eyes of another, a being who sees by displacement, where I see you through me, or you see me through visions of a free-floating "I," or through the "eye", the organ of sight, that floats freely ... A free-floating "I" that in any particular moment presents any number of vantage points. That's partly what can fuel resistance from a good borderline patient ... this "anything" that anyone says, anyone could have said something else ... any "I" could have acted differently, at any given time.

So a good borderline patient can always say, "Well, why should I listen to what you're telling me ... it is after all *you* telling me." But there can be an impact between patient and analyst, through which I, the analyst, develop a truth of the moment, a truth which grows out of the impact, that I somehow select and through which I become aware, in an aesthetic way, of the impact's growth ... I become aware, then, of what it might feel like for the patient to be impacting on me in this way. And I'll develop trains of words or images that grow from the aesthetic nucleus of the impact which, without functioning as a definitive truth or perspective, can still give rise to an infinite number of other possible perspectives ... Then the one truth, the one perspective I select and present to the patient, becomes a poem, my song of the patient at that moment: and through it, I can access the patient's feeling states. We impact each other with our momentary dream presentations.

You've written of yourself: "From the outset it seemed clear that I could never be a strictly orthodox analyst." It's uncommon to find an analyst truly free of the shackles of schools and doctrine, one able to embrace – and I mean the term "embrace" rather literally – figures as diverse and far-reaching as Freud and Jung, Lacan and Kohut, Winnicott and Bion. What is the process, what is the attitude that allows for your incessant efforts at synthesis, and how have those efforts been accepted in the greater and often rivalrous communities of psychoanalysis?

From early on, it was never a theoretical or technical matter. It was desperation. It was a hunger, a need, a personal need that I met, in reading each of these people at a given time. In an inner sense, I was reconstituting an aspect of myself or area of myself. If I read Jung, or Freud, or Winnicott, I felt that some other part of me was coming into being, or was being mediated into life through these various midwives. So it was, in essence, a salvation quest ... or a matter of integrity as a person, getting more of myself into being and developing more of a life for myself. I gravitated towards the people who, at different phases of my life, seemed to be midwifing what needed to be midwifed at that particular time ... And as I have a sense of loyalty, I remain loyal to all my various loves from those different phases of my life. I read Jung before Freud. For some reason I didn't understand Freud when I was younger. I tried and tried and tried to read him, but it was too painful and didn't make much sense. But Jung was easy to read, Erich Fromm was easy to read, and I devoured their writings in my late teens and early twenties ... So in a way I did it backwards. I evolved into a Freudian later ... I was a Jungian before a Freudian, instead of the reverse, which ought to be the case, developmentally, according to Jung. Of course, I couldn't be a Freudian either because of Freud's anthropology and reductionist picture of what particular fantasies were important. Not being a formal theorist, it wasn't much of a problem to go through these different so-called schools or theoreticians. It was actually a matter of dire need ... It wasn't a theoretical matter, it was a concrete personal matter involving the constitution of the self ... of my own self.

How has it played out in the field at large? I really don't know. I don't know what position I have, I don't really see myself in the field at large ... This much is somewhat clear to me at any rate. When I was in graduate school and going through training, and I stumbled across people like Searles or Winnicott or Marion Milner, I felt inwardly very much like William Carlos Williams describes himself in medical school ... He said that writing poetry got him through medical school. My having fallen upon people like Searles and Winnicott very early on, long before they were popular, got me through graduate school ... They got me through training. It's as if discovering them made me feel it was okay for a guy like me to exist, because it was hard for me to get that kind of validation, in the formal training that existed at the time. I like to feel that I've encoded, in my writings, the message that it's okay for people to be and develop in their own way: that we mutants are very real and have a very real contribution to make, and that the world would be poorer without us. We have a right to walk around in the sunlight and to stretch and to play our music and to sing and dance ... And maybe it's okay for grown-up children, for analysts like us, to help keep the balance, to help keep things afloat. I have, thank God, gotten confirmation from diverse sources: from many good souls who've read my writing and have been deeply stirred or affected by it. I've gotten numerous calls or letters or invitations from people who have had the experience, in reading my writings, of hearing their own voices in a deeper way, of feeling they had a right to be in their own particular way ...

Of these influences, Bion and Winnicott seem to stand out as being particularly dear to you. You've studied both for decades, and Bion you knew personally. Can you say something about these two men?

Two great mutant men! Winnicott, I suppose, one wouldn't ordinarily think of as a mutant because he had this myth of normalcy about himself. But, you know, in his writings, especially in his writings about Jung, in his "splitting headache" dream related to reviewing Jung as well as in his actual review of Jung's autobiography, Winnicott talked about having been somewhat liberated, of having been able to achieve a degree of madness in his work. Whereas I don't think Bion had to go through that process of apology for his madness. I think he worked more explicitly with and from his madness pretty much from the onset. I got the impression from his biography that he probably knew quite early that he was quite mad and didn't know what to do with his madness. At a time when people weren't all that concerned with problems of madness and the role of madness in human life, Bion, especially, offered some of the most stunning portrayals ever of the mad dimensions of life.

Winnicott? I visited him in 1968, I think, when I was in London. I was having a terrible time in graduate school, especially with one clinical teacher who'd wonder how I would come up with the things I'd come up with. She would always feel they were right, but didn't know how I got them. So she was put off by me because she didn't get my methodology, even though she seemed to agree with the results. So during this horrible time in graduate school, I go to meet Winnicott, and he greets me at the door saying: "Hello, Dr. Eigen. I'm sorry I haven't read your work." He greeted me as if I were someone. I was quite thrown because my experience of my life in New York didn't exactly convince me that I was someone or, for that matter, anyone. So, here I am, being treated like a king by this old man, who seemed very gentle and sweet, who offered me sherry and then went on trying to convey to me something about the sort of work he did. In the meantime, he felt free to move about the room, or sat at the end of his couch in a corkscrew kind of way, which seemed rather awkward ... He didn't seem shy, so much as awkward ... What would it mean to be awkward without being shy? His was a kind of awkward intensity, in which he was digging, digging for the experience that he wanted to convey and the way he wanted to convey it, the way that he could feel it could be conveyed to me. And as I looked at him all corkscrewed up in this awkward, intense way, I found he looked very much like an old woman, in his old age ... So here he was, screwed up in this awkward intensity, when I had this feeling and thought: "Oh my God, he's sort of like me!"... that somehow we shared this awkward intensity in our attempts to get at something, in trying to get at the thing itself and find a way of conveying it. I wouldn't be so delusional as to put the two of us on the same plane, but it was a freeing moment for me ... It was as if he was not afraid *to be* – in this unsmooth, rough-hewn way, in order to try to get at something ... Ultimately, something about him conveyed permission. It's as if his message was: "If I can be Winnicott, you can be Eigen!" It was a beautiful moment ...

It was a different experience entirely when I went to have consultations with Bion. I walked in, and the first thing I felt, that took me quite by surprise, is I felt he looked like a bug ... He looked like a bug! ... He looked frightened ... like a frightened bug. It's as though he were putting himself under me somehow, in order to understand ... He was putting himself below me, and I felt for that moment empowered. It's as though he were empowering my narcissism by operating from a position of dread. As the session went on a lot of his pronouncements seemed to me oracular, or orphic, and I felt he could be talking to anybody. I felt that I, as a person, didn't exist for him, and I felt very uncomfortable with that. I found him rather joyless, and began telling him how joyless he was. Then, as things went on, we talked about Plato, and he talked about his analyses with Rickman and Klein, of how his earlier contact with Rickman helped save him from Klein. Then out of the blue he started talking about the Kabala, asking me if I'd read it. I told him yes, I had, but not very much. And he was quick to say that he too hadn't read it much. But it dawned on me as the session went on that he was implying ... that he was talking to me at a level that I wasn't used to being talked to. I write about it in the afterword of *The Electrified Tightrope*, actually, how he anticipated my development by almost a decade. Anyhow, by the time I left him after the session, again I had a parallel feeling, though not at all like the one I got from Winnicott, because Bion was more bug-like with me, more cryptic ... But again I had the feeling that if it was okay for him to be Bion, if he could do his thing with me the way he did, then perhaps I could discover a way of finding out what my thing is and to do it with a sense of freedom. Both men had this capacity, I felt, to give permission, to give permission to be different, to be in one's own way.

Were your consultations with either man anything like a traditional analytic or supervisory relationship?

I only saw Bion when he was here in New York at the IPTAR Seminars, and everyone was presenting cases to him. I figured I would try to get the most out of the situation, so I presented myself as a case. He told me to get married, and to stop psychoanalysis. He told me I had been overanalyzed, that I'd been in analysis long enough; that I should break away, and get on with the nasty business of finding my own self. In retrospect it's touching and odd and uncanny and inspiring, uplifting, that many of the ingredients of the conversations we had, while he was here in New York, about Plato, about Klein, about the Kabala, about the weirdness of one's own idiosyncratic nature ... that many of these ingredients turn out to be generative bits and pieces of my own inner world. It's as if the riches that he spontaneously shared about his own life matched a few gold pieces in my own treasure chest. His words, then, hadn't been random; he wasn't talking only about himself. His own unconscious mind was making selections that resonated with treasures buried in my own being, treasures that our sessions helped animate. It was something like psychic acupuncture, where he was getting to certain nerves, certain pressure points that could be stimulated.

There are two other figures who seem to have left their mark on your work and life. I'm thinking of Marion Milner, with whom I understand you've corresponded for years; and of your first analyst, Henry Elkin. Your admiration for Elkin seems filled with generosity and gratitude, and yet, you write that your analysis with him did not end well.

Henry had a strong destructive side, in terms of being intuitively dogmatic. But he had depth and weight, and I had a very deep attachment to him. Implicit in our contract was the sense that something would come of this attachment. And as I began seeing him when I was quite young and quite hopeful, when he left New York I found myself feeling abandoned, looking, perhaps, for a way I was going to survive without this relationship, to carry on without a dependency that had seen me through some decades. How does one resolve a transference of this nature? I don't know. It's not all that clear to me even now.

Milner? I originally loved her appendix to On Not Being Able to Paint. I taught it in my seminars for many years. My reading of Milner was, again, like the other people I'd read, really for my own life. It wasn't, however, her concept of undifferentiation that helped me to reconstitute myself in any way. It's when she couched her findings in terms of a paradoxical formulation, in an "I-yet-not-I" kind of structure or dynamic or process, that I felt moved along. It was the "I-yet-not-I" feeling I got from her formulations that led to the first article I wrote about her work. It was one of the first major articles published on her work, and I thought it was a positive article, a helpful article. Pinchus Noy wrote me from Israel at the time saying how helped he was by it. He told me I'd put my finger on elements of Milner's work that had bothered him, that he couldn't grasp, so that he now felt released to assimilate what he had always loved about her in a more undiluted way. That was the effect I had hoped for, generally. My article on Milner's work, however, apparently precipitated antagonism from Margaret Little who, unbeknownst to me at that time, had used the concept of undifferentiation to couch an awful lot of her own work. Apparently, she felt that I had hurt Marion with this paper. I felt badly about that, because I was trying to help midwife a process, help catalyze a process further. Marion and I had written to each other, and her surprise baffled me, since I'd already sent her my review of On Not Being Able to Paint, which contained some of the main ideas spelled out by my longer paper. So I explained to her that what I wrote was the result of a process for me, and that it seemed, from the letters I'd received, to have had some use, at least for other people. So I had, then, to simply find a way of standing by my own reality, by my own experience, while at the same time tolerating, or finding a way to go through the flak, and all that it precipitated.

Well, Marion and I kept writing back and forth for quite some time over the matter. Then, much later, she wrote to me saying I was right in what I'd said; that she felt the article had also been helpful to her, in that I had actually freed her from a dead language that wasn't necessary for the experience she was trying to convey. I think that our love for each other survived whatever it was that momentarily came between us. Our love and what we get from one another survived the viscissitudes of that time. I think in a way that's a good model for therapy, and for living ... that we lived through the pain and agony of a broken union. We very much value our contact with each other.

One striking aspect of your work, already present in The Electrified Tightrope *and, more recently, in* Coming Through the Whirlwind, *is the candor with which you convey your own history and inner realities. In your books you highlight elements of biography, early experiences of religion, family, sexuality, college. In* Whirlwind *you portray the rich world of the analyst's internal struggles with two tremendously engaging patients. Were these kind of revelations difficult for you, or did they issue very naturally? It's not common for analysts to write about themselves so frankly and openly: especially, for example, about their erotic reactions to a patient, as you document in your* Whirlwind *case study of Cynthia.*

What's more difficult is how much I haven't done. I would be happier if I could do more of it. Each time another shell is shed and I come out of the closet a little more, I get so much more out of it myself, and so do my patients. Therapy, I suppose, has not simply been a profession, it's been ... it is my life. Therapy has been less of an external, professional process than it's been an internal birthing process. I wonder if more therapists wouldn't benefit from being more open about how much they get from their patients.

I think we get an awful lot from our patients that helps us grow; our patients help organize us, and we grow an awful lot through the work we do ... or at least I and certain other people that I know do. Therapy can be unlike other professions in that there's less of a separation between what one does and what one gets out of it. For example, I've seen writings in the literature about therapist burnout, and I'm wondering what it means for a therapist to burn out. Perhaps the person was using the wrong model for therapy, was trying to be more external to themselves to make the work more of a "profession," like a lawyer would make it. I get many lawyers who come in and hate what they do, who feel unreal about the ways they have to make themselves function in the external world. A therapist has a chance to have much more of a connection with the work that he's doing... Part of doing therapy is that one is always in therapy, one's always in one birth process or another, or is evolving in a deep, inner way in connection with other people. As I can see so far from the effect on others and on myself, the more openness of a certain sort the better, I would think.

You write in The Electrified Tightrope: *"In the long run my work as a patient is what made me an analyst." Can you talk about that experience, and about that dimension of "the work"? Of the work that is intrinsic to any authentic therapy, and to the fashioning of a life through the interweaving or marriages of our many selves?*

Jung said a long time ago that a great psychologist doesn't have much of a choice: that his only choice, so to speak, is whether to spend his life inside a mental hospital as a doctor or a patient. That's kind of tongue-in-cheek, I would think, but the truth is that, for the therapist who lives and "professes" his work inwardly, being a therapist is being a patient in a way. One is always engaged in this kind of evolutionary experience, always working on oneself, and that doesn't make for much of a distinction. The distinction between patient and therapist fades away. Of course, I have to do something for the patient in order to feel justified for earning money for my work. But very often I'll take money from a person and thank them for it, and wonder what I did to earn it: because I probably got at least as much from the experience of being with them as they may have gotten from me.

Actually, as I become a little less frightened of being open, I become more and more aware of how I grow with certain people, and how interacting, especially with so-called "difficult" patients, promotes my own development. For example, if there's a person I cannot help, for whom anything I do strikes out, that person is forcing me, if I'm going to help them, to find a way of being with them that I hadn't exercised before. And if I fail to find it, it will be a failed treatment ... In a way, it's like a baby bird pecking at the mother, pecking the mother into developing the maternal urge to feed ... Well, there are certain patients who have to keep pecking away at the therapeutic field until, somewhere along the line, the field develops the capacity to help this particular set of birds develop. And when one of them arrives in the office and you cannot help them, when you can feel their anger or their drive to get help pecking away at you, it's not always easy to recognize that we've yet to evolve a corresponding capacity to respond to their particular kind of pecking. But if one does stick with the process for a long enough time, whether it's ten years, five years, two hundred years or a thousand years, sooner or later, that capacity will evolve or get pecked into existence by the bird's own persistence. By not giving up, that bird, somewhere on this earth, will evoke the particular set of responses that it requires and is looking for. And when that actually happens with a patient, after weeks or months of being stuck, it's marvelous! When all of a sudden, because of an internal shift in one's own being, the case moves on: because the therapist's being has actually changed, and has entered another phase of living, in response to getting pecked at in a way never experienced before.

Thanks for letting yourself be pecked at.

You're welcome, I'm sure!

Works Cited

Buber, M. (1970). *I and Thou* (tr. by W. Kaufmann). New York, Scribner.
Calvino, I. (1981). *If on a Winter's Night a Traveler* (tr. by W. Weaver). New York, Harcourt Brace Jovanovich.
Derrida, J. (1978). "Freud and the Scene of Writing," in *Writing and Difference* (tr. by Alan Bass). Chicago, University of Chicago Press.
Dewey, J. (1959). *Art as Experience.* New York, Capricorn Books.
Fromm, E. (1957). *The Forgotten Language.* New York, Grove Press.
Gendlin, E.T. (1962). *Experiencing and the Creation of Meaning.* New York, Free Press of Glencoe.
Glass, J. (1993). *Shattered Selves: Multiple Personality in a Postmodern World.* Ithaca, Cornell University Press.
Lévi-Strauss, C. (1963).*Totemism* (tr. by R. Needham). Boston, Beacon Press.
Milner, M.B. (1979). *On Not Being Able to Paint.* New York, International Universities Press.

MICHAEL EIGEN: Selected Bibliography

Psychic Deadness (1996), Northvale, NJ: Jason Aronson. Inc.
Reshaping the Self (1995), New York: Psychosocial Press.
The Electrified Tightrope (1993), Northvale, NJ: Jason Aronson, Inc.
Coming through the Whirlwind (1992), Wilmette, Illinois: Chiron Publications.
The Psychotic Core (1986), Northvale, NJ: Jason Aronson, Inc.

ADAM PHILLIPS

Maybe it's because I'm writing this sketch shortly after arriving in Italy, as I prepare for a rare six weeks of art and leisure in Rome ... maybe it's the swirling richness of the city's baroque heritage, its full-bodied lavishness, that has me thinking of cherubs and Bacchus in the same psychic breath with Adam Phillips. Innocence and extravagance. Precision of detail mixed with boldness of style. Perhaps that's why, when I think of Adam Phillips, I again and invariably recall Michael Eigen's words: "Nowadays, I think of psychoanalysis as an aesthetic, as a form of poetry. You have all these psychoanalytic poets and singers trying to express their aesthetic experience ..." For Phillips, after all, is a singer, a minstrel, a painter and aesthete: not only of the written word, but of the art form that is a human life, and of the decorative masterstrokes, the improvisations, we call stories ...

An Italian poet I've translated, Valerio Magrelli, has a poem that goes like this:

> And what if these turns of the key
> never ended?
> And what if I were locked out
> left turning the key my entire life?
> And what if I lost the key? ...

For me, this is the place where Phillips, the pragmatic aesthete, and his faith in stories, come in. Where the anxieties of relentless questioning, of emotional and existential fixity, find relief in the arabesque flourishes of the imagination. In the therapeutic occasions that stories evoke and nourish, in response to the paralyzing "what if's" of life. Ultimately, the idea of the story is the key Phillips himself turns, time and again, systematically, even obsessively, but happily, unconcerned about ever losing the key because its loss would only open another story, another dream. Another lifetime. Or, perhaps, another of our Sistine chapels of the mind, with plenty of cracked and discolored recesses to replenish and restore.

The following interview, which took place in Phillips' London home on January 6, 1996, focuses on themes developed mostly in *Terrors and Experts*, recently published at the time.

AM: *You open your latest book,* Terrors and Experts, *with a quote from Andrew Marvell's* The King's Speech, *where he writes: "I am a changeling." Yet the changeling that is the unconscious seems continually to provoke authoritarian, or fixed, understandings among the schools and "experts" committed to its study. What do you make of this general picture, and what are its implications for the practice and politics of psychoanalysis?*

AP: This is a big question. I think that there is something inevitably, potentially authoritarian, or just authoritative, in formulation. I think that once we institutionalize psychoanalysis, there will invariably be people whom we trust as authoritative voices about this thing or practice called "psychoanalysis." But this is the place where Winnicott is very useful, because Winnicott's preoccupation, it seems to me, is not so much with the given thing but with what one can make of it ... not prioritizing the value of the analyst's interpretation so much as the use the patient can make of it. By the same token, I think the risk of an authoritative statement becoming authoritarian occurs when it's unuseable, when people can't make something of their own of it, when they can't use it to dream something up. What we're really talking about, then, is the way people use and transmit so-called knowledge, or so-called information, or so-called technique. Both what their words invite, and what, by way of response, they can enjoy.

Later in the book, you seem to speak to this same phenomenon when you write: "Psychoanalysts run the risk of believing there is a King's English of the psyche and everybody is, or should be, speaking it." Is it accurate to suggest that there is something akin to a totalitarian impulse that much of our profession is all-too-ready to accommodate?

I wouldn't want to put it that extremely, but I think that the anxiety, the self-doubt and the uncertainty that's integral to what we're doing prompts people to extreme solutions. It's not surprising that in something as uncertain as psychoanalysis, people are drawn to conversion experiences or to forms of idolatry, because there is a lot of anxiety in this game. To call it *totalitarian*, however, ups the stakes too much, and the risk is that if we start speaking like that we start creating unnecessary antagonisms. I think that what we need to do in psychoanalysis is to see the points in theory, or the points in its institutionalization, at which people become authoritarian, or become something that makes us think of them as totalitarian. We need to see what it is at that moment that makes people feel the need to be absolutely convinced of something, or to have other people agree with them in some absolute sense ... because in a way you could see the apparently totalitarian moments as the most interesting ones. They're the moments when there really is something profound and powerful and conflictual going on, that create a preemptive strike called an authoritative statement.

You ask in your preface to Terrors and Experts: *"If the unconscious is that which does not fit in, why has it been so difficult to sustain non-compliant versions of psychoanalysis?" For me, this begs a prior question: what are the forces that have exacted compliance? Compliance with what? And why has it been so difficult for alternative versions and visions to take root?*

I really feel inadequate to answer these questions, because I haven't got an overriding view of the matter. If we take the situation in Britain, which I know at least a little about, you will find a lot of prejudice about Kleinian psychoanalysts and Kleinian psychoanalysis. It seems to me that one of the things the Kleinians represent – insofar as there could be such a monolithic group – is the tyrannical parents. There is a sense in which compliance starts at home, if you like ... and I think what there is to comply with has to do with the fear of what will happen if we don't comply. That is to say, there are fears of catastrophe here, imaginings of some kind of catastrophic primal scene. The scenario is one in which, if I don't comply with somebody I need, I lose the relationship with them. So, at some fundamental level, if I want to become a psychoanalyst, I have to abide to some extent by the rules of the game, otherwise I don't know whether I'm a psychoanalyst or not. This poses an inevitable conflict, as the question becomes: at what point is something an innovation? Or at what point is it a change of the game? What do you have to do to stop being called a psychoanalyst, by the owners of psychoanalysis?

I think it's perfectly fair enough that psychoanalytic trainings should set out their game. That is to say, if you want to call yourself a psychoanalyst trained by our institution, then these are the things you have to abide by and believe in. The question then becomes how people deal with dissent. I don't want a situation in which dissent is dealt with in some absolute, dismissive way. But I do think it's inevitable for parameters to exist. Beyond a certain point you are no longer playing our game. It's suddenly turned from draughts to chess, but then you have to go somewhere else to play it. Ultimately, I think there's a lot of bellyaching and spurious rebellion that goes on in relation to psychoanalytic institutes, where adults are simply contracting into a specific game with specific parameters. At that point at which the game becomes unacceptable, one should go and do something else.

Now it's not all that simple of course, because not only are there strong emotionally empowered beliefs and convictions about authority, or what it means to live a good life, and so on. There's also a very powerful economic factor. That is to say, if I want to practice as a psychoanalyst, I have to get this qualification. In this light people have to develop what we might politely call compromises, and what less politely we might call false selves. I think in order to do a psychoanalytic training, you have to have a repertoire of false-self solutions available to you.

Your comments lead nicely to my next question. You conclude your preface to Terrors and Experts *with the following words: "The psychoanalyst and her so-called patient share a project. The psychoanalyst, that is to say, must ask herself not, 'Am I being a good analyst?'... but, 'What kind of person do I want to be?'" Is this project, then, concerned as much with ethics as with desire – which you yourself define as "morally equivocal"? And how does the analyst's own answer to the question consequentially involve her patient in what you call a shared project?*

I think that desire is inextricable from questions of ethics. In a way, it is the ethical imagination that constructs the notion of desire ... that we can't separate what we want from people from our obligations to them. The very word *desire* has become a bit of a free-floating counter, since morality only seems to make sense if we have, as it were, a counterforce to it, something amoral, or that undermines our ethical positions. But this is only if we think of ethics as a monument, rather than as an ongoing process, in which we are continually coming to localized accommodations – within all our relationships – about what we want to do together and what we want to be for each other. I think it's both the worst kind of psychoanalytic theory that glamorizes a certain kind of ruthless unconcern, and the best kind of psychoanalysis. We're never going to be able to avoid, nor should we be trying to, the question of what kind of people we want to be. Our ideas about desire are integral or subsumed by that question. For example, you might say a lot of modern people ... the kind who might read a book such as this one ... will want to think of themselves as having or being involved in something they call desire. I think it's a very exciting, exhilarating notion. But it's not some kind of deep truth about the human condition: it's an historically and culturally located "regulative fiction."

In contrast to the inherited, and still dominant figure, of an Enlightenment Freud committed to a project of self-mastery through knowledge, you play in Terrors and Experts *with the idea of a "post-Freudian Freud" intent on questioning "the very idea of the self as an object of knowledge." In your words: "The post-Freudian Freud suggests that the project of self-knowledge is itself the problem, the symptom masquerading as the cure ... (P)sychoanalysis can now help us unlearn this modern religion of selfhood." What is it that now enables psychoanalysis, and her patients, to forsake an idolatry of the self – especially within a culture that is ideologically invested in supporting that idolatry?*

Concerning the possibility that we might want to undo the idea of the self, I prefer to put the question pragmatically. What do we use the idea of a self to do? For example, we need a self to vote with, but selves are not always useful in love affairs or in writing. It seems to me that a lot of descriptions and formulations about pathology have to do with the creation of certain kinds of reified internal monuments. It is as though people become addicted to a version of themselves. They begin to have convictions that they are a certain kind of person. That's what a symptom is. I mean, if I'm agoraphobic, I'm the sort of person who can't go out. This is, so to speak, a *truth* about me – until I can see it as merely an aspect of who I am. For those of us daunted nowadays by all the people existing in a state of fanatical conviction about one thing or another, it might be quite important to think up or dream up alternative ways of being, alternative versions to fundamentalism, whether psychoanalytic or religious. It might be quite important to produce a counter-culture that questions states of conviction, and explores what we're using states of conviction to do, why we might want to be convinced of things, and what it is that we find in states of certainty. One thing you might say is that there is, potentially, a form of megalomania in such states. At best, of course, there's also a form of political commitment. This is to say, then, that to question states of conviction does not necessarily presume an absence of belief. The issue, rather, involves finding a way of believing that is not a form of domination, primarily of oneself. Belief is a form of cruelty.

The critique you put forth seems to share much with the Buddhist contention that it is the very dualistic structure of human knowledge that, in making the self into an object, institutes an essential aliena-tion – or what we might call "the symptom." In this regard, has Buddhism informed your thinking at all?

I'm very interested in Buddhism, but I think of myself as a tourist in relation to it. What little I know of Buddhism inevita-bly comes out of a very specific set of historical and cultural contexts. When I'm reading Buddhist texts, I feel myself to be reading at least at one remove. In a way, the reading is part of a project of finding other ways of thinking about the things that preoccupy me ...

I do feel that there's a sense in which you can only under-stand a body of ideas when they aren't a body of ideas for you, but are simply a form of life, the way one lives. So I have to preface this by saying that I really feel very much of an outsider here. I don't want to appropriate Buddhist ideas to what I do, but they can't help but interest me because of my preoccupations. For instance, I find very interesting descrip-tions in Buddhism of states of addiction: addiction not only to certain versions of oneself, but to the very idea that there is a self or selves to be addicted to. That is to say, there's a capacity for imaginative self-idolization. I like the absurd idea of a Buddhism that isn't about escaping from desire: conse-quently, I can't possibly believe in anything that anybody's calling Buddhism. I do think, though, that the questions Buddhists ask about one's relationship to desire can't help but be interesting. Lacan's point that man's project is to escape from his desire is integral to this picture, as is Jones' concept of aphinisis – about the fear or death of desire. In other words, we're organizing ourselves around a relationship that feels extremely difficult to manage – personally, ethically, and politically. I would prefer to produce, as it were, better stories about that relationship than those that are either concerned with eluding desire, or that wholeheartedly celebrate and romanticize it. To this end, what I find intriguing is the Buddhist preoccupation with the states of mind consequent upon the abrogation of desire. What it would be like, for instance, to not be preoccupied by desire? What would we be thinking about? What does desire fill the space of? These seem to me to be very, very interesting questions.

What has been the price, in your view, of the inherited Enlightenment model of the psychoanalyst as scientist? At what cost have other models also present in Freudian theory – you yourself list the lover, the comedian, and the mystic – been repressed, and how can they be recovered, not only theoretically, but in the practice of psychoanalysis?

I'm not anti-science. What I am "anti" is the idea that there is one dominant criterion of value which is, broadly speaking, scientific. I think science is for people who love science, and they should do it. The risk is that it does tend to occlude or make the other possible criteria look rather trivial or silly. I think it's very interesting how little mysticism there is in contemporary scientific theory, as well as in psychoanalytic theory. I think psychoanalysis is, in a way, intrinsically mystical or bordering on what would once have been called mystical experience. That's why Michael Eigen's work is very important to me. Bion's work is less important but of interest. Lacan is obviously interesting as is Winnicott, again in a different sense. But I would much prefer a world of lovers, comedians and mystics to a world of scientists who find such people beside the point.

... My sense of the pleasures of science is that they are too much about the pleasure of consensus, and I suppose I'm more interested in the possibility of shareable private languages – which is obviously a contradiction in terms. I'm more interested in the possibilities of pleasure: of sensual and erotic pleasures. It seems to me that what the comedian and the lover and the mystic all keep very close to is a notion of the erotic. I don't really know what that word means, but it conjures for me something that's to do with a certain kind of ease. It's not conflict-free, but is somehow akin to a joke... a joke is the easiest pleasure in the world ... getting a joke, for me, would be the model of a good interpretation ...

What interests me about mysticism is that it is unavoidably preoccupied with certain kinds of intensity. That is to say, the project in mysticism is not to escape from or to cure the intensity; minimally, the project is to acknowledge that intensity, but it also involves finding representations for it and of it, to bring those intensities into the shared world. That, for me, is obviously something wonderful ... We can't help but be lovers in the broadest possible sense. But I would want erotic love to be our model of what it is to love things and people. I think the cliches about science, about its detachment, its domination and capacity for exploitation, are really very frightening: partly because they're true, partly because my guess is that they stop us from looking at the actual erotic components of scientific inquiry. And of course this is where Freud is quite interesting. When Freud talks about infantile curiosity, that's where we are as scientists. I would like scientists to give us accounts of the infantile nature of their curiosity and enjoyments, rather than to be producing apparently superordinate or transcendent accounts of the way the world is. I'm not at all interested in the way the world is. I'm very, very interested in what people make of the world. Psychoanalysis, unlike science and religion, does not offer us something to merely submit to.

What do you see, then, as the pleasures or erotics that science brings to psychoanalysis? Or why does psychoanalysis remain so captivated by the erotic lure of the scientific paradigm?

I think fantasies of prestige are erotically exciting. If one lives in a culture that is dominated by scientific prestige, where science defines what real knowledge is, and where scientists are the people who possess that knowledge, you can see the implications. But if we were to drop the idea of wanting to know the way the world is, we wouldn't be that interested in scientists. Personally, I'm more interested in local knowledge. It's much more interesting for me to know how to get to work in the morning than it is to know whether the sun goes around the earth or not. For example, I think that space travel is almost totally uninteresting. Sure, I enjoy the pictures of what it's like up there. It's absolutely astonishing that there are universes as big as ours, and that it's all infinite. But this, for me, is of the order of day-dream. It's like knowledge about evolution – very interesting, but about which we can do nothing. We're just going to evolve. Knowing about evolution, in a sense, is rather gratifying, because it shows us something absurd about knowing things ... because whether you know about evolution or not you are going to evolve. You can't start evolving differently. I also think we underestimate how much we take on trust. That is to say, there's a very interesting and widespread election of scientists as people who know things. And yet we're clearly not the ones going over their experiments. Most of us couldn't possibly do so. But there is a very powerful idealization of people whose knowledge we couldn't possibly possess, or of whose knowledge we couldn't possibly trace the process. They're like magical parents. We can't possibly imagine what it would be like to know what they know, or to get to what they've gotten to. I think that's very exciting.

On the matter of the lover, the comedian, and the mystic: the psychoanalyst's recovery of these models, or genres, *as you call them, would similarly necessitate a critique of the* expertise *to which a scientific psychoanalysis aspires. In your words: ...(A)ny form of expertise is going to recreate that crisis of authority and language that is at the heart of both infancy and the acquisition of language ... The act of knowing – as opposed, say, to be absorbed in someone or something – is itself more of a problem than what there is to know." It would seem that analysts have been traditionally more comfortable colluding with patients' attributions of omniscience than becoming absorbed by the experience of a patient ...*

I think that to be preoccupied, to be involved in a knowledge project, is to be involved in an omniscience project. I also think that one of the striking things about being in a good conversation is that you forget you're having the conversation. The conversation has a life of its own. It's like time when you lie in a hot bath. It kind of disappears. The project of knowing another person is of a different order, and is inevitably a distancing one, with its own agenda. Clearly, to be lost in thought with somebody, or lost in conversation, to be in a sense absorbed in what you're talking about together, seems to me a more engaging project, which also sets a rather different agenda. You can work out what it was all about later, or maybe never, but there is something mutative or generative, or just in itself moving, about being absorbed in a conversation with somebody. I think that's a good way of spending one's time. I also think it's something you cannot simulate or produce through technique. No amount of refinement of psychoanalytic technique is going to create a good conversation. Conversations between people are really about chemistry between people. You can call it unconscious communication, you can call it lots of things, but sometimes something happens between people that suddenly preoccupies them together. It's as though they're lost in thought together, but it's called a conversation. Those for me are the moments when something happens. Of course you need the other moments too, and there's always a lot of awkwardness between people, and a lot of uncertainty and wariness. But every so often there are spots of absorption. Spots of self-forgetting, mutual self-forgetting. That seem to me to be a good way of being with people.

Is the conversation then, as you describe it, the ideal of what you would call a psychoanalysis?

Yes, it is. Psychoanalysis for me would be an ongoing conversation that is of interest to both parties, who don't know why they like it, but know they want to go on doing it.

On the matter of science: given the entwined histories of psychoanalysis and its founder, the persistence of the Enlightenment Freud, and the invaluable contributions of studies in infant and child development, what do you see as the role of science in the configuration of a psychoanalysis amenable to the "post-Freudian" Freud?

I really think it's important for people to follow their curiosity. Some people, for all sorts of reasons, most of which they're not going to know about, will find scientific inquiry fascinating, and it will be preoccupying for them. It will engage them on some very deep level. Those are the people who should do science, and they should be part of a multiple conversation about what's going on in the culture at large. I want and like scientific stories when I can understand them, when they feed into the kind of conversation that I imagine for a culture. I don't at all envision a demise of science, nor would I want people to stop doing science. To the contrary. I would want people who love science to do it, and to feed their findings back into a public discourse. But I also would like people to feel free not to be impressed by it, or to submit so readily to it.

To be more specific, can science coexist with, and contribute to, a psychoanalysis no longer invested in the exaltation of knowledge?

Where traditional notions of cure are similarly called into question?

I think so, because some of the most interesting theorizing is being done in the philosophy of science. One of the things that science brings in its wake is questions about its own project, so that it inevitably raises all sorts of issues about what we do when we're knowing, how we go about knowing, and what it is that knowledge is in the service of. When you read Roy Porter, or John Forrester, or Steven Shapin, science seems irresistibly intriguing. This, I think, is one of the values of science, which leads me to believe that those people who know about this form of knowing might be very good at telling us about the process itself and the motivations for engaging it. For this reason I wish there were more autobiographies by scientists, or even biographies of scientists. I am not of the opinion, however, that we should start believing that infant observation is going to tell us about what people are really like. While some accounts are really lyrical and interesting and evocative, most of them, I think, are fantastically banal and boring. But of course, these are prejudicial tastes, and clearly there are lots of people who are ready to swear by it all.

The issue of science and the kind of knowledge it fosters would seem to bear directly on the question of consensus. As you put it: "... It is the Enlightenment Freud that always pushes for consensus, that is willing a community of more or less shared knowledge ... The psychoanalyst is an expert on the ways in which the patient pretends to be an expert on himself; the ways, that is, in which he gravitates towards consensus, towards fitting in ..." It's a short leap, it would seem, from consensus to what I call "normalization." Would you agree?

Yes. In a way the purpose of consensus must be to create fantasies of normality. The use of fantasies, or standards, of normality is that it enables us to see difference. At its most coercive, it enables us to see deviation. I think we have to be very careful about what we're using our norms to do. That is to say, if they're coercive, if they demand our agreement, they seem to me to be dangerous. If they function as possible guidelines, then they can be useful.

We should be enabling people to tolerate disagreement. There's a terrific idealization of agreement, which I see as an idealization of togetherness and symbiosis. Instead, to tolerate difference means, potentially, tolerating other people's envy. One of the things consensus tries to do is create a group of people who, by

agreeing with each other, need not be envious of or competitive
with each other. I don't think that's a bad aim at all, but I do think
it's never going to be the whole story ... There is a pressure on
people to abide by the cultural consensus, because we all inevitably want to be part of the culture. Any cultural group is going to
somehow be based on trust, or on fantasies of shared knowledge.
It's not that I think there shouldn't be such fantasies; indeed, these
are essential to any group. What's crucial, however, is the kind of
difference a group allows, and what its relationship is to the people
who speak that difference ...

Clearly, on one end of the spectrum, you've got scapegoating. Personally, I'd like to live in a world without scapegoats,
but a world without scapegoats means a world with more conflict. We'd have to assume that eventuality, because we will get
crosser with each other if we stop scapegoating people. Still, I
think there are a lot of pleasures in conflict. It's underrated.
One of the things we might be doing, then, is to enable
people to tolerate fear.

*Similarly, do you see political implications deriving from the
particular way in which the analyst deploys her expertise: i.e.,
whether she does so in an enlightenment or post-Freudian scheme of
things?*

Yes, I think the risk is that if the analyst needs to be believed or
agreed with, the analysis recreates a certain kind of childhood
trauma, of a relationship in which if you don't comply or agree
then you're abandoned or rejected or punished. That, to me,
seems a bad sadomasochistic model of a relationship. But, there
is, of course, a problem here that psychoanalysis makes very
vivid: if there are such things as resistances, and it seems to me
that there are, then the analyst doesn't merely capitulate when
the patient disagrees. That is to say, the analyst has to be tena-
cious without being authoritarian. And there might have to come
a point, at times, where you as the analyst say, "We disagree
about this. I think this is what it means." Or, "I think it's about
you and you think differently. I don't need you, however, to
agree with me." The analysis then continues despite the disagreement, but we do need to put the difference on the table,
without having to decide now, or necessarily ever, which one of
us is right. In fact, the question of right and wrong is exactly the
problem. What we have to see is who can produce a story, or a
version, that we can make something of that we want.

Throughout Terrors and Experts, *one of your strategies is to engage the reader with a series of questions which, without being rhetorical, may very plausibly remain unanswered as they point to the inherent ambiguity of the analyst's predicament. And yet they provoke a kind of mental fuzziness, or vertigo, which prompts me to want to reflect them playfully back to you. With your permission, then, I'll be interspersing the rest of the interview with an occasional question of yours, taken directly from the book. For starters ...*

Could I just say something about that? Obviously, one can't help but write the way that one writes. I'm not interested in having theories. I'm interested in making sentences. Even if I could organize the experience, I wouldn't want people to come away from my books knowing my theory of worrying or boredom. I'd want them to come away as if they were humming a tune. That is to say, that something, for whatever reason, stuck with them ... perhaps a sentence, or a thought. I think of my essays as pools that you fish in. None of it may work for you. You might think the whole thing is pretentious, or dull, or you might think a whole series of things. But you may find a sentence or a few sentences that resonate and stay with you. That's what I'm after. I'm not after having lines on things ...

Is it OK to toss a few questions back your way ... after having fished them out?

Sure.

For starters, then: "If, as Freud, suggests, to 'have' an unconscious is to be, or make oneself, radically odd to oneself – to be always in and out of character – what is the analyst supposed to be doing to (or for) her patients? To make them more knowing, or enable them to tolerate, or take pleasure from, their clouds of unknowing?..." What is an analyst to do?!

I think the not entirely glib answer is both. On the one hand, one of the things the analyst does is to show patients the ways in which they think they know themselves, what they use that knowledge to do, and what it's used to protect themselves from. On the other hand, inevitably, a story, or a whole set and repertoire of stories about the past, gets produced: stories about how a patient has come to be who we, at this moment, think they are or might be. We're also going to be showing our patients how they construct certain stories in order to make certain futures possible ... how making a story is to produce a relationship to time, to future selves. I think what's really being shown is that: (a) things are always much more muddled than they appear; (b) the repertoire of possibilities is always more extensive than we believe; and (c) we often don't know the grounds of our inclinations, or tropisms, or whatever it is* we call them. We are making choices that we are inclined, by something, to make.

In "Authorities," the opening chapter of Terrors and Experts, *you claim that "psychoanalysis as a profession has always been resolutely committed to the mainstream" – distancing itself from "discredited things like religion, glamor, mysticism, radical politics and the paranormal ..." What, if anything, is changing from within psychoanalysis to make room for what has traditionally been marginalized?*

I find it very difficult to talk about psychoanalysis, partly because I don't mix at all in psychoanalytic circles. I have very few friends who do the job. I can only assume that there are generational things going on now, what with the gradual dying out of the second and, to some extent, the third generation of analysts. There is now an inevitable acknowledgement that psychoanalysis goes on in a world, that the attempt to freeze time or to live in Vienna in 1910 has stopped, that inevitably things move on, that as certain cultures become in a sense more fundamentalist, certain others become more pluralist. And I also think – or perhaps this is a wish – that younger people who have grown up in different political, economic, intellectual environments are going to have less time for, and be less impressed by, people telling them what psychoanalysis is, or claiming to own psychoanalysis, or assuming that they are in a position to legitimate whom or what is a psychoanalyst. What we're seeing, then, is an inevitable return of the repressed, as everything that was pushed out now comes back. As Freud said to Jung, everything you deny returns from outside ... All analysts should be trying to find something better than psychoanalysis, something more suited to their particular tastes.

There's a diversity around that cannot help but infiltrate the profession, as all sorts of people are gradually going to be interested in psychoanalysis who don't want to be psychoanalysts.

That's where the new life is going to come from. The people who want to be psychoanalysts are already up to their neck in it. Paradoxically, I think the people who can see there's something useful in psychoanalysis, but who otherwise want to do other things, are the people from whom psychoanalysts might benefit the most. Inevitably, when psychoanalysts mix with each other, they end up doing the same thing... they either totally disagree with each other, or they altogether agree... and it doesn't matter which they do, since the end result is the same. That is to say, they're basically keeping alive a certain consensus ...

Along these lines, I also think people get bored with ideas. I mean, ideas have a shelf life, just like relationships. You can't go on and on and on saying to yourself, "where id was there ego should be." It just isn't interesting beyond a certain point. Habits of reading, habits of interpretation, change ... A life devoted to reaching the depressive position, or experiencing mature love, can't be endlessly crippling.

On the matter of "authorities," it seems to me that one of the reasons for such discreditation is the reverence that the "Holy books" of theory inspire in psychoanalysts. This is a concern you take up in a later chapter called "Symptoms."

I think psychoanalytic training should be not only teaching people psychoanalysis, they should be teaching people how to read ...

But if our books proscribe something – that is, if they can't systematically account for a phenomenon – marginalization is sure to follow. What do you make of the "religious attitude" and, for that matter, of the generally conservative "nature" of so many psychoanalysts?

I think we should start from a position that theory has nothing to do with practice, and work backwards. I think people should be reading the psychoanalytic theories they're drawn to for whatever reason and be doing psychoanalysis. I'm not worried too much about the connections between theory and practice. The risk is that in a scientific–technological culture, psychoanalytic theory becomes a kind of how-to book. I think this is a very misleading way to read psychoanalysis ... any more than you read novels or poems to tell you how to live or what to do tomorrow. You read novels and poems and you live your life, and of course there's an interdependence, but you don't know what it is. It's not programmed or scheduled. It's completely unpredictable. So I really believe that in psychoanalytic trainings people should only read the psychoanalytic theory they like. I think people should follow their inclinations and read theory like they might read novels or newspapers, and see where they go with it, without worrying particularly about how they're going to use it. The risk, you see, is that psychoanalytic theory becomes simply a question of direct use value. In other words, a psychoanalytic training should be not only teaching people theory, it should be showing people what they might be using theory to do, and noting the ways in which people are inclined to use theories. Students should think of themselves as pragmatists and dream-workers.

How is it, then, that advocates of "free-floating attention" can, through the lenses of their theories, be so selectively perceptive about what they hear from their patients?

I think we can only be selectively attentive, but I do think it's important that we notice that this is what we're doing. I find it astonishing that there should be this story called "psychoanalysis" that puts something called "free association" right in the middle of its picture as a form of truth-telling, only to kill it dead as soon as possible in order to produce theories. The problem, of course, is that there is nothing more boring than a book of free associations. That is to say, free association in and of itself is not necessarily artful enough to be a good form of transmission. There's an uneasy relationship, or let's say a relationship that hasn't yet been worked out, between listening to and valuing free association in clinical work and the writing or the speaking of theory. I think that theory should be more artful than most free association is. It should be a reworking, a working over, of free association. When theory gets too far from free association, it becomes stultifying. When it gets too close, it then becomes incomprehensible, or just too irritating, because it is only really in the psychoanalytic setting that we agree to be interested in free association. We agree to be interested in dreams, we agree to be interested in people's masturbation fantasies. Outside of the setting these can be the dreariest things on earth, and this has to be acknowledged. That's the point of what analysis is doing. It's setting a place apart where we can give such matters a different kind of significance.

Several times in your book, you point to the "defensive functions" of different aspects of the psychoanalytic enterprise. What is it that psychoanalysts so desperately need to defend – or defend against? To refer to the book's title, what are our terrors?

I really don't think it's viable to generalize about psychoanalysts, but I do think that psychoanalysts should be interested in such questions. That's really the point that I'm making: not that we can be anything other than defensive, but that we might be interested in what our own defenses are for. That is to say, we might really be more interested in our fantasies of catastrophe, and we might be more wary of our inclination to idolize and fixate and idealize. All psychoanalysts are different, but some are more different than others.

I loved your chapter on Freud and Ferenczi, by the way. One of the dynamics you explore, through a revisitation of the Freud–Ferenczi correspondence, is the role of Freud as Master and Father to the first generation of psychoanalysts. Noting, for instance, the fates suffered by Jung and Ferenczi, you write: "When it came to radically dissenting views, and unusual ways of living, the (original) psychoanalytic group – not for the last time – showed itself to be expert at character assassination. The unconscious was not allowed to be counter-culture. It had to be assimilated." It's as if, on one level at least, Freud was more identified with Laius than Oedipus ...

I think one of the interesting things about Freud was that he was capable of sustaining such split identifications. I think he was capable of identifying with both. I like a lot who I imagine Freud was. I find him very appealing, often very moving; and there are also aspects of him that I imagine I don't like ... I don't think it's entirely surprising that he was worried about the way in which what he had described was going beyond him. He was discovering something very obvious but no less traumatic: that when one goes into the world, or when one writes something and puts it into the world, it is subject to an uncontrollable multiplicity of interpretations. This is what otherness is. There are other people in the world. You write books. People get all sorts of things out of them. It's very, very strange. They don't even pick out the bits you think are good. That's what other people are. That's the point.

So Freud goes on to produce a body of theory that is astonishing in its capacity to make people want to interpret it, to invite people to use it in many diverse ways, and I can see why he might have felt protective of it. I can see why he might have wanted to try to circumscribe the interpretations available. I can see, as he was clearly a man with a great deal of moral integrity and prejudice – two things one can't always tell apart – that he wanted to make sure that his theory reflected what he took to be the best available version of himself. I don't think we should be dismayed about this, nor do I think this is grounds for outrage. And I similarly don't think we have to idolize Freud. I think we can admire him. I certainly admire him a great deal. Like Wordsworth or Wallace Stevens or William James, reading Freud changed my life. I'm so pleased to have lived a life in which I could read books by Freud. It seems to me astonishing. But, as ever, the very reading of Freud poses, at one and the same time, a kind of Winnicottian as well as a pragmatic question: what are we using Freud to do? We can use him to stop ourselves thinking. Or we can use him to have all sorts of thoughts, and in this sense, I really do believe that the Freudian thing is not remotely over. In fact, it's just beginning. I think it's just beginning to dawn on people what they might be capable of thinking, as a consequence of noticing Freud.

In this context, you go on to explore Freud's dismissal, or indeed suppression, of Ferenczi's fascination with the occult, and his dismissal of telepathic phenomena as nothing more than "thought transference." In a more virulent polemic, Freud demanded similar allegiance of Jung with regards to the unassailable authority of his theory of sexuality, which he actually referred to – if I'm not mistaken – as dogma. *How has this authoritarian strain of Freud's own personality influenced the one-hundred-year history of psychoanalysis?*

One of the things about psychoanalysis is that it gives us a story about what people are doing when they virulently hate something. So Freud, of course, like all of us, hated the things that you described. But he also gave us a story about what we might be doing with such hatred. In other words, why certain things might evoke such hatred in us. To say Freud is dogmatic might be saying no more than that Freud was a person. There were certain areas or moments or ideas or tones of voice that aroused him to a state of conviction that was domineering and inevitably aggressive. In other words, he was a passionate man ...

I think there's a sense in which people are as powerful as we let them be. People who want dogma can find in Freud their dogmatist and repudiate him. I don't think those are the most interesting things about Freud, but I think the places where he begins to get dogmatic are the places where there's new growth, where there are new things around. Perhaps I should add, however, that I don't think psychoanalysis is simply a process of filling in the gaps in Freud's sensibility.

If this is in fact the case – and my assumption may be mistaken here – how did the dogmatic strain of his personality come to be privileged, if you think of the allegiances he still inspires? If, in fact, the legacy of the Freudian canon is such that it also readily evidences Freud's own contradictions, hesitations, and disavowals of certainty?

I think it's not at all strange that we want heroes and heroines. I certainly want people to admire, and to be admired myself. What I don't want is people who require unconditional admiration of me, or whom I have to admire in an uncomplicated way. Another of the very useful Freudian insights is the power and pervasiveness of ambivalence, that we know that when we're idealizing somebody, something else is up. Not that we don't value these people a great deal, but something else is also going on. I don't think Freud made psychoanalysis anything any more than Lacan has made Lacanianism anything in and of itself. I do think that one can have a more or less sadomasochistic relationship with one's admirers, with one's audience or followers. But I still think that the onus is on the followers to sort that out. I don't think we should look to Freud as the omnipotent parent who would give us not only his present but our future. Instead, we should be thinking about what we're wanting to make of that legacy. I think the onus is on us, not on Freud or Lacan, to produce different versions of the theory.

You close the chapter on Ferenczi extolling his life and writings as examples of "something too rare in psychoanalysis: the fluency of disorder, the inspirations of error ..." "Ferenczi," you continue, "exposed the defensive function of professionalism in psychoanalysis, and, by implication, the posturings of any professional identity unable to acknowledge (or enjoy) what it is organized to exclude." It's as if Ferenczi unmasks the element of paranoia, the posturings, that Freud establishes in his treatise on group psychology. In light of this premise, can a highly technocratic and bureaucratized society such as ours make room for, and not seek to police, the vagaries of disorder and error?

These are very difficult questions to think of, because it's not always clear what we're talking about when we talk about order, or what these fantasies are of things being in place or fitting together. It seems to me that psychoanalytic theoreticians oscillate between idealizing what they think of as order and idealizing what they think of as disorder. Basically there is a kind of lurking chaos theory at one end of the spectrum, and there's a lurking kind of bureaucratization at the other end of the spectrum. I think the important thing to remember is that these are fantasies, that they're mostly unconscious stories about and pictures of what might be going on inside us. So when analysts or other people talk about fear of chaos or fear of confusion, I think we should ask, along with Wittgenstein: "What's the picture here? How do we see that which we imagine is going on?" It is in this sense that representations are always *outside*. There's a sense in which we're producing pictures and metaphors and analogies of what we think of as internal space. All these pictures have consequences attached to them. In speaking more directly to your question, I was very surprised during my training to see how pompous and self-important many of the people who claimed to be teaching me were. Although nowadays my dealings with psychoanalysts are minimal, I think there is the promotion of a certain official version of the psychoanalytic personality that is sufficiently composed, sufficiently wise and, as a consequence, often rather unfriendly. I would want to get back to basics about how friendly people are prepared to be professionally, and with the links they allow themselves to see between their so-called private and professional lives. I mean, if one believes there's an unconscious, then there is no such thing as a professional life; there are just different representations, as it were, inside or between one's selves. I would like there to be less of a gap ... albeit with an inevitable difference ... between what we psychoanalysts are like with our friends and lovers and how we are with our patients. The psychoanalysis I value is done in an atmosphere that is closer to friendship than to a doctor–patient relationship. Friendship, rather than anything medical, would be my model ...

I also think that psychoanalysis can perform a useful function in offering alternative versions of professional selves. In cultures which are overprofessionalizing themselves, that idealize a certain kind of bureaucratic competence, the analyst is somebody who might speak up for another way of being. A way, for instance, of being a responsible civic person, but not some buffoonish caricature of a bank manager ...

You've anticipated my next question. On the idea of identities: since identities are established and maintained through processes of differentiation and exclusion that are often antagonistic, is there another way to conceive of and look at identity formation?

Again, I think these things are terribly difficult to speak about, because it's very difficult not to have a picture of an inside and an outside. It's very difficult not to think that life is about including certain things and people and feelings and thoughts and excluding others. One of the good projects now would be to work out a way of thinking about what a person is, without needing the idea of exclusion ... that is to say, without our ideas about the self being informed by notions of purity. All versions of the self that I can see are versions of not getting one's hands dirty, not being in free association with other people or with certain parts of oneself ... The risk is that we're too clean, that our ideas of selfhood are forms or ways we exempt ourselves from circulation. Another way of saying this would be the notion that we are essentially political animals, that we only live and thrive and have the idea of selves in a group ... It's interesting to imagine a democratic culture where there was no idea of a self, or where we were not trying to have identities. We might be, as it were, trying to participate in a communal good life that didn't require us having something to think of as an identity. So, I would like good descriptions of people not preoccupied by having identities, but who still have passions, moods, thoughts, feelings, whims ... without prioritizing the extremes of this imaginative spectrum ... For example, I think we should value whims as much as we do passions or hints, or as much as we do orders. We shouldn't be too impressed by what are fundamentally militaristic ideals of character.

In preparing for these interviews, I'm inevitably involved in an imaginative conversation with my interlocutors. To help illustrate the process, I'd like to relate an anecdote, and some associations of my own. When you say, in the chapter on Ferenczi, that the uncon-

scious was not allowed to be counter-culture, but had to be assimi-
lated, I think of Dostoevsky's parable of the Grand Inquisitor, and
of recent developments in the psychoanalytic politics of a country
like Italy. I'd like to cite this as a concrete example of what happens
when the totalitarian impulse is indulged.

In recent years, legislation was passed there requiring any and
all practicing psychotherapists – including psychoanalysts – to be
nationally licensed as psychologists: that is, to hold a university
degree in either psychology or medicine. What's astounding is that,
in exchange for group licensure under a "grandfathering" clause
(since few if any analysts held degrees in psychology – a discipline
only recently incorporated into academia – and not many more
were medical doctors), the entire psychoanalytic establishment has
agreed to accept for training only those candidates with degrees in
psychology or medicine. What makes this all the more startling is
that the law itself makes no specific reference to the practice of
psychoanalysis! In one fell swoop, the entire history of "the ques-
tion" of lay analysis, expressive of a different strain of Freud's
personality, was obliterated, with the knowing complicity of every
psychoanaltic group in the country. Can the kind of psychoanaly-
sis you advocate even hope to take root in climates where the
dominant impulse is to regulate, and where selling one's soul to
the devil is seen as the hallmark of a kind of "professionalism"
meant to protect the "consumer"?

Well, obviously that's a very dismaying story. But then I think
we can't yet imagine a group that doesn't organize itself
around exclusion. I think the onus is on the people who are
appalled by such a state of affairs to make other arrangements, which might need, in the extreme, to be against the
law – although not necessarily as the first solution. People
might need to find ways of lobbying to change the rules, or
they might need to simply change the game. You see, for
example, I would prefer in many ways to be called a conversa-
tionist rather than a psychoanalyst. It's silly, which is why I
don't do it. But I think the risk is that the name or the word
psychoanalyst becomes honorific. I don't think there's any big
deal about the word, frankly. I think it's given a certain aura
by stories like the one you've just told, for example. Stories
like that reinforce the aura of the name. I think it's possible
for us to call ourselves other kinds of things. I think it's possible to involve ourselves in all sorts of practices that we
might think of as psychoanalytic and other people won't.

That's fine. I think that any group that wants to legitimate itself in that way would be unacceptable to me and would, in a sense, by that very act delegitimate itself. But the onus, in any case, is on those people who are appalled by certain situations to say as much, as publicly and eloquently as they possibly can. I would want this to be done by democratic process, whereby people work to persuade other people why and how it is that certain versions that make a mockery of psychoanalysis are absolutely unacceptable.

I have one question – one of many, actually – that I'd like to ask concerning the literary aspect of your writing. I find there is a seductive, almost bewitching elegance to your essays: a quality nourished, in a way, by the lightning-quick resonances of the aphoristic markings interspersed throughout them. I wonder if there is a certain tension that gets played out in this way, precisely between your own Enlightenment and post-Freudian Freuds. More specifically: while the concessions to the pleasures of writing, to its aesthetics and erotics, are everywhere evident, there is also a quality of definitive "pronouncement," a knowledgeable *quality, if you will, that inheres in a more subtle way. For example, to state as you do that "knowing becomes rather literally the process of jumping to conclusions" involves inevitably a claim to knowing as much ... Is this a fair and accurate assessment of your work? Can you comment on this tension from your own perspective?*

Yes it is. I think that there is a sort of internal conversation, if you like, between something free-wheeling and something more formulaic. The trouble is, of course – even though it's cute to say so – that it really is true that one doesn't know what one's doing, and that this is the way I write. On the one hand, I'm the ventriloquist's dummy of the culture; on the other hand, no one has ever written these sentences. This is also the way I love to write, as it happens; this is the way these sentences turn up on the page. You see, I don't think about psychoanalysis consciously very much. I don't talk about it to people very much. I never go to meetings. But when I sit down to write, it's as though I've been thinking about psychoanalysis all the time. I mean, there's plenty to say and I'm always surprised by my preoccupation with it. I think there are inevitably influences at work here, although of course they're memories, as influences always are. You could probably find most of what I think about psychoanalysis in *Paradise Lost* and Keats' letters ...

But I do think that what turns up in the writing has a very powerful effect on me ... When people accuse me of being provocative, they have no idea how provoked I am by what I write. It's almost as though the aphorisms, or the pulling-up short, or the knowledge claims are partly an anxiety about the free-wheeling nature of what's being written, for which, I think, there's a sort of containing function going on ... because aphorisms are very contained ... they're overcontained, if you like. They're like a stun, they pull you up short ... It's almost as if what one deals with in one's writing is one's own internal delirium ... where there's a potential one tunes into that can't be unbounded, but feels as though it is ... something with no end to it ... something that goes in all sorts of directions ... It's almost as though, every so often, I have to remind myself that I'm writing!

The way I do remind myself, I think, is by producing aphorisms. I don't do so deliberately, but they just turn up every so often. I want them to turn up, I should say, but they also happen to turn up. I want to write things that I'd really want to read, things that by implication my friends and the people I like will want to read. I want what I write to be entertaining. That's my primary wish. I want my writing to be a pleasure to read.

... Where the process is concerned, there's actually very little revision in my writing. It's mostly as you read it. What I revise are the sentences where the tension you've described goes out of the writing, where I begin to get ponderous, or to lecture. Or where I become too facetiously clever at the cost of something else. I love being clever. I don't want to disparage that at all. But I do think you need both of the elements you've described to give any writing life.

Switching back to your preface, for a moment. You mention how the language of psychoanalysis still gets "snarled up with the old-fashioned language of 'will'." Later in the book, in a chapter entitled "Fears," you mention a certain "antipathetic view" of the existentialist take which sees fear as a route to authenticity. Is will, or agency, altogether alien to the psychoanalytic project?

Yes, I think it is. Or to put it another way, it may be that whatever ideas of will have been used need to be rethought in the light of psychoanalytic ideas. In certain ideas of will, it's as though we have an inner agency, or a god within, that is somehow under our control, that we can make do things for us ... or who prompts us to do things. One of the liberating

things for me about psychoanalytic thinking is that it does
away with the idea of effort. You can't try to be psycho-
analyzed any more than you can try to have a dream ... In
other words, we have to rethink the ways we describe what we
call making choices, or our capacity to determine things. I do
think that the worst kind of psychoanalysis, often covertly, and
sometimes unawares, returns to ideas of will ... when it gets
really frustrated with the absence of will in its discourse, psychoanalysis returns to it, or tries to smuggle a bit of will into
the picture. I think this is true of some Kleinian theory, for
example, whereby we really should try to be good. I think it's
a very interesting project to imagine living a life without will-
power, or without the idea of a will. Or, to live a life imagining choices but with no concept of will. These are the kind of
things psychoanalysis invites one to work out.

Back to Buddhism ...

Back to Buddhism.

*If I might be provocative, this raises for me another question. Isn't
the recognition of one's desires a prelude to the kind of ethical
action Sartre invokes?*

I think that must be right, but I also think that's exactly where
the conflict is ... the idea of choice without desire. That's the
kind of puzzle I'd like to think about.

*The point I made clicked in when I read the following line of yours,
again in the essay entitled "Fears," where you say: "We must locate
our fears and act accordingly." Arguably, this is also a way of
saying that we ought to recognize our desire, and act accordingly. Is
there a contradiction here?*

Well, in psychoanalytic terms there isn't, and in existential terms
there is. And maybe that's a way of formulating the distinction.

*Towards the end of the essay you write: "Freud's authority, like all
authority, is constituted by knowing what people are frightened of" –
in other words, as you yourself suggest, by knowing what people
want. Earlier, in a different context, I mentioned Dostoevsky's
parable of "The Grand Inquisitor." With these echos in mind, what
can politics, and politicians, learn from psychoanalysis – if indeed*

*they can learn anything at all? I remember Christopher Bollas tell-
ing me that in Europe there is generally a greater readiness to
invoke, or at least to listen to, the "authority" of psychoanalysis
than there is in the United States ...*

Psychoanalysis hasn't got anything to teach politics unless politicians and journalists are interested in it. I think there's a lot of
grandiose speak about psychoanalysis and politics, which is part
of the idea that psychoanalysis is terribly important. Now, I do
think it's terribly important to the people who are interested in
it, but I think it isn't terribly important to an awful lot of other
people. I think that it can be very misleading to produce a
picture of the world as a civic society based on psychoanalytic
ideas ... There's a famous story that John Cage told in which a
friend of his has composed a new piece of music and invites
Cage to attend the concert. Cage obliges, and at the concert he
reads in the program notes written by his friend: "I hope my
music goes some way to diminishing the suffering in the world."
Cage listens to the music. After the concert his friend says to
him, "What did you think of the music?" Cage replied: "I loved
the music but I hated the program notes." "Why?" the friend
asks. To which Cage said: "Well, I think there's just the right
amount of suffering in the world." Now, as a political story, I
think that's a terrible statement to make. It's hair-raising. But as
a personal story, or as a story in a psychoanalytic context
between two people, in a certain sense you might say that from
the patient's point of view there is just the right amount of
suffering in the world ... I think we have to be very careful
about making the link between what goes on between two
people and what goes on in groups.

   If there were politicians and journalists interested in psychoanalysis (I say politicians and journalists because I think their
respective professions are now inextricable), or if psychoanalysts
wanted to interest such people, one of the things that would have
to be considered would be the relationship between two facts:
namely, that in psychoanalysis decisions do not have to be made,
while in politics they do. In other words, the grounds, the ingredients, of decision making would have to be considered. That would
be the first point. Additionally, there may be politicians and journalists interested in the psychoanalytic picture of what a person is.
The result might be an interest, then, in the kind of politics we'd
have if politicians believed that people have an unconscious. Of
course, politicians might be better able then to manipulate people.

But they might also be better able to take into account ambivalence. It might also follow – and this for me would be the Utopian version of such a dialogue – that it would be impossible to have an oppositional politics because all politicians would have to acknowledge how every position is implicated in every other position. So that in England, for instance, the Tories are the disowned parts of the Labour Party and vice-versa. Now if we could imagine, in some preposterous way, a politics in which each party took back its projections, we'd have a very different picture of civic society. Such a version seems to me absolutely preposterous and unlikely, but interesting, nevertheless, to circulate, in order to see what happens to it. Who knows? I think psychoanalysis gives us very good stories about why people might, for example, become fascists. I don't think it gives us stories that are going to make any difference to people who are becoming fascists.

Working from the same premise – that to know what one fears is to know what one wants – what does it mean "to assent to our repertoire of fears"? And where does Adam Phillips stand on what he calls "the question that haunts psychoanalysis": namely, should wants be understood (Freud) or met (Ferenczi)?

I think we should be wary of people who are telling us what we are frightened of, because I think that is a very, very insidious form of control and domination. I don't think analysts should be in the game of imposing fears on people. I think they're useful as people who might have a sense of what the cultural repertoire of fears are, but I also think fears are very idiosyncratic. Some of the things one might be listening to, or hearing about in spite of the patient's intentions, are the specificity of someone's fears and their relationship to fear itself, or what they think fear is ... A lot of abstractions, like fear and love and hate and so on, are often used as collusive counters ... In a psychoanalysis, then, what one is really looking at are people's implicit pictures, or questions, of the sort: "When I feel guilty what do I really mean by this?" Now the risk, of course, is that psychoanalysis becomes a philosophical seminar of sorts. Well, I'm interested in a psychoanalysis that isn't frightened of being a philosophical seminar, but can't help but take as part of what's going on the emotional impact of these preoccupations. One of the things we're looking at, in an embodied way, and not at all in a disembodied way, is a person's language ... It's a patient's language that we're hearing. It's not only verbal language, of course, it's bodily language too. We're hearing, in some very vivid way, people's words, while at the same time looking for and trying to understand where these words come from ... That is to say, we're exploring the history of a person's vocabulary. We're exploring what people think they're doing with their words: what they're doing to other people as well as to themselves.

In a chapter entitled "Dreams," you recount a parable of Kafka's about leopards in a temple ceremony, which you use to make a rather confounding argument about the place of dreams in a psychoanalysis: namely, that the privileged place of dreams in analysis may indicate nothing more than the patient's all-too-ready compliance with both the process and the parent-like figure of the analyst. In your words: "Whose ceremony (treatment) is this, and who decides? And who do the dreams really belong to?" Though power is a word you rarely use, these questions raise its spectre in a way that Foucault, for example, might call a totalitarian exercise. I'd like to put these very same questions to you: whose ceremony is a psychoanalysis, and who decides? And who do the dreams really belong to?

I think all those questions are what the analysis is about. That is to say, the process of the analysis has to address exactly those questions, because these questions obviously go back a long way. They go back to questions like: "As a child, whom do I belong to? Who am I? Who's in charge? Who decides how I spend my time?" Everybody, at the beginning of their life, lives in a very odd time space, which is the overlap of their internal biological rhythms with a regime or a schedule imposed by parents in a particular culture. In a sense, one of the things one's hearing about in a psychoanalysis is the relationship, which isn't always one of conflict, between those two time scales. It's as if one lives in the crossfire between those two time scales. Questions, then, of ownership and belonging, which are also partly questions of compliance, are integral to the treatment. And ownership and belonging, of course, are very different things.

I also think that all one's bodily products, of which of course dreams are one, have an inevitably ambiguous status because they are *between* people even as they belong, in a certain sense, to the person whose products they are. Such products cant't be private because if they were they'd be totally unintelligible. One of the things we might be analyzing now is the patient's relationship to what they assume to be

the analytic situation. That is to say, by now people have all
sorts of transferences to an analysis itself. These transferences
come from all sorts of places, of course; they come partly
from the culture, but they're also informed by a person's relationship to her parents, or to her parents' home, or to the
setting. In other words, somebody comes into my room and
feels she is permitted to be certain versions of herself and not
permitted to be others. Well, somewhere this is a derivative of
what the person felt in her own home or relationships of
origin. So, in a way, it's exactly those questions that one is
analyzing, in order for one to dispense with them. Ultimately,
I would look to dispense with the idea that either the analyst
is in charge or the patient's in charge. What we're aiming for,
I think, is a position where the question of being in charge
disappears. That's what collaboration is. It isn't an abrogation
of authority. In a collaboration, it's just that the question of
who's in charge disappears. It ceases to be significant.

*In the same chapter you make the interesting point that psycho-
analysts often fail to see their dream theories as anything but the
final word – ignoring the fact that for centuries, and across countless cultures, any number of other, similarly serviceable "theories"
did quite well. When you ask, "What will the dream be for us
tomorrow?", I assume you ask this not only of your individual
reader, but of psychoanalysis as well. Were I to invest you with
an "oracular" function, what about the dream tomorrow – in terms
both of theory and of its place in clinical practice?*

The point I'm getting at is that all these theories are essentially
culture- and context-bound. So that, as you've said, and as
Freud himself says in *The Interpretation of Dreams*, dreams have
different functions and uses at different times in different
cultures. I wouldn't want to predict, nor could I, what they'll be
used for in the future, but I do want to show the sense in which
that is precisely what we don't know. The advantage of acknowl-
edging this is to see that our present-day beliefs about dreams
are not fixed, they are not set forever. One of the things I
suppose I'm persuading people to do in that chapter is to listen
for a very idiosyncratic dream function. That is to say, people
are going to have very particular relationships to their own
dreams, and psychoanalysis is, if you like, its own culture of
dreaming. In this light, one of the things that's going to happen
in analysis is that a person moves from her own culture of

dreaming into another culture of dreaming ... which may not be dissimilar to an anthropologist going to speak to another culture. It looks as though it's the same. It looks as though it's completely different. It looks as though we're sort of all on the same wavelength. I think we aren't. And so we need to know that dream theory changes, that the uses of dreams change, and that it's quite unclear where what we think dreams are for feeds into another person's understandings. In other words, I think dreams, as bodily products, are subject to all sorts of unknowable influences.

I'm trying to phrase this question as I think of it. In light of what you've just said, would the same hold true for our understandings of the unconscious – if we assume it to be a product and construct of our own culture that might easily be alien to others?

Yes, I definitely think that. But one of the signs of the way in which the idea of the unconscious is now embedded is that it's impossible for those of us who believe in it to imagine a person who doesn't believe as we do. That seems to me the sign of an idea becoming absolutely encoded in the culture. It's as if it's taken for granted, to the extent that alternatives seem preposterous. In this sense, the idea of the unconscious is a bit like a religious concept. It's as though you're either in this faith system or you're out of it. But, of course, like every other idea or description we make, the idea of the unconscious must be time-bound and context-bound.

In this way then, does the future of psychoanalysis hinge on preserving the privileged dimension of the dream as the royal road to the unconscious?

I think we really shouldn't be interested in preserving psychoanalysis at all. I think that we should be interested in finding languages for what matters most to us. So far, for some people, psychoanalysis is one of these languages. It doesn't have to be. But I think the whole project of protecting, conserving, promoting psychoanalysis is absolutely irrelevant. I think psychoanalysis should be seen as one of the languages in a culture that is useful to do certain things. We should really be asking prior ethical questions about how we want to live and who we want to be ... When we look around us, it's easy to see that there are pop songs which, in many ways, are much more influential than psychoanalysis ... "Blood on the Tracks" and "Eat a Peach" have been much more important to me than *Playing and Reality* or *Envy and Gratitude* ... There's politics, psychoanalysis, anthropology ... I mean, there are millions of things. I don't think psychoanalysis is there to be protected. It's there to be used and then dispensed with when something better comes along.

You remind us in the essay that the dream is always overdetermined; that it can never be exhausted, as it is always dreamt for a multiplicity of purposes. Does the dreamwork, in a way, provide you with a model for a certain parallel understanding of the self – which you later define, in another essay from Terrors and Experts, *as "a miscellany ... never one thing or another ... but always provisional and circumstantial"? In other words: is the self that we cling to an interpreted dream?*

Yes, I think it is, and I think that the dreamwork is the best picture going of what it is to be a person. It's the picture I like most, I should say, because it's about a process of transformation that we can't know very much about. It's very extraordinary because we neither know what goes into the process – what the raw material is – or the consequences of what comes out. In a way, we don't even know what we've made! And so we really are like a way station in a process. That for me is what the dreamwork is about, and that's one of the many reasons I value Bollas' work.

In the closing lines of the essay entitled "Dreams," you invoke a humbler, more modest function for the psychoanalyst: "(What if) a psychoanalyst is no more nor less than a person one tells one's dreams to, a person one knows to be interested in such things." Do you think psychoanalysis can forsake the authority that goes with this presumed "expertise"?

Well I hope it can forsake the authority, but I also hope it doesn't forsake the pleasure. I think that interpreting dreams is fantastically interesting and useful and moving and engaging. Dreams really are, as far as I can see, bulletins or news from elsewhere. They are extraordinary objects on which we can perform interpretations, like poems and novels and events for the satirists. I would want a world in which people go on being interested in dreams, and where there were a place in the culture for people who are known to be interested in them, no matter what their ideological or psychoanalytic persuasion.

Earlier I had invited your reflections on what might happen to the practice of analysis if the analyst were divested of any number of traditional claims to power or knowledge. What I'd prefer to ask now is this: in a situation where such claims persist, and where an analyst consciously or unconsciously clings to them, what power does a patient have to divest the analyst of those claims?

The bottom line here is the patient can leave the analysis. I mean, children are the people who can't leave. I think that has to be made quite clear. I think that there's an obvious difficulty here, which is integral to what's going on, insofar as the so-called patient comes in need and therefore in a state of vulnerability. Of course the analyst, by virtue of being a person, is also in a state of need and vulnerable, but in a different sense. This, in my opinion, is what's always potentially dangerous about psychoanalysis: namely, that it can disable people's capacity for criticism by infantilizing them. I think that if people have real doubts about their analyses or their analysts, and if these doubts are not satisfactorily met by the analyst in the analytic situation, then they should go see someone else to discuss their doubts, or have another, parallel analysis.

The next-to-last chapter in your book is entitled "Sexes." Already in its first few pages you intimate the question, inspired by Judith Butler, which anchors the essay and which I'd like to ask you outright: in light of the quasi-religious status psychoanalysis accords to the concept of mourning, is it possible for us, in some sense, to mourn the sex that we are not, that we all may well have "lost"?

I don't know whether it's possible, but I don't think we should want to. I think that psychoanalytic theory prompts us to be a bit too keen on mourning, and to be rather too eager to engage in it, because it's supposedly so deep or generative or mutative or useful or morally good for us or whatever ... I don't think we should be necessarily mourning the sex we aren't. I think we should be more or less able to acknowledge the possibilities, in a certain sense, of being the sex that we aren't, and the senses in which we can't be that sex. That is to say, this is like an ongoing unfolding of the consequences of bisexuality ... or of the consequences in the relationship between psychic bisexuality and anatomical unisexuality. That's the dialogue. I don't know that we should be in a hurry to mourn either of the sexes. Mourning is a form of violence, too.

Here's the question you ask specifically: "What would have to happen, in the so-called psychoanalytic community, and in the wider community, for an ethos to be created in which people were encouraged to mourn the loss of all their repressed gender identities (or to consider their resurrection)?"

I think there would have to be a genuinely lived acknowledgement of psychic bisexuality on the part of the analysts themselves. In this sense there would have to be ... the worst word is tolerance ... the best, enjoyment ... of their own homosexuality. That's what would have to happen.

Significantly, you refer in this context to "the cost, the deprivation, involved in all gender identities, not to mention the terror informing these desperate measures." We're back to the title of your book, with a phrase that echoes, for me, the paintings of the German abstract expressionist Munch. That's harrowing language you use to describe who we all are, or what we somehow make ourselves out to be ...

I think that there are very powerful, terrifying fantasies of contamination in the way gender is lived, organized and described. If we believe and/or experience masculinity and femininity as being at war with each other, or as mutual saboteurs, then there's going to be a real terror about being the other sex, whatever one conceives it to be. That's one bit. The other bit is, I think, something that could be called psychobiological – which is the experience of having begun as part of somebody else. The resultant process of differentiating from the mother involves, as it were, a kind of life and death struggle. The risk, I think, is that we have too stark or too severe an idea of what it is that differentiates or separates.

I don't think we should talk about separation. I think we should be talking about enabling or acquiring the requisite distances to do the things we need to do that we can't do when we're too close to somebody. I don't think we separate from people at all. I think that sometimes, in order to do certain things, we need to be far away from other people. I think there are terrors connected with these distances, which I imagine to be biologically based somehow ... The cliche version is that, unless one separates, one fails to become oneself ... but aside from any biological destiny, there are, as it were, environments that thwart our projects of selfhood ... and when these projects are thwarted, even though we often don't know what they are, we do know what we feel: it's as if we can't bear to live, out of some really profound dismay or despair or sense of futility. These are the indices, this is the register we're looking for internally. In a way, then, the message is: "listen for your resentment and hear it early, because it's a clue about you're being somewhere you don't need to be." I think there are great terrors involved in being compromised.

I don't know if I read you mistakenly, but what I gathered from the line I quoted was that the very sex that we are, or the gender identity we somehow come to assume, in and of themselves constitute desperate measures.

Yes, that is what I mean. I think they are desperate because they are, in a sense, the consequence of being on the run from the other sex. It's as though there's always a sex to escape from.

Throughout the chapter, you give lovely – and compelling – expression to the postmodern concept of multiplicity, to the idea of preferred or privileged selves we perform. Indeed you suggest, citing Valéry, that there may well be a psychic necessity to the staging of such a plurality. And yet, you remain keenly aware of the point where theory comes up against the wall, not only of actual clinical practice, but of the human being and life of one's patients. How would you answer your own question: "But how many lives can the analyst recognize in, or demand of, his patient, and what are the constraints on this recognition that so easily becomes a demand?"

Putting the matter constituitively is a bit misleading. In a way this question can only be answered specifically for each person. I think the risk of a kind of fundamentalist pluralism is that it says there's no constraint, that we can be anybody and everybody. That's one end of the spectrum. The other end of the spectrum postulates a true self against which everything else is, as it were, a compromise or betrayal. There are risks on both sides. On one, the risk is that the analyst, in a certain sense, is too happy to settle for too limited a version of the patient. The other alternative, just as bad, is that the analyst is too demanding of the patient to be many people. Again, this is something that has to be negotiated very specifically between the analyst and the patient ... because what we're looking at here is an idea of a repertoire ... a repertoire of possibilities ... a repertoire of possible versions of oneself. Of course one of the ways in which this can be shown – and seems to be often the case in analysis – is that our aims or ideals are really descriptions of what people are doing anyway ... So that one of the things an analyst might be doing is showing someone in treatment an unfolding multiplicity of selves which the patient is straining to call a singular *me*. It's as though, in this case, there's a diversity available to be disclosed ... But I do believe that analysts ought to be very attentive to what a patient seems to want for herself. For some people the idea of having a true self is very, very important: it's an idea that can be challenged, but not violated. For others, the idea itself is a tyranny, a part of the problem.

Throughout the book, and again in the context of "Sexes," you raise the issue of authenticity. While "the analyst who believes in the unconscious can hardly set herself up as a representative of (any) authentic life," how can this positioning be averted? Arguably, it is the very sense of inauthenticity that prompts people to seek out treatment, in a context where, as you yourself acknowledge, "the repertoire of possible selves can only come from the culture." Given the ubiquitousness of processes of identification, how can psychoanalysts contend with this dilemma?

One way is for them to get out of speaking the language of the "real" or "truthful." I think it would be better to promote the idea of preferred selves rather than authentic selves, because the idea of an authentic self already prioritizes a certain version, and that could be used very defensively. That is to say, I might want to think of a certain version of myself as authentic, as a way of managing or concealing other selves that might be, as it were, less legitimate but more preferred. The other essential task simply involves the endless process of showing people how they identify with other people, what the reasons are for their identifications, and why a rather specific repertoire of people comes to be privileged.

Towards the end of the essay, in the context of discussing "more and more versions of people," and thus of sexualities, you raise the question: "If we banned the word love, it would be interesting to see what we found ourselves saying (and doing) to each other." Curiously, it was this very phrase that alerted me to the fact that the word love

had been "banned" from your book, so to speak, until this very appear-
ance. Is there a reason for so inconspicuous an absence? Of a word
whom another psychoanalyst you admire, Julia Kristeva, places at the
beginning of her psychoanalytic cosmogony?

I think I'm wary of the larger abstractions, or of what Frost calls
the larger excruciations ... words like love and power ... because I
think they create certain kinds of complicities that I can't be sure
that I'm part of or want to be part of. I can't help but think that
not using the word *love* in my writing must be a repression ... that
is to say, it has to be symptomatic. I am aware that it's not something I'd want to be glib about ... it's also something that seems to
me to be less and less ... how can I say, it's a bit like religion ...
Any word that a lot of people have found useful over a long period
of time cannot help but be terribly important and interesting. But
it also can't help but be rather daunting as an inheritance, because
you don't know what you're inheriting from ... This is another way
in which I think psychoanalysis is rather useful, because it opens
up the question of love so much that it's as though the word *love*
might disappear. It might be interesting to imagine what a life
would be like in which we don't use the word, because I think our
lives would be very, very different. But as with any real symptomatic repression I can't say anything very interesting about it.

You end the essay with an impassioned and unequivocal statement
of just what is at stake in our work, politically and morally:
"Understanding sexuality," you write, "as if such a thing were
possible – is just the beginning, if that. The difficult question is
how we decide which kinds of loving are acceptable. Understand-
ing does not inform our morality, our morality informs the ways
we have of understanding. The language of pleasure and the
language of justice are inextricable. By being a new way of saying
this, psychoanalysis can be recruited either to consolidate our
prejudices or to show us what our prejudices are for." Can you
say something more specific about this?

Since I think every sentence is a different essay, there's too much
for me to answer in this case. So I'll just pick out bits. I'm
reminded of what we were saying at the beginning of the interview
... that nothing we say is going to be exempt from an ethical
position, so that there's no outside to ethics for me ... I think the
risk is that we lose the psychoanalytic point that it is as if sexuality
is something that is both outside culture as well as inside it. We

need both dimensions. This is where I think relational psychoanalysis might be rather misleading, because everything gets too socialized, everything gets domesticated too quickly, or instrumentalized too quickly – as Laurence Jacobson has shown.

I think we really are dealing with something recalcitrant in ourselves which, for want of a better word, we can call sexuality ... something that is not easily acculturated, something that is rather vagrant and disruptive ... something which, it seems to me, the notion of justice attempts to deal with. Such a notion is a way of dealing with something in ourselves that is asocial, or doesn't care enough about other people. So that when we're talking about pleasure, or talking about the erotic, we're always talking about acceptable ways of loving people; about ways that people can be together that will not damage something very important inside us – something which, for want of a better word, we can call a moral sense. But there's a sense in which this is incredibly difficult because we're living by incompatible criteria. This is what Freud means by conflict. If we use Freudian language, from the id's point of view and from the superego's point of view, these are two different universes. I mean, what we don't want to start believing, or what we're frightened of feeling, is that pleasure and justice are two incommensurate universes. Ultimately, psychoanalysis is part of a human project which is always and inherently ambivalent: a project which, on the one hand, aims to increase the range of the human community, of the intelligible, the consensual, the shared. On the other hand, it acknowledges what cannot be shared ... what simply isn't subject to intelligibility, what is in excess of our capacity to join together, what is uncivil. That's what I'm getting at in that essay.

Finally, you end the book with a renewed discussion, from a different perspective, of the two psychoanalytc projects outlined earlier. In an essay entitled "Minds," you map out the the historical trajectories and differences between a Cartesian tradition that exalts the mind as the very seat and determinant of our human being; and the intuitions of Winnicott, who sees the mind as the telltale sign of original trauma, "an attempted self-cure," in which we all share, for what you call "a too-problematic dependence." Whereas the first, to which Freud was heir, inspires a psychoanalysis that quests after reliable knowledge about the self, the second aspires to "the facilitation of the psychic time before there was mind." To rephrase a question I've already asked: in a way, is the future of psychoanalysis already present in Buddhism?

No, I don't think there is a future for psychoanalysis in Buddhism. But I also think there's no future for psychoanalysis – and I don't think that matters very much, I should say. There's no future for psychoanalysis if it doesn't look to other places for regeneration, and particularly if it doesn't look to the places it wants to exclude. By its own logic that's where the life is, that's where the action is. In the sense in which you're intimating, Buddhism has a lot to offer the kind of psychoanalysis I would value, because of its very preoccupations, because of the kind of grandeur it gives to relinquishing what we think of as the mind, of what's possible if we don't think of ourselves as having minds. And it seems to me this is where mysticism, or a version of mysticism, begins. But also a version of what I take to be a common-sense acknowledgement that we're part of nature, you know, that we're more like trees than cars. That's really what we're like.

WORKS CITED

Freud, S. (1900). *The Interpretation of Dreams*, in J. Strachey, ed. *The Standard Edition of the Complete Psychological Works of Sigmund Freud*, 24 vols. London: Hogarth, 1953–73, S.E. 4–5.

Klein, Melanie (1957). *Envy and Gratitude* London: Tavistock.

Marvell, Andrew (1990). "The King's Speech," in *Andrew Marvell* (F. Kermode and K. Walker, eds.). Oxford: Oxford University Press.

Milton, John (1972). *Paradise Lost* Cambridge: Cambridge University Press.

Winnicott, D.W. (1971). *Playing and Reality* London: Tavistock.

ADAM PHILLIPS: Selected Bibliography

Monogamy (1996). London: Faber & Faber; New York: Pantheon.

Terrors and Experts (1995). London: Faber & Faber; Cambridge: Harvard University Press.

On Flirtation (1994). London: Faber & Faber; Cambridge: Harvard University Press.

On Kissing, Tickling and Being Bored (1993). London: Faber & Faber; Cambridge: Harvard University Press.

Winnicott, (1988). London: Faber & Faber; Cambridge: Harvard University Press.

NINA COLTART

This book closes with my conversations with Nina Coltart. In the sketch I had originally prepared, I remembered how our time together had alchemized quickly into a golden trust. I also noted the intimations of death that echoed after reading her final book, *The Baby and the Bathwater,* as well as the gracious knack with which Dr. Coltart, in the course of our discussions, made the ominous rather ordinary. "Not only did memories come alive," I'd written, "but also the precious experience of somehow being granted permission, by Dr. Coltart, to visit death and the dead with her." Clearly, for all of the intimations I and other readers may have perceived, no one expected so sudden a passing. I consider it a fateful privilege to have been entrusted with this final testament of sorts. It is my hope that anyone who reads it will, like me, be graced with its wisdom.

The following interview took place over the course of two days, September 12 and December 7, 1996, in Dr. Coltart's home outside London.

AM: *I'd like to move from the preface to your most recent book,* The Baby and the Bathwater, *where Christopher Bollas situates your writing in the context of a literary tradition in psychoanalysis. In his preface, Bollas talks about the particular literary challenge of a final group of essays. Can you discuss that particular challenge?*

NC: While not easy to formulate, part of my attitude to producing books has been to write the way I speak and teach, as well as the way I analyze. Patients of mine who've read my books say they heard me all along in them; this pleases me, because I don't have to tell you that an awful lot of analytic writing is extremely heavy, turgid, pompously theatrical, and quite boring ... really terrible stuff! And although I never deliberately decided, "Now I'm not going to be like that," I am sufficiently conceited to think that I really don't write in that sort of turgid, heavy, humorless way. I've wanted my writing to flow, to have a certain lightness about it – not shallowness, but light-heartedness – because that's the way I think about a lot of things. It's probably thanks to the influence of

Buddhism in my life that I don't regard psychoanalysis as desperately serious. I think it's important, and it has been very important for me for a good many years ...

Psychoanalysis has given me a very good life. It really has. All along I was a round peg in a round hole and I felt that this was the life for me – that it was absolutely right for me. And I do stress that – particularly in my second book, How To Survive as a Psychotherapist. I want people to enjoy their work. I want them to enjoy my writing, but more than that, I've always wanted to convey the sense that if they're not enjoying their work, if it's so heavy and ponderous and a great worry to them, if they lie awake at night anxious about their patients, then somehow they're on the wrong wavelength ... Not that the work shouldn't be like that, but that it need not be.

Well, I have to confess a disservice I've done you.

You have? What have you done?

When I heard the title of your second book, amid the craze of self-help and pop psychology books one finds in America, I didn't purchase it out of dismay. I remember asking myself: "How can the same woman who wrote Slouching Towards Bethlehem now be writing a how-to manual?"

Oh dear! So you haven't read it?

No, I haven't ...

Well, I wouldn't say it's a laugh a minute or anything of the sort. In that sense it's perfectly genuine. But as I say in the first chapter, in reference to the title, I'm not talking about grim survival. Survival has become such a feature of the twentieth century in a terrible and tragic way, particularly for people like the Jews, that I thought I must convey straightaway that by survival I mean survival with enjoyment. I stress that over and over again during the book. Otherwise, it is a sort of how-to book. It was actually commissioned. The publishing firm got hold of me and asked me to write it. It's the only book I've sat down and written, as my other books built themselves up from papers. It never really occurred to me to write a book. But on this occasion the invitation appealed to me. I thought, "Yes, I could do that. And I could do it in a way that matters to me." But I do see what you mean. There's such a rash of psychotherapies, and such a proliferation of all sorts of conditions and counselors ... God knows you've only got to run into a bus or the back of somebody else's car, and there's counselors pouring out of the woodwork in hordes! I don't know where they all come from, or who they are, or even who trains them ... Or whether they do any good. I don't think they're giving people time to work things out on their own, to have their own grieving processes, to struggle to be _grown up. It's a trend I disapprove of strongly.

You've often suggested that you rarely write with no internal incentive. And yet The Baby and the Bathwater *seems to have been inspired by a series of external occasions ...*

It's perfectly true that there's always been an incentive, an occasion, people writing and saying, "Will you come and speak to us, on such and such a topic?" For example, people from the Washington School of Psychiatry used to come to London every summer for meetings at the Tavistock. On one such occasion they were interested in psychosomatic medicine and asked me to present a paper. For some time I'd been vaguely thinking of writing about a doctor with ulcerative colitis whom I'd treated, hence the paper "Blood, Shit and Tears," which appears in my last book. Actually, there was quite a bit of excitement over whether it could be published in America because of the word *shit* in the title. I remember asking David Scharff, the director of the series in which the book appeared, "Well what do you suggest instead?" And he said, "Well, there's feces." I said, "'Blood, Feces and Tears'?!... I mean, it's ridiculous!" The whole thing, you see, is a play on Churchill's pronouncement. You know: "We will face them with blood, sweat and tears." Anyway the title did get through in the end. But it's that sort of stimulus that I've always responded to with my writing. Somebody would ask me to write or deliver a paper, for which a topic had already been knocking around in my mind that could well lend itself to the occasion. But I can't say I would have got round to the writing without the invitation. That's how my second book got written, as a result of an invitation that I found very appealing.

But what about the process that stems from the invitation? A talk or paper is one thing, but your essays – as Bollas suggests – are marked by a distinctly literary form and quality ...

Yes. I suppose so. To tell you the truth, I was a bit taken aback when Kit wrote that preface ... because his contention wasn't something I was very conscious of, or could readily identify with. But I can tell you about the process through which I produce my papers. They hardly change as they move from talks to book form. Because once a paper's done, I forget about it. But when I'd first start thinking about a theme on which to write, I'd often say to myself: "Oh, I can't do that. I've got nothing to say about the matter, nothing at all. It's just an interesting idea." So then I would shove it to the back of my mind and leave it there, stewing around, marinating, often for months. My schedule, then, was always so booked up in advance – which was fine by me – that it allowed for this process to happen. And then one day, probably quite near to the date of my speaking engagement, I would always end up in a panic ... That's another thing about the production of my papers. I'd suddenly think, "I've got to be able to do that paper in a fortnight." And I would settle down – I always write in longhand, I can't do typing or word processing – and pick up a pen and think, "Well it's now or never." And out it would all come. That's literally the process, and it's one I've always relied on. I knew, even when I was getting into my necessary panic, that the idea was stewing away all along, and that it would be there when the time came to put pen to paper. But I can assure you, there's nothing about my writing that's fashioned as a literary work. I don't know whether this sounds conceited or not, but it's simply the way I write. I have always been a great reader, so that must have unconsciously influenced me a tremendous amount. I have read and read and read all my life. I don't mean psychoanalytic texts. I mean novels and biographies and studies and memoirs, all of which I've enjoyed.

Is there any element of "strategy" you rely on?

Well, I always look to achieve the greatest simplicity of expression. Always leaving out, as far as possible, technical language or specialized language, so that lay people can read the stuff with some enjoyment. I mean, quite a lot of my friends read my books, and most of them aren't psychoanalysts; they're ordinary doctors or historians or people from other walks of life. The fact that my books are intelligible to them gratifies me. It really does. Of course, in a paper like "Handling the Transference," there has to be some technical language because it refers to a peculiar aspect of working with the unconscious that is specific to psychoanalysis. But overall, to the extent that there's any strategy at all, it has to do with simplicity and love of the English language – a language which is extremely expressive, as well as extremely plastic and flexible.

In taking issue with some of Lacan's writings, Janet Malcolm suggests that Americans and the English, when they write at their best, have a way of tempering theory with analogy, whereas the French resort to more theory in order to address questions of theory ... I thought of your work in that context ...

Oh did you? Oh good!

... in fact, two passages from The Baby and the Bathwater *come to mind, two wonderful English sentences where analogy works precisely to temper the theory ... May I read them and invite your own reflections?*

Please do!

One is from the chapter on vocations, where you write: "Giftedness is hard to define and even harder to write about. We are in the borderlands of the invidious and the unspeakable." The other is from your description of the man with two mothers: "Nevertheless I visualize Mr. A's ego not only as split but, even in the adequately functioning area, as having some rotten floorboards, and under severe stress he is at risk of falling through them into a terrifying underworld of violence and part-objects."

Yes, I remember. Actually it's many years since I wrote that paper, but I remember having that image so clearly. I could see this man constantly endangered by the rotten floorboards through which at any moment – unknown to himself because he was a careful man – he could fall through. I like Janet Malcolm's comments. What she says in the quote you cited strikes me as quite true. I haven't read much French psychoanalysis, but I can imagine that theory piled on theory is a way of trying to handle it, and that wouldn't suit me.

Again on the matter of Bollas' preface. He places you squarely in the company and lineage of Winnicott, Rycroft, Khan and Milner, "who as a literary movement comprise the best expression of the independent thought typical of this psychoanalytic sensibility. This work is a literary spirit of place." How do you see yourself within that literary movement?

Think of that! Amazing. Well, I can tell you for sure I didn't put myself there with any degree of intention. But it's true. I mean, Khan wrote beautifully. It's such a pity he went off the rails because we lost a really great expounder of psychoanalysis. *The Privacy of the Self*, for example, is a wonderful, wonderful book. Rycroft is an extremely cultured, educated man. You never have met Rycroft, have you? He's an extraordinary man. And he couldn't write an ugly sentence if he tried, nor one dripping with psychoanalytic solemnity. He really couldn't ...

Do you know that Rycroft and Peter Lomas and I are the only three people, so far as I can tell, who've ever actually left the Psychoanalytic Society? People just don't leave the Psychoanalytic Society, even when they've had it really, even when the time has come. Personally, I felt that the time had come for me to do so. I didn't need the Psychoanalytic Society anymore. But when I left it quite a lot of people were very upset. Long ago Rycroft left. He describes his reasons for doing so somewhere in a paper that appeared, I think, in *The British Journal of Psychotherapy*. He got so tired of the internecine warfare and the ugly sniping in scientific meetings. That was also one of the things of which I tired. I ceased going to scientific meetings years ago. The people there all behaved so badly. This affected Rycroft so much that he left the Society as a relatively young man. But of course he made his name, established quite a practice, and even today everybody respects him greatly. His example goes to show that you don't have to be a member of the Society to be successful ...

A lot of people were quite upset when I left. Two or three people actually came to see me to ask why I was leaving. Several wrote to me at the time of my decision and then again the following Christmas, saying, "We could hardly believe it ... we do hope you'll join us again. Why don't you come back?" I think this still attests to the enormous gulf that existed between me and most of my colleagues. It really does. It simply would never have occurred to me to return. One of the people who came to see me was a former patient of mine. She was very cross. I recall her saying, "What is the matter with you? Are you depressed or something?" I said, "No, on the contrary, I'm delighted and very happy." "Well then, why are you going?" she insisted. And I said, "Why would I stay? I'm finished here, I'm going." She settled down after a bit. I think she was frightened. I understood what was going on, but she'd got hold of the wrong end of the stick ...

What were your reasons for leaving?

I didn't need the Society anymore. I had no more need of it
at all. I'd long made a name for myself as a consultant. I'd
been seeing prospective patients for assessment interviews, and
referring them on to other therapists, for years and years. So I
hadn't needed the Society to refer patients to me for a long
time already. I've told you about the scientific meetings. And I
no longer felt that I needed the library. People who were
going to remain my friends would remain my friends anyway
... and have. So why would I continue to need it? I was
actually turning my back on my identity of a psychoanalyst. I
think that's why a lot of people don't leave. I think they're
frightened of remaining without an identity ... So many
analysts are so very strongly identified with the notion of *being*
a psychoanalyst that, as far as they're concerned, maintaining
that identity means belonging to a society. That's something I
didn't feel.

Also, many analysts go on working far too long, which
suggests to me that their lives are rather barren. In my eyes, I
see them wandering on, dementing steadily behind the couch,
running the Society with the kind of ghastly authoritarianism
that old people develop. I mean, I could see that happening to
me. One of the reasons for not being in power in the Society
any longer is that one gets bossier as one grows old. People
develop the awful habit of throwing their weight about, thinking they know everything just because they're old. I was
always very clear about not wanting to go down that path.
There's plenty of people doing it. I shall name no names. I'd
love to but I won't.

*You've mentioned the internecine warfare at the Society. I've
gathered that there's a political dimension to the Society – what
with the "forced" cohabitation of Kleinians, Independents, and
Freudians – that never suited you well ...*

No, it didn't, I'm afraid. Another reason I wanted to leave the
Society was because of all the hypocrisy and phoniness there,
all those people tip-toeing about being charming and polite to
each other. But as I remember thinking, in preparing my last
book: "Oh, to hell with it! This is my last book, why not say
it?" Why not say that there are plenty of people in the Society
who would appear perfectly amiable and friendly towards you

while you were in the Society, but if the occasion arose, they would as soon stab you in the back? They really would, and I don't like that ...

I don't like that feeling of potential mistrust and disloyalty which does exist in the Society, and it's no good for people to skirt it or pretend it doesn't exist. Of course, it's existed since the 1940s when the so-called "controversial discussions" took place – which you may have come across in Pearl King and Riccardo Steiner's book. They bravely compiled and published them, and quite rightly too, I think. And of course, it was all meant to settle people down, so that we could resolve our differences and get on well together ... But it was like putting together chalk and cheese. It's a great pity the Society didn't split back then. I think I say as much in my last book, and I don't mind being known to say it. It jolly nearly did split, but didn't – which somehow was taken to reflect a sort of triumph for British diplomacy. Well, so much for British diplomacy ... If the Kleinians had gone off and formed their own Society, and if the Independents and the Freudians had been left to get on with their view of things, I think the situation would have been far better. We're the only capital city in the west that has only one Society. It would have been quite alright to split. We would have been spared this constant nagging, this semi-underground warfare between people and groups ...

The Kleinians are religious. They are a religious movement, while the rest of us aren't. And fanatical religious movements believe that they possess the truth, and are prepared to impose it at practically any cost on other people. That is going on all the time in the British Society ... under a veneer of civility which is so phony I can't tell you.

Would you say that such a "religious" element is somehow intrinsic to Kleinian theory, as well as to the personalities that adhere to that particular group?

Oh, indeed I would. I think it is intrinsic to the theory. That's why the theory attracts the personalities it does – people who, for some reason, are presumably in need of a religion. It's a pity that the Kleinians don't actually go and found one, starting with Mrs. Klein herself – who was an extremely imperious old lady – and her heir apparent, Hannah Segal ...

... A lot of powerful personalities are one-sided and obviously in need of a religious conviction, of a sort of missionary lifestyle.

Such people were often attracted to the Kleinians. Quite a lot of
students were drawn to them because they didn't know any
better. God help me. I might have been drawn towards them
myself. Because if you start absolutely green, you don't know
how to choose an analyst. You don't know where you want to
go. I didn't know anything about psychoanalysis when I started,
and I might have easily been directed to a Kleinian analyst. I
don't know what would have happened then because, in my
younger days, I was fairly suggestible. I might have become a
Kleinian myself, I suppose. I'd like to think I'd have risen above
the theory's initial appeal, or seen through the group's shenani-
gans, but I might well not have.

Nowadays, the rest of us are up against that group because
we find ourselves arguing with people who *know* they are right.
They embody a religious atmosphere. So when I say that the
Society is politicized, it is in a very specialized sense. It's
religio-political. Of course, ultimately, the entire agenda of the
Society is political business. I was Chairman of the Board and
Council for three years and that was a pretty hefty job ... The
religio-political nature of much of the stress and strain and
struggle in the Society would be evidenced in the long,
exhausting Council meetings. Council is a very powerful body
in the Society, it runs the Society completely. Sure, there are
sub-committees, but they all answer to Council. That was a
trying time for me; and yet I enjoyed it, I thrived on it. But,
God, I had to be very tough.

*In your view, what are the stakes that have sustained this forced
cohabitation? Why the reluctance to split?*

That's a very good question. I haven't really considered it
because, after living in the middle of the fractiousness for so
long, I guess I took its reality for granted. In looking back,
though, in the wake of the war and our own controversial discussions, I think there was a tremendous need and longing for
peaceable solutions, especially as a lot of the immigrant analysts
were Jewish refugees. There might have been quite an uncomfortable feeling among the rest of the Society ... subdued but
strong ... Certainly when I joined the Society, the Gentiles were
in the minority. As most of the Kleinian analysts were Jewish,
I'm sure we didn't want to have any feeling of appearing that
we'd booted out the Jewish analysts or got the better of them. I
think I'm right in saying that. At the time there were plenty of

Freudians, of course, but not so many Independents. I did come to notice, however, that most of the Gentiles in the Society clustered into the Independent Group ... In any case, I'm sure that what we see today has something to do with that history, insofar as it helped foster quite a phony layer of harmony and amiability, in which every point of view was to be and could be respected. But it's simply not true.

It was striking to hear you refer to the Kleinians as "imperious." It doesn't seem, however, that a truce is conducive to the creation of an empire ...

No, no. But the situation in the Society can possibly be seen as owing to the British capacity for diplomatically appearing to go along with something while not quite endorsing it in actuality. That's possibly why quite a lot of Britons make good spies ... And perhaps that's why there isn't a Kleinian empire. There's just constant, quiet sniping. But certainly in a local way, some of the Kleinians are very imperious. I'm perfectly certain Mrs. Klein was. But this isn't to say that, aside from the Kleinians, some of the rest weren't, or aren't. Anna Freud was imperious, there's no doubt about that. She had her own little gang at the Hampstead Clinic. Similarly, there are certain well-known Kleinians who have their own little groups today ... who keep on running seminars and appealing to people when they're getting on to eighty, I may add ... So there are all sorts of tiny, little sub-empires, but as a group, no, the Kleinians have never established a hegemony over the whole of the Society.

Where did Bion fit into the picture?

Oh, that's a good question. Bion was a law unto himself really. For one thing, Bion hardly ever spoke ... which is such an attractive trait. Did you ever see Bion? He was a big, solid man with the most magnetic dark brown eyes ...

Michael Eigen describes him as a bug ...

As a bug? Oh no! To me a bug is a small thing. I may not understand what Eigen means, but to me a bug is a little thing, and Bion was something big. We had seminars with Bion when I was a student. I remember twelve of us all sitting around in the common room, and he'd come in and sit down and stare at us. He didn't speak. This, I was to learn, was such a typical Bion entry to a seminar. He just stared, at us, with an expressionless face. I don't know what a basilisk is, quite, but I would describe him as a basilisk. I've got the greatest admiration for the man. I like his writing. I don't understand the grid and never have ... but some of his writing is positively inspiring. And unlike many psychoanalysts, he understands about faith and mystical experience ...

I can't remember the seminars, to tell you the truth. I can't remember what happened when Bion began to speak. I'm so absolutely fixated on that beginning which was dramatic ... even traumatic ... And because he was like that, he was nobody's follower. Nobody's at all. I've always wanted to have my second analysis with Bion. I never got around to having a second analysis because, by the time I thought I could fit it into my life, I didn't feel in need of it. But I remember telling my analyst that I had Bion in mind for my second analyst, and she was delighted. She was a wonderful old lady, and she was very impressed by this choice. Now though, looking back, I'm not so sure ... I don't think Bion would ever have taken me because he'd started traveling to America by the time I'd begun to consider the prospect. But one or two people who had analysis with Bion were for me a focus of envy. I would have loved to be in analysis with him.

Was it mostly that stare of his, those eyes, that captivated you?

His capacity for silence. You know, an awful lot of analysts simply love the sound of their own voices ... a bit like me going on now! They're very authoritarian, as I've said, and they like to lay down the law – particularly at the Kleinian end of the spectrum ... which Bion himself belonged to. But he was Bion. He didn't belong to any movement and, to give him his due, he didn't really found a movement either. He didn't try to. He had lots of admirers, but that's a slightly different situation.

In the course of this first hour together you've mentioned Klein, Rycroft, Anna Freud, Bion. If I remember correctly, your own analyst was Freud's own last analysand ...

Yes.

... which makes you a granddaughter of Freud!

(*laughs*) And, I must say, of Mrs. Klein's ... I've got the most extraordinary lineage. Because Mrs. Rosenfeld, Eva Rosenfeld, my analyst – whose last student I was – to the best of my knowledge had two years with Freud, in Vienna, shortly after the First World War. She came to England with the Freuds, and was good friends with Anna. Of course, those were the days when you could have analysis with the old man and then pop into the drawing room and have tea with Anna. It was all so much more ... how can I say? ... it was cozier in those days ... When Mrs. Rosenfeld came to England, she was depressed. She'd had a tragic life, and I don't suppose Freud had really got anywhere near the core of her experience ... nor am I sure that her worst tragedy had happened as yet ... of which I'll soon tell you. But she went for some therapeutic analysis to Mrs. Klein. She was with her for two years, and always said that she'd been helped a great deal. And I'm sure she was. I'm sure Mrs. Klein was a most careful and concerned therapist. I have no doubt about that, and I would never, in all my criticism of the Kleinians, include Mrs. Klein in my criticisms – apart from her imperious personality. As a therapist, I think she was probably very caring, and I know she helped my own analyst a lot ...

The two women also had a great tragedy in common. My analyst had four children – three boys and a girl. Two of the little boys died during the First World War of some form of dysentery. Her daughter, whom she adored, was nearly grown up by the time she came to England ... But the girl died as a result of a mountain climbing accident. And Mrs. Klein had a son to whom the same thing had happened. I may be making this up, but I'm not sure they weren't both in the same accident ... Anyway, it was the greatest tragedy of my analyst's life. She'd left her husband, come to England, and was left with only one son ...

I must say, I think this considerably influenced her counter-transference to me. I have no doubt about it, and after all, why shouldn't it have? – as long as she was aware of it, and I'm sure she was. At the time I began my training she had already retired, and Ilse Helman – who'd interviewed me and thus learned my history – got hold of Mrs. Rosenfeld and said, "Look, you've got to come out of retirement. You've got to analyze this girl. You're the one for her." So Ilse Helman persuaded her out of retirement ... Mrs. Rosenfeld was getting on to seventy when she started my analysis. But she had, because of her story, a peculiar sympathy with my own life story ... which also had a traumatic tragedy in it. From that point of view, because I hadn't yet metabolized the results of my story, Mrs. Rosenfeld was very helpful to me. I mean, my analysis did a lot for me, getting me over the tragedy in my life. And it trained me to be an analyst, of course, which as I say gave me a very good life.

Where does Nina Coltart see herself in the history of psychoanalysis? Your lineage, if nothing else, warrants the question. But I also ask this because your book conveys a sense that you have a message to impart. It is, in a way, a testament. And, I would argue, it's only a person with a genuine sense of their place and importance who can presume to impart any kind of message ...

Well, I suppose it's rather a contradiction in terms, but I would say that if I have been consciously sensitive to my place in the psychoanalytic tradition, it's been as the most independent representative of the Independent Group. I couldn't possibly have belonged to anything but the Independent Group. And I suppose if my message has been anything, it's been to follow your gift ... Absorb your training. Winnicott always used to say, "Learn the basics, and then do what you like." It's pretty much like St. Augustine saying: "Love God and do what you like" ... meaning that one should know properly how to love God. And I do think analysts should absorb the whole of Freud ... I was always keen for my students to read as much Freud as possible during their training. Again, absorb your training. Expose yourself to as much good teaching as you possibly can. Cast off the one-sided, politicized adherence to certain viewpoints, and follow your gift ...

That's why I make rather a lot of giftedness and vocation. I suppose, if anything, that I would follow Bion on that score. Bion always advised people to trust their intuition. In the last resort, you're left with nothing but your intuition, facing what he called the final, ineffable, unspeakable experience of another human being. That is a stance that I would regard as being truly independent. I wouldn't say I'd been at all consciously influenced by knowing that Freud and Mrs. Klein hovered like Easter Island statues in my background, I can assure you. But I always felt a devotion to Freud's writing ... I still do, because he wrote so beautifully, and I so admire the courage and independence with which he forged on and on and on, changing his mind quite a lot of the time. And although I wouldn't say, by any means, that you have to use all of Freud's theory, I do think if you use his attitude, his work method, then you can't go far wrong.

Earlier you made reference to analysts who hang around too long. I got the impression, while reading The Baby and the Bathwater, *that you wanted to make sure that those who didn't know of your own retirement would now know through the book. I also got the impression – if you'll pardon my frankness – that you may have even wanted to get a sense of whether those colleagues who did know of your retirement were missing you ... and that if they didn't, well they ought to! What about your retirement? And am I reading too much into it?*

I certainly wanted people to be perfectly clear that that's what I was doing: that I was moving on and away from psychoanalysis; that it has served me very well; that I loved it, but that it was over. I did want people to know that. I think it's important because I really, deep down, feel that people should not drag on, throwing their weight about, well into their seventies and even – God help us!– into their eighties ... I received a letter the other day from an old friend of mine in the Society, a woman younger than I. She'd been to the retirement party of the Society's recent president, and told me of a number of people who were there and what they were still doing. Well, I was simply horrified. Here are these old people who were training analysts when I was a student and are still at it! You cannot help but get arthritic in your ideas, old-fashioned, self-important. You can't help it. It goes with old age. These people should be shifting over and out, and giving younger people a chance to come up, run the Society, become training analysts themselves. The most ludicrous power is still invested in who's going to be a training analyst. Only very recently, I happened to meet someone, an extremely good clinician, who hadn't openly done, as you might say, a great deal for psychoanalysis. She is a very independent person and hadn't been known to settle on either side of the Society's divide. Well into her fifties, she had applied for the second time to be made a training analyst, and was again turned down ... which suggests to me that the wrong people are doing the selection, and that their selective powers are creaking. That's why I wanted people to know that someone who was well-known, and whom they might respect, was turning her back on the whole setup.

As to whether they miss me, I don't know. I haven't consciously thought of that, though I suppose I hope that they would. Of course, I have left three books of which I am very pleased. I'm proud to have written them, and they say pretty well everything I want to say. So people needn't really miss me. "Me" is in my books. I don't think I should be remembered, not in the way that Winnicott and Bion and others are remembered ... I haven't got that sort of stature. I was always a bit too eccentric, often up against quite a lot of the authorities, a bit too critical. Kit Bollas would support this. He knew that I was quite openly critical, and of the battles I'd fought. So I can't tell you whether I will be very long remembered or not ... I don't think I will ... and I don't think it matters two pence if I'm not. My books are there for people to read and enjoy. Then again, everything is transient anyway!

In what ways do you consider yourself an eccentric?

Why do I call myself an eccentric? Going to Oxford was a bit unusual for a woman in my days, as was my later switch to medicine and the efforts to finance my education – although I did manage mostly on scholarships. And I didn't get married. I didn't particularly want to be married or want to have children. That's eccentric in middle-class culture – perhaps not in the sense that people point at you or tap their forehead at the sight of you, but my choices in no way reflected the predominant expectations for a woman my age. Especially in my childbearing years, it was certainly quite difficult to defend those choices. People find it very difficult to understand that you have prepared not to want children, and to accept that you didn't want children. I actually like children, and I like being with them. My own parents had died in an accident when I was eleven, and that left me with what you might call a neurosis, albeit a rational one at that. I always had an anxiety about having children, and about possibly leaving them with such an affliction as being orphaned. In a way, like everyone else, I too was scarred by the events of my childhood ...

Additionally, on the matter of my eccentricity, I have a religious temperament. I can safely say I believe that such a thing exists. For many years I had been a devout member of the Church of England, but ended up leaving it, long ago. Personally, I couldn't sustain being a Christian, yet I still wanted to have a religious system within which to operate. I spent a lot of years rambling around, searching, until I found the one that suited me: Buddhism.

Such a choice is also mildly eccentric in English, white, middle-class culture ...

Then there's the fact that I've always lived alone. The fact that I didn't want to be married and didn't want children, didn't mean I wanted to live with women either. I didn't. I wanted to be on my own. I've been quite a recluse. And even to this day to admit to such a lifestyle is regarded as a bit odd. People don't know quite what to say. For example, I've traveled a great deal on my own, which always and absolutely horrifies people. "Won't you be frightened going alone?" they'll say. And if you ask them what of, they can't tell you. There must be a sort of fantasy that arises out of a cultural pressure to be coupled, to live with other people. Well, I must say I've never shared in it. Quite possibly parental loss in early life removes all those conditionings from you. I think it probably does. Well, so much the better as far as I'm concerned. So that's why I think I'm eccentric.

Apart from your issues with the British Society, what were the more intimate moments or milestones in the latter part of your career that convinced you that it was time to retire?

I know exactly what they were. I can speak to that. I retired in December 1944 ...

Fifty two years ago!!!

(*laughs*) Yes! I hadn't even got going then ... 1944 ... what was I doing? I was at boarding school, God help me! Let me start again. In February 1994, one of my oldest and dearest friends, whom I'd actually been to school with and kept up with ever since, rather suddenly developed a very bad case of cancer of the lung ... Then again, what case isn't a bad one? When she discovered it, she had an enormous lump in her neck. God knows how she'd not noticed it before. Anyway, she lived in Cornwall, which is quite a long way from London, and I very badly wanted to go and visit her straightaway. And I couldn't, because for the immediate future – for the next ten or twenty days or so – I not only had all my patients, but I also had Society commitments.

As it happened she lived for ten months, and I managed to visit her for seven long weekends during the rest of her life ... So I did see quite a lot of her. But it was this situation that first put the idea of retirement into my head. It hadn't been there before, and marked for me a considerable change of heart and mind. I suddenly wanted more time in my aging life, if necessary, to visit friends and see more of them. Until then, I had always said I could never retire, that I should be one of those dreary old analysts who die in harness. I hadn't really thought about it then ... now it's perfectly clear as I've come to disapprove of such people. But I had thought that I wouldn't be able to tolerate retirement. I'd thought that I wouldn't be able to do without the identification as a psychoanalyst ... only to discover I perfectly well could. I didn't need that identification any longer. I didn't want it ...

I was so clear on certain things. After my friend's cancer, I wanted more time for my friends in the evening of my life. I began to realize, in 1994, that I was sixty-six. I felt my memory failing pretty rapidly – not in enormous ways, I wasn't dementing or anything like that, but it was the ordinary memory loss of old age, which comes in leaps and bounds. Quite suddenly mine got quite a lot worse. And whereas I used to pride myself – as I'm sure many analysts do! – on my ability to recall a week's worth of material for patients who saw me as many as four or five times a week, I suddenly began to find that I couldn't even remember what a person had said yesterday. I began to find I could no longer recall where we'd ended, I couldn't pick up things. Well, this concerned me. It hurt my pride as a worker.

Much more importantly, however, I found I was decathecting the work. I've written quite a lot about vocation and my own work in psychanalysis. For me, the decision to become a psychotherapist had a strong vocational component. I believe in the concept of vocation. I'm aware it has a religious connotation, and I'm quite prepared to accept that. I'd always worked vocationally. I always felt a huge commitment to, and cathexis of, the work. I always loved it, no matter what was going on. As soon as I got over my youthful tendency towards depressiveness and anxiety - which I managed to accomplish in my forties – every day would seem lovely to look forward to, precisely because I was going to see nine or ten patients. I simply adored the work. Then, in recent years, I found I was getting bored. I started getting fed up with my patients. I was still fond of many of them – most of them, really, as they'd nearly all been with me for some time. But I was decathecting the whole process. I wasn't so good at it any longer. I was losing my subtlety, my intuition was not so sharp – signs which, for someone like me, were very powerful. I put them together and decided I'd leave at the end of that year. And so I went.

So the decision wasn't one that was long planned or meditated ...

No, absolutely not. On the contrary. I had always thought that I would go on and on, but I began to look forward to being free. When the work becomes a burden ... when something that has been a joyful vocation begins to weigh on you ... it's time to go, and I recognized it. And I've never regretted the decision. There were some people – you know, the sort who want you not to be happy, as well as quite a lot of patients and other wet blankets – who said: "You'll suffer bereavement, I know you will" or "You're bound to miss this life." I heard all sorts of gloomy prognostications. But they simply didn't prove true. Nor do I think I entered a state of denial. I believe I was simply ready to go. And the sense of liberation, of real liberation that came upon me almost as soon as I'd gone, was wonderful. I didn't regret the decision at all, and I haven't since – not for a second.

As I just recently left my country of origin, one of the things that astonished me was the incredible ease with which, when the moment came, I just got on the plane and moved on. We seem to have this amazing plasticity, above and beyond our capacity and indeed the necessity for mourning, to get on with our lives ...

I think so too, Anthony. I do. I don't think you would repress or deny the mourning process. You've thought the decision through. You wanted to do it. And you are! There are times in everybody's life when a page just has to be turned, and you know you've got to the end of a chapter. The next one is there to be written ... so let's start writing it, already. That's exactly what it felt like ... the sense of knowing, not doubting, not wondering, not thinking, "Oh dear, I wonder if I'm right ..." Knowing you've come to the end of a chapter ...

In this light, do you think of yourself as being particularly brave?

(*laughs*) No, no I wouldn't ... because I felt that I was going into something much more empty, more peaceful, less demanding, less burdensome ... The Buddhists, you know, value emptiness very greatly ... Whereas I think of someone like yourself as brave. You're still a young man, but you're not in the first flush of youth when one tears off at nineteen and rushes about the world. You've got a wife, you want to start a family, and your immediate professional prospects are uncertain in your new country. No, I think my case is quite different ...

Your concern with "vocations" touches invariably on the matter of purposefulness. Along these lines, I'd like to redirect your attention to the place of writing in your life. Why does a person who considers writing and its joys as a "central and confirming element" of her profession – as you acknowledge in the chapter entitled "Why Am I Here?" – let fourteen years go by between essays? Why such a gap between your first paper, "The Man With the Two Mothers" – written in 1967 and only published now, thirty years later! – and the 1981 "Slouching Towards Bethlehem"?

Yes, it does sound rather contradictory, doesn't it? I have to say that my sense of writing as something central and confirming is one I get when I am actually writing, or when I become aware that I'm writing. But, although this sounds very paradoxical, I've never felt the need or the urge to write. As I've said, when somebody offers an incentive or a title or a subject to address, then I take great, great pleasure in the process. But I've never felt – like I'm sure Kit Bollas feels – that "I've got to write at all costs. I've got to shut myself up in my room and write and write." I'm sure Kit feels that way. It's why he can go on. The fact that I don't feel it is why I've stopped. And I know I've stopped. Hysterics will say, "I never know what I'm thinking until I open my mouth and say it ... "

A lot of writers would say that too ...

Exactly. To that extent, I'm an hysterical writer. It's only upon reflection, after I've already written something, that I realize, "Oh yes, I do think that." That's what I mean by the confirming element. Something comes to my mind, or reaches the tip of my pen, and I realize it's something I'd thought for ages. So these "thoughts," if you will, are not pre-formulated ... they are not thought out, by any means, and I think that's obvious from my books. I'm not an intellectual. Kit has this idea that I'm part of an intellectual literary tradition, but I don't think I am. As I've already suggested, very often writing makes me aware of a deeper level, perhaps an unconscious level, of thinking – so it's been very valuable to me. It's helped shape up quite a lot of my ideas. But it doesn't mean I feel an impelling urge to go on and continue writing.

But my question remains unanswered. How do you explain the four-teen-year hiatus between your qualifying case history, "The Man With the Two Mothers", and "Slouching Towards Bethlehem"?

I did answer you in a way, and I'll tell you why. A parallel consideration to my response is that I disapprove of youngish practitioners who start writing straightaway. Unfortunately some of the older analysts urge them to do so. They direct writing seminars and encourage students to get going as soon as possible. Now I think that's ridiculous. Such students are in-experienced, and no one wants to read callow stuff from younger analysts – which is obviously not deeply felt or experienced. Surely I don't want to. It's phony. Such writing doesn't teach me anything. It doesn't give me any sense of a wise, thoughtful person at work. To this end, you see, I consciously held back for quite a number of years. I had to do the qualifying paper for membership because that's what was done in those days. And yet I now realize, looking back, and as I've said in my book, that the direction my writing was to take was already in embryo in that paper. Still, I don't like shallow, inexperienced people starting to try to write. I don't think they can do it, and I think it shows. So I wanted to wait until I felt I'd got a lot of experience under my belt.

Is it safe to assume, then, that from the very start – from as far back as 1967 – there was an element of reticence that may have kept you from publishing?

That's precisely what I did feel. I was always quite reticent about publishing. Having produced three books, I know that sounds odd, but a lot of my papers aren't anywhere to be found. They aren't in journals. I've only ever published one paper in the *International Journal of Psychoanalysis*, and only one or two others in journals that commissioned a piece. But an awful lot of them haven't been published. One or two were solicited for books and then published. "Endings," for example, was intended for a book, in honor of Rafael Moses. *Slouching Towards Bethlehem*, my own first book, was all thanks to Bob Young, who was then at Free Association Books. He started me off in that direction. The idea had never occurred to me personally. I always wrote a paper for a purpose, and once that was done, it was done.

In his preface to The Baby and the Bathwater, *Bollas talks*

about travel literature as a literary tradition of which the British
are fond, and picks up on your description of yourself as an
"armchair traveler." What about the genre and your relation to it?

It's true, I have read quite a lot of travel literature. I'm reading
something at the moment, *A Merry Dance Around the World*, by
Eric Newby. I enjoy travel literature, and have also travelled a
great deal. It's one of the great bonuses of being single, not
having to worry about a family and the money a family requires.
I've traveled an enormous amount in my life. I've been all over
the place. And I do think that writing a clinical paper is like
sitting and following somebody's life journey. That's what is so
incredibly privileged about our job. We simply sit there listening
to people, and to the most extraordinary tales. And without even
moving, we get to enter our patients' imaginations, we get to
enter those tales and stories and events and be where our patients have been. After that, all you've got to do if you want a
paper is to write the material down. It's really not that difficult.

You do make a distinction, however, between two kinds of psycho-
analytic writing. You distinguish between the case history and the
"occasional" paper, that might result from an invitation where a
talk can give way to your own free associations. On this very
score, a colleague of mine, upon reading your work, remarked that
you had a way of beginning an essay from a clear starting point,
only to digress, meander and detour back to the matter at hand.
In a way, it's a process you yourself recognize when, towards the
end of The Baby and the Bathwater, *you discuss what you call*
your "free associative musings" ... What of these two different
writing strategies?

Your observations are perfectly true. I love writing case histories
because they're so much easier. You just summon up that
internal object and focus on it and write his or her story. But
the other papers ... I think they're of the sort that prompted
Kit's remarks. They're the ones in a tradition of essay writing
which goes back to Montaigne and also develops very much as
an English literary tradition. I'm thinking, for example, of Hazlitt
and Lamb, both of whom I was educated on in my youth. Essay
writing was very much part of the sort of education I had before
I went on to medicine ... First when I studied English literature,
and then when I did Modern Languages at Oxford, I had to
write essays every week. As a result I got very used to the genre

of essay writing and loved it. And that's what my other papers are. They're essays. I mean, you learn to free associate, long before you become a psychoanalyst, by being a writer of essays.

Can you say more about the British tradition of the essay, and of your own experimentation with the genre?

In the course of a British public school education, when you get into the sixth form, you write essays every week. You also read essays, by people like Hazlitt and Lamb and so on, and you get the hang of this particular sort of free associative style which embroiders, even as it keeps to, a main theme. We used to be set essays on absolutely everything! I remember one, from my last term in the sixth form: "Nature is too green and badly lighted." Well, that's an astonishing idea really, and that one could even say twenty words about it is amazing. I mean, one says either yes or no. But I remember loving writing that essay ... Off you go, wandering about, citing a few clever quotes that make you look as if you've read a lot more than you have – intellectual stuff, you know? ... Then, when I'd finished at Oxford, I went to St. Bartholomew's Hospital, one of the few places that accepted women, where they had what was called an Arts Scholarship. I thought, "I'd better go in for that because I haven't got much money to pay for this new venture." And it was so much after my own heart. It was the only hospital that had such a program. For it I had to write an essay, as well as a general English paper. Another requirement, unfortunately, was a maths paper. Well, as I'm innumerate and can't do maths, I eventually got a letter from the dean saying: "Dear Miss Coltart: We are happy to offer you the Arts Scholarship, but feel we should tell you that you scored only 7% on the math paper. We would like you to have some coaching before you come up ..." So it was pretty clear that it was my essays that got me the scholarship. I should have got it. I had already got a degree, and most of the people going in for the scholarship were straight out of school ... But what a great help it was. It paid all my tuition. I don't know quite what I would have done without it. And indeed I did get some coaching, and a fat lot of good it did me! I don't know how I got through the first two years of medical school, I really don't ...

You've touched on an idea I'd like to explore further with you, regarding a particular relationship, in British circles, between the essay and psychoanalysis. Somehow the essay seems to have become a privileged vehicle for the transmission of a certain kind of psychoanalytic knowledge. Can you comment on this phenomenon? I'm thinking, in addition to your work, of Khan, Bollas, Adam Phillips ...

And well you might. That's a very good point you make. I hadn't thought of it at all like that before, but now that you make the link, I do see that a lot of these people do indeed write essays ... I'm not so sure about Winnicott, although if you look at *The Maturational Process and the Facilitating Environment*, that too is a series of little essays. There's one in that very collection, I think, called "String" ... where he just free associates and writes a delicious, little, elegant essay on string, of all things, in a psychoanalytic context ... And of course there's Khan's writings ... Khan was an extremely knowledgeable and cultured man. He was steeped in culture, and couldn't help writing essays. And I think Kit Bollas can't either. His two earlier books are more of a mixture of technique and highly individual, original thought ... *Shadow of the Object*, I think, is a superb book ... as is *Forces of Destiny* ... They're both filled with wonderful ideas ... But they're essays alright ...

I'm not so sure you could say that Freud wrote essays. Freud was very pedagogical. He always wrote to teach. Now if you're just writing to teach, I think it's a different matter. What comes across is a lesson – which is something different from an essay. So while Freud wields language in such a way as to verge, on occasion, towards beautiful literature – and the Strachey translation is so exquisite! – I don't think of his papers as essays. Take Charles Rycroft: a lot of his work is in essay form ...

Adam Phillips I'm not so sure about. I do think, I have to say, that an essay should be easily intelligible. I've always aimed at that in my writing. After reading Phillips's second book, *On Kissing, Tickling and Being Bored*, a friend of mine and I – both admirers of Adam, mind you – agreed that we'd found him so exceedingly clever. And that he is, he's very clever. And it makes reading him rather hard work. It really does. I don't know if you found that when you were interviewing him but, my God, he's bright! And I think he sometimes overdoes it in his books ... Anyway, in his latest book, *Monogamy*, he's either lost the essay knack or abandoned it in favor of the aphorism. And the more he abandons the essay style, I think, the less popular he risks becoming ...

In such a context, however, I'm beginning to see more of
what Kit meant about me and a certain tradition of literary
psychoanalysts. It's the first time I've given it much thought,
and I didn't really understand it before ... but I do think
there's a strong tradition of essay writing among British
psychoanalysts. To tell the truth, Kit rather put me off
initially, because he read his Introduction to me over the telephone from New York, when it was actually 11 o'clock at
night here, and I was standing in the hall here in my pyjamas
... I nearly fell to the floor, I was so overcome by it. And
then he said, "But there's one thing you must do. You simply
must change the title of the book." "To what?" I said. "You
must call it 'In My End is My Beginning,' because," he said,
"you're so literary ... you're a T.S. Eliot lady." But I couldn't.
I just couldn't. I mean, pleased and grateful as I was, and
indeed still am, for that Introduction, I think it is a bit exag-
gerated. I remember saying to Kit: "I've had the title of this
book in my mind for two years. It swam into my mind. I trust
my title. I can't change it." Kit really wanted me to. But to
call it anything like "In My End is My Beginning" wouldn't be
true to me. I'd be true to an image that Kit has of me, to an
image which – while perhaps an aspect of me – is not to my
mind a central one.

*In your opinion, what is it that has made the essay a privileged
vehicle, in British circles, for the transmission of psychoanalysis?*

It's partly to do, I believe, with the independently minded people
in Britain who were attracted to psychoanalysis in the Thirties,
or shall we say as soon as James Strachey's translation came out.
A fascination with the new use of the unconscious was coupled,
I think, with an admiration for the literary quality of Strachey's
translation. I think this aspect attracted quite a lot of people,
like Rycroft, possibly Bion, Alex Stevens and others I can't call
up right now ... people who were never, first and foremost,
banner-waving psychoanalysts, but went on to become members
of the Independent Group. These people appreciated literature,
they liked the civilized, leisurely feeling of the pursuit of psychoanalysis. Psychoanalysis in Britain has attracted many such
people, much more than it has in other countries. And in the
process it's also produced a few eccentrics, people like myself! ...

On the matter of your eccentricity, some might find eccentric the

way you've declared your most recent book, The Baby and the
Bathwater, to be your final one. But throughout the book I noted
other intimations of finality which I'd like to explore with you ...

Isn't that interesting? I really was not conscious of the book
being such a finale, such a farewell ... mostly because it wasn't,
so to speak, "written" as a book, but as a collection of papers
spanning the last four years. The only exception is the first essay
– which we've already discussed – written many years ago and
identified as such. The last piece was definitely written as a final
paper, to close the book and to close my writing life. But that's
very interesting ... that you felt the sense of farewell, of closure,
throughout the book.

... in fact, upon receiving the book from you, no sooner did I open it
than I was struck by the stark black-and-white photograph of you ...
That faded, dated quality of the photograph had something grim
about it ... I was in a way relieved, when I finally got to the chapter
entitled "Endings," to see that it was about death ...

Oh my goodness!

... I do hope I can be so frank as to talk this way with you ...

Yes, I'm delighted. I'm very interested, of course. I mean, when
I say delighted, I'm delighted because I am utterly fascinated. In
a sense I don't know what you're talking about, and yet it rings
quite true to me at the same time. You've picked up on something ... But with regards to the photograph, it was the only one
I could dig up. I had it taken soon after I bought this house,
which brings us to about five years ago. For some reason, I've
almost forgotten now why I had it taken, together with some
others. I just went to somebody up the road and said I needed
some photographs. I think it was originally intended for my last
book, *How to Survive as a Psychotherapist*, which dates it 1993 ...
for which, by the way, they later decided not to use photographs
... But that's very interesting, Anthony ...

Actually, I was also somewhat perplexed by the book. While you
declare it to be your last, it left me with the sense that you somehow
had more to tell. Repeatedly, in fact, all throughout The Baby and
the Bathwater, *you only hint at crucial experiences which are*
rarely, if ever, more fully disclosed. You'll make fleeting references to

people or events, only to have that reticence of yours take over ... Might we revisit some of these instances together?

I'd be glad to, although I don't quite know what you mean!

You've mentioned here the traumatic, early loss of your parents. In the book, you make a reference to an early experience of death and handling it alone – but you go no further, and leave the reader in anticipation of a story that remains vague and untold. Similarly, in talking about Buddhism: you mention, almost in passing, twelve years of Buddhist apprenticeship – but nothing more is said about those years, which one would assume were pivotal in your development. You mention discovering, relatively late in life and in the context of an amazing group experience, a long-repressed anger towards your mother – but here too, as a reader I felt slightly teased, as if the autobiographical evocation were merely incidental ... And there are other instances as well ...

Yes, I can see how all this would appear very enigmatic. I agree with you ...

... finally, then, to round out the list, the book left me with the impression that there is a lesson, a kind of wisdom, that you'd like to impart at the close of your career ... and that you'd perhaps like to do so less discreetly, more directly ...

That's very astute because it's barely conscious. But the minute you say these words, their meaning feels familiar to me. I can recognize what you mean. I must immediately say, however, that I don't quite favor the idea of sitting on a mountaintop, like some hunched-up old sage, with some secret wisdom to pass on. I assume you don't really mean it that way ...

No, not at all.

But you are very astute the way you've picked up things in the book. I must say that nobody else who's read it has said to me anything at all similar to what you're now saying. And yet you may well be right, because I do think that the experience of losing one's parents is traumatic. My sister and I were evacuated to Cornwall because of the war in 1940, together with our old nanny who'd been in the family for generations. She'd been my mother's nanny, and she was a wonderful, wonderful person – a salt of the earth person. It was in Cornwall that my sister got very sick with an illness that to this day is undiagnosed. I suppose it may have been glandular fever. But the local doctor, who lived twelve miles away, got very worried and said that my parents must be sent for. My father was also a doctor, a general practitioner in London, where he was practicing out of our house because he was in a reserved occupation. Upon being summoned for my sister, he and my mother got on the night train to come to us. I went to meet the train at the local station with the local taxi driver, who fortunately was an old friend. The train never came. The station master by then knew that there had been a horrendous crash up the line. But he only informed the taxi driver, not me. The taxi driver, a very paternal and nice man, didn't tell me either, and eventually after four hours we went home.

As Gill was very ill and Nan was very busy looking after her, I began to man the telephone. Various messages came through, but we didn't get the final message, that my parents were actually dead, for nearly twenty-four hours ... They'd been taken to hospital, where somehow people either couldn't bring themselves to tell us or couldn't sort out the identities of the victims. Well my sister, thank God, recovered ... I don't know what my life would have been like if she had also died. I'd have been a lunatic, probably, if she had died as well ... because we've been such very good friends ... She's my only sibling. She was four years younger than I, and it was in the wilds of Cornwall that we became very close companions. Anyway, a tragedy like that fractures your life completely, and from there on you're a different person, you lead a different life. You've got a secret life. And as in those days there was no such thing as psychologists or counselors – thank God, in a way! – my sister and I were sent off to boarding school ...

Generally speaking, this story is not one I've readily disclosed with people. I did hint at it in my book because it's such a powerful influence in my life ... It's from such events that one knows about handling death, about handling grief and trauma ... or rather, about not always handling them successfully ... I became very depressed and disturbed when I was at boarding school, and nobody really understood what was happening to me. It was a difficult time. One woman there was, however, very good to me. She had an instinctive understanding of my situation, and I've been friendly with her ever since. She's very old now, but I still visit with her occasionally.

Eventually I managed to totter and lurch into the world of psychoanalysis. I didn't know how to look for it. I didn't know enough to know that it could help a person so. But it helped me a great deal. Later in life, you could say that the practice of Buddhism finished off the healing for me. But it took me twenty, twenty-five years to heal – and one does end up with a sort of superiority from such a prolonged struggle with survival ... Whether to call it wisdom, though, I'm not so sure ... I would prefer to call it wisdom ... But I used to feel secretly that I knew a great deal more than other people. I don't know if this much affected my behavior, except I'm sure that it turned me into something of a loner ...

My sister dealt with the aftermath quite differently. She got married, when still quite young, to a man twelve years older than herself. It's been a very happy marriage which lasts to this day. They instantly had four children whom she raised. They've all grown up and got children of their own now, and my sister is quite the happy grandmother! So she did the family bit, whereas I went in the other direction, inward, working things out in private. So if there are messages along such lines in my book – and you can see I very rarely talk about this, because I can tell that I am flushing! – then you're quite right to have picked them up.

Aside from the tragic story of your parents' death, there are – as I've suggested – any number of other stories or events which you hint at in your last book but leave undeveloped. Would you also consider revisiting them in greater detail?

Yes, I think so. It's very alert and sensitive of you to have picked up on those sorts of half-remarks and strung them together. You've got an interesting collection there! I must say, as I listened to you pick them out, I did wonder where you headed ... But after this last book, *The Baby and the Bathwater*, only then did I notice something of what I think you're talking about. I mean, quite a lot of my patients die. That is to say, in my books I write about quite a number of patients who actually die. There are two – one in my second book and one in this, my third – who commit suicide, which is not exactly a distinguished outcome for an analysis. Others die relatively young, like the "the man with two mothers," for example. Then there's the man in "Blood, Shit and Tears," whom I assume by the end of the essay is probably dead. And then there's the paper called "Endings." "How interesting," I thought.

Unwittingly, I was up to something, saying something that I hadn't quite fully realized ... You know how difficult it is to read one's own unconscious – I've always thought it much more impervious than anybody else's – but I can only deduce or, rather, I now know, that from early on in life I've known more about living with death, or Mr. D, as the Dutch doctor Bert Keizer called him in a wonderful book entitled *Dancing with Mr. D*, than most people do. Consciously, I wasn't aware of having any particular message to impart to others about it, but from a very young age I have always thought that I can tolerate the idea of my own death far more easily than a great many people can. I do think one should acquaint oneself with the idea of one's own death. I believe one should contemplate ending. And I suspect that in this book that is the half-message I'm trying to deliver.

With regards to Buddhism, I referred to twelve years of Buddhist practice insofar as it took me that long before I realized the third sign of being. There are three signs of being in Buddhism: *dukkha*, which is suffering; *anicca*, which refers to the transience or impermanence of all things; and *anatta*, which means no self. In an essay from my first book, *Slouching Towards Bethlehem*, I comment that *anatta* is the one sign that westerners find hard to swallow. We're all so ego-bound. The whole of psychoanalysis is bound up with the concept of the ego. The whole idea of being a no self takes the Western mind ages to penetrate, to be realized. And yet, as I think I said in *Slouching Towards Bethlehem*, I initially didn't bother about this very much. I thought, "Well, if I practice Buddhism faithfully and listen to the teachings, I will probably come to that point of realization. And if I don't, I don't." And in twelve years, really, of very regular practice and listening to teaching, I did come to it. I'd realized that I had realized it. *Anatta* had become real for me ...

Now this, of course, has considerable impact on what was, let's say, already an "interest" of mine: namely the idea of one's own death. If one is not a self, if the ego is a construct, the result of a conditioning we come to accept, well then, what is there to fear? In any case, it's always been my impression that people fear dying much more than death ... but that too hasn't been much sorted out in the West. I mean, it does require a lot more contemplation and attention. I myself continue to practice. It's not that I got to the point of realizing *anatta* only to think, "Alright, that's it, now what should we do next?" To this day I continue my Buddhist practice; insofar as it centers on meditation, it is interminable.

In speaking about death and Buddhism, you've actually anticipated the two final topics I intended to discuss with you. But if I may ask, what of your anger towards your mother and the unhealed wounds it's left?

I was really very green when I started my analysis. I wasn't somebody who was steeped in the process from early on, not at all. Anyway, you can't be in analysis for very long without realizing that it's not as if an idyllically, blissfully happy childhood of eleven years was suddenly fractured by a nasty trauma, and that only thereafter did everything go wrong for you ... I mean, Winnicott says the dreadful has already happened. And however dreadful the death of my parents when I was eleven, that had to be preceded by what the Buddhists call "pre-conditioning". Looking back, I have subsequently realized that I was in many ways an anxious child, ready for depression. And the trauma of my parents' death slotted rather neatly, as you might say, into that predisposition. I used to get very anxious and cry easily as a child, probably because my mother was very inexperienced when she had me. I was her first child ... Looking back, one of the less obvious difficulties of losing one's parents at eleven years old is that you can't later find out much about them. I think, however, that my mother was prone to depressiveness herself, and may well have been an anxious and somewhat depressed mother, particularly for her first child ...

Her own mother became our guardian although she didn't look after us. She was a rather demonic old lady. My sister and I still have a legend in our family that we had a wicked grandmother. She had a fearful temper and was very jealous, and my mother was by no means her favorite child. My grandmother had lost her favorite child in a very tragic way. In fact, her entire life had a tragic quality to it. Her favorite child was her firstborn son, who was older than my mother. He'd fought in and survived the First World War, only to come home and be killed in a motorbike accident just up the road from where the family lived. To have survived such a savage war, and die as he did – that was an extraordinary tragedy. Ten years later, my grandmother's relatively young husband – a handsome, dashing general practitioner – dropped dead beside her in a theatre queue. Ten years after that, her only other child, my mother, died in a train crash. All these deaths couldn't have done her soul much good ... One tragedy after another, her entire life was one of tragedy. Surely, one would hardly expect such a life to make of my grandmother a nice old woman ...

As my mother's brother and father predeceased her, she had her own increasingly difficult mother to cope with, who lived nearby. I don't think my grandmother helped my mother to be a more contained and mature person. I think all this came to be evidenced by the fact that I was, to put it mildly, an anxious child with a tendency to cry ... My primary love object – and saviour of both my and my sister's sanity, after my parents died – was our nanny, who had also been my mother's nanny. It was a feature of Edwardian England to have a nanny – a good, solid, reliable nanny. Like I said earlier, ours was a salt of the earth type. Funnily enough, here at Leighton Buzzard I've landed up close to where she was born, just up the road from us. Her father was a gardener in the Woburn Abbey Estates. I now go to Woburn Abbey as a room sitter. It's extraordinary, in my mind, to have something like this come full circle in one's life! It's so fortuitously lovely. But then again, who knows how truly fortuitous it is? ...

But anyway, my nanny was always my primary love object. I realized this much more during my analysis. I was rather afraid of my mother, rather in awe of her. I loved her, of course, and was actually quite devoted to her ... But my nanny was also a certified midwife who worked in my father's practice. In those days a midwife would go out on cases and live for three to four weeks on end with the recently delivered baby and its mother. So my nanny would disappear from time to time. I don't think I ever quite got the hang of her disappearances; certainly I never knew when she was coming back, or if she was ever coming back. You well may not believe this, but it took even this psychoanalyst many years to work out her preconditionings ... the undercurrents of the comings-and-goings of someone so loved, who'd disappear and often fail to return. So in a way, my parents never getting to us in Cornwall from London on the night they died, was the culmination, an apex of sorts, of a dynamic that had always been for me a source of great anxiety.

If we're talking about unhealed wounds, then this is the deepest one of my life. I've talked about this only to one or two friends rather than in my analysis. I never really got near this core in my analysis, as my analyst, I think, was too classical. I am somewhat reconciled to the fact that it's a wound from which one never recovers. I think my ego has had to grow various defenses or skins around it, because the pure anxiety of waiting for someone whom I love and depend upon to come to me, is still, at times unbearable ... God forbid they fail to show up! ... Even if they've been held up because of fog at Manchester Airport ... as far as I'm concerned the anxiety is psychotic. It's intolerable. It's an unhealed wound, and I can't heal it. I simply have to weather it, and fortunately that sort of thing tends to happen less and less because you discover defenses, you grow up, your love objects become aware of the wound and try to look after it for you ...

My analysis was extremely classical, old Freudian stuff. I'm not knocking my analysis, so far as it went it helped me a lot. But there's no doubt in my mind that it didn't go far enough, and many analyses don't. My analyst would often say that I was angry with my parents, or that I felt guilty about my parents ... But the words simply never clicked with me. They did not become real ...

Years later, though, I had a powerful experience – to which you've referred – which I documented in a paper entitled "Two's Company, Three's None." In the course of a training in group analysis, I had an anxiety attack during a session in which, because of some empty chairs, we were discussing absent group members. Up until then I had been the granny of the group, an owl of sorts who'd keep her distance ... Old wise eyes, you know?! Instead, I suddenly became the vulnerable one, a person who develops symptoms like the rest. I realized then that I had been all those years stewing away a sort of fury at my mother, from long before she died. I was furious with her for letting me down, for being so absent. In a rather circular way, it was through her death that I later discovered she'd been an absent mother in life. When she died and became totally absent, of course, I'm sure that any awareness of her shortcomings first needed to go into profound repression.

When I talked to Christopher Bollas some time ago, he mentioned his father several times in the course of our discussion. It was one of my first interviews and, as I felt somewhat tentative, I decided not to ask about his mother. At this point, however, I don't want to make the same mistake and not ask about your father ...

You reckon it was a mistake, do you?

Perhaps not at the time of the interview ...

Is there anything specific you want to ask me?

I simply wouldn't want to leave your father out of the picture ...

No, let's not. I'm one of those people who thinks that fathers do definitely come into the picture later than mothers. By later I mean around the age of one, one and a half. The notion of the father playing just as much a part as the mother simply didn't operate in our family. I mean, we were a very conventional, old-fashioned family. My father was a busy general practitioner. I don't think he had any part in our early upbringing. He was always a distant figure. He was Scottish, and Scottish people can be extremely reserved. So was he. Reserved, and ironic.

Interestingly enough, years later I discovered that in his consulting room he'd kept Freud's early books. This, mind you, in an ordinary general practice in South London, in the 1920s and '30s. So he was picking up on Freud pretty early. I found that fascinating, because it had had no influence on me becoming a psychoanalyst, as far as I knew. But I always felt rather afraid of my father, rather distant from him ...

I never felt I got to know my father very well, except insofar as what became patently clear during my analysis, when I learned that I was strongly identified with him. Now I don't think you can strongly identify with somebody without coming to know them very well. Many people who knew my father – who have, of course, become fewer and fewer over the years – would all say how exactly like him I was. I thus began to rethink the whole business of not knowing him very well. As it turns out, I knew him, of course, extremely well, down to the bones ...

My first degree was in Modern Languages at Oxford, and all the time I'd wanted to be a doctor. I fought tooth and nail and worked extremely hard, harder than anybody could possibly imagine, I think, these days, to take a second degree in medicine. I spent six years, after I'd finished my Oxford degree, in order to become a doctor. I hadn't done any chemistry or math or physics, and the first two years were an absolute nightmare. But it never occurred to me that I was going to fail. I absolutely knew that I was going to become a doctor. And it was only, again, later in my analysis, that I developed any inkling of the fact that this was the most profound enactment of an identification with my father. But the interesting thing was that, as soon as I became a doctor, I realized that I didn't particularly want to be one. I'd achieved that. I had become him. I'd restored him to

life. I really didn't want to go looking at people's sore throats
and binding up their wounds. In fact, I wanted to be a psychiatrist, which I became. But ultimately I could have done psychotherapy and psychoanalysis without becoming a doctor at all.
Becoming a doctor had nothing to do with my chosen profession. In a way, then, a whole segment of my life had to do with
knowing this father of mine, whom I'd always thought I didn't
really know.

*Having never practiced Buddhism, I'm intrigued when I hear
someone like yourself say that she's realized the no self, only to
acknowledge her own ego's historical need for defenses, as well as
her own psychotic anxieties. How can a person who's realized the no
self speak of an ego that is still so vulnerable?*

And so well functioning, a lot of the time! It's a question of
levels of attitude, of levels of experience. The Buddha himself,
if you read some of the scriptures or *suttras*, as they are
called, was very good on this score. He was a very astute
psychologist. He realized the difficulty of the question you've
just asked. Here we are, we're cast into the world, we all have
our cultures and languages and personal histories to contend
with. We have to talk to each other. We have to be. We have
to function. Increasingly in the world we're asked to cope with
cultural inputs. We can't turn our backs on the world and say,
"Well, sorry folks, I'm a no self. I don't take part in that sort
of thing." We have to observe the conventions of the culture
that we live in, or else we'd have no life. I guess we would
crouch in a corner meditating for twenty-three hours a day,
possibly managing to totter to the shops and get a bit of food
to sustain ourselves ...

For the longest time, we've had tools for thinking about the
self, and the way the mind operates. Freud himself, of course,
gave us a way to understand the structure of mind – one
which, while thoroughly flawed and subject to countless revi-
sions, I quite accept. Conventionally, of course, we all are
selves to ourselves. Other individuals are selves to us and, as
individuals, are different from the next individual. Such a view,
indeed such an experience, is all part of the convention that
life and living demand of us. It doesn't alter in the least the
fact that the three signs of being – suffering, impermanence,
and no self – are still fundamental truths, with a capital 'T.'
Everything else involves the conditions of going from day to

day, of putting one foot in front of the other – from communicating with our friends at a micro-level, to trying to make sense of all sorts of global phenomena on a macro-level of existence.

Is it this recognition of social and cultural realities that keeps Buddhism, in your view, on this side of nihilism?

Buddhism is not, as is often thought, nihilistic. Not at all. It is the recognition of precisely what we've been talking about that keeps it from being so. Nor is it lugubrious. I mean, it's very serious and, at heart, actually pretty austere. There's a great deal of laughter in Buddhist monasteries – real, genuine heart-felt laughter. A lot of life is seen to be very ironic and very funny. Personally, I've never laughed so much as when listening to some of the abbots' sermons or talks, at the monastery just up the road. And yet, Buddhism is basically an austere religion. Contrary to Christianity, it doesn't have much, for example, in the way of consolations or comforts – except, that is, for what I regard as the three bare truths, which prove themselves through one's own efforts, as one tries to live out the fundamental precepts of the Middle Way. Such efforts make you happier, as the Buddha always said they would. In fact, the Buddha's message, in short, was: "Be good and you'll be happy." It's what all the Victorian and Edwardian nannies have been saying for years!

On the matter of Buddhism and the self, I was flipping through a copy of Anthony Burgess' autobiography recently, a book called Little Wilson and Big God, *when I found the following quote:*

What do we mean by the ego? It is an existential concept, I believe, and the ego I examine is multiple and somewhat different from the ego that is doing the examining. Even the ego that began this book in September of 1985 is not the one that has completed it in 1986. In other words, the book is about somebody else, connected by the ligature of a common track in time and space to the writer of this last segment of it which cheats and looks like the first.

As a Buddhist, what do you make of Burgess' remarks?

That sounds remarkably like the sort of sermons I've heard from advanced monks! Certainly, if you've gotten as far as thinking that there is no self – or, I would prefer to say, as *realizing* that there is no self, because you don't get that far by thinking – you're going to accept fairly readily that the self who got up this morning is not, by any means, the self that you experience yourself as now. Of course, we go on experiencing ourselves as selves because, as I've already suggested, you can't not do so. But between then and now conditions have changed, hundreds of thoughts have been thought, hundreds of moments have been lived through. Burgess is quite right. There is a kind of ligature, possibly called memory, which connects the first part of his book to the last, or the beginning of our conversation to where we are now. But nothing much less tenuous than that.

How did you chance upon Buddhism, and what has been the history of your attraction to and involvement in it?

I talk a bit about that in *Slouching Towards Bethlehem*, insofar as I see myself as having a religious temperament. I do believe such a thing exists. I mean, there are people who go through their lives absolutely cold to religion. It doesn't mean anything to them at all. There are also people who, quite the opposite, have religious temperaments and look for worship, belief ... dependence, if you like ... elements that are usually associated with religion. Early on, from my late teens until I was about thirty, I was quite a devout practicing Christian, and it did a great deal for me. During that time I knew some good, decent Christians, and that was certainly a help. And, of course, I believed in God, and took Communion regularly.

And yet, as soon as I developed an active sex life – which was rather late for me, not surprisingly, in my late twenties – almost overnight I stopped believing in God. I think this happens to a lot of people, except it doesn't really get talked about very much. It's a phenomenon I've encountered in other people as well. And when I say stopped, I really mean stopped. Suddenly, and unequivocally. I haven't ever quite worked out why active sexuality should stop making a person believe in God. I mean, I've got some ideas about it, but not very many. In a way, I don't really care any longer. It all seems so long ago. But of course I still had a religious temperament. I was also a depressed young woman, and I wanted to be an analyst. So then I had an analysis; and though I never indulged a fanatical credulity in psychoanalysis the way some people do. it did occupy my attention for several years. But almost as soon as I'd finished I started looking around for something to sponge up my religious proclivities. It's not that I leapt out of one and into the other, however. There was a gap of four or five years, before I became actively involved with Buddhism ...

I remember having an instinctive feeling that I wanted to learn to meditate. This was because my analysis, although it helped with my depression, didn't do much for my anxiety. I felt that if I could learn to meditate properly, I would be helped to manage my anxieties. I remember learning of a weekend retreat, run by a Buddhist monk as part of an ongoing adult education program. I applied to attend it, and did. The monk running the program subsequently turned out to be one of the greatest Buddhist teachers in the West. He virtually brought Theravadin Buddhism to this country, and set up the first Theravadin monastery, of which there are now six. Many people think this sounds rather ironic, but I regard my life as a series of strokes of luck. I had one or two strokes of bad luck, sure, but I've had some real strokes of good luck in my life. One of them was that weekend – at which I not only learned the rudiments of meditation, but came to be taught by someone who subsequently became recognized as a great Theravadin teacher. Sheer luck! I remember thinking, "I want this man to be my teacher." And I've never looked back. That must have been twenty-five years ago ...

Have your practice and commitment been as unwavering as your early Christianity? What about the evolution of your Buddhist practice over the years?

By the time I started in Buddhism, I was older. I'd been analyzed, I was established in my career, I was moving towards being successful in my career. In many ways I was grown up and more mature, and I brought far less depression to it. I did bring with me need and a capacity for anxiety, but I think the evolution of my Buddhist practice has been altogether peaceful, much more so than my earlier years as a Christian. It's not true to say I didn't go into it with the kind of devotion I'd brought to Christianity, because I did. But then that's part of having a religious temperament. But my Buddhist development and practice have been quieter. Slower, and gentler ...

You can listen to countless Buddhist teachings or sermons and many, if not all of them, say the same thing. They all evidence how the Buddha was a great teacher, precisely because he knew that, for the few things in this life that really matter to sink in and be properly taught, they've got to be repeated over and over again in different ways. Moreover, if you've got a good teacher, as I've had, a lot of the teaching is very amusing to listen to. There're lots of jokes. Teachers all hammer home at the same themes, always from slightly different angles, until you really begin to simplify your heart. By purifying your heart and simplifying your mind, you come to realize that you don't have to keep scrambling about like a monkey thinking your important thoughts. You learn to get deeper into meditation, where the whole aim is to empty your mind of thought. Meditation in the Buddhist tradition is not thinking, contrary to the Christian tradition, in which you're literally given a theme to think about. The two traditions couldn't be more radically different in this way. Buddhist meditation is a sustained effort: watching the breath to clear the mind, getting behind the scrambling monkey of thought in order to stop it. Being able to do so, ever more and more profoundly, and experiencing its effects, has been for me a slow but steady process.

Increasingly, many parallels are drawn between psychoanalysis and Buddhism. What are the principal ones you've found? And what application, if any, has Buddhism found in your clinical practice?

At the risk of sounding like my own salesman, I'd have to send you to buy my first book, *Slouching Towards Bethlehem*, where there's a chapter on Buddhism and psychoanalysis in which I talk in some detail about the ways in which they've never clashed for me. I've always seen them as potentiating and strengthening each other. That was always my experience. In the early stages of both, you might say, the paths have much in common. Many people who go into either, or both, are in more-or-less anguished states of mind for which they want help. Along both paths you begin to look into yourself: reflecting on your past, in analysis; and on your conditioning – which after all is your past – in Buddhism. Through both you learn how very influential those early effects were, and you learn to begin to examine them by free association. There's no clash here, none whatsoever. The paths tends to diverge further on because Freud always said he was not setting out to develop a religious system. He was not trying to provide a philosophy of life, nor was he trying to teach morality. Far from it. In many ways, he was trying to undermine morality as he and his times knew it. And this is where Buddhism and psychoanalysis begin to diverge, but in a way that never seemed to me to matter all that much ...

Whatever analysts say about being non-judgmental, or about being neutral on matters of morality is, of course, absolute bunkum. Analysts are making judgments all the time. The entirety of one's moral fibre, one's whole moral outlook, is involved in every single session, and in the tiniest of clinical judgments one makes. It can't not be this way. Therefore, the fact that Buddhism aims, on one level, to help establish and strengthen a moral base, doesn't seem to me to be in conflict with psychoanalysis. Not at all. At least not as long as analysts don't start imposing their own strong moral judgments on patients. Again, I don't see how there's any conflict, because analysts can't help expressing indirectly their own morality to patients. Patients aren't fools. They're going to hear the echos of that morality. They're going to pick it up. They're going to know if an analyst is trying to impose that morality on them, or not ...

With regards to any clinical applications, I think they are indirect at best. If you go into Buddhism and stick with it, you can't help having your way of thought influenced. But you have to be careful about not becoming a moral teacher or a pedagogue. A lot of my patients would probably be surprised on finding the chapters I've written on Buddhism, in both my first and last book. That is to say, it's only indirectly that they'd come to know that Buddhism was something I practised. I would not extol Buddhism or teach Buddhism to a patient. Only very, very occasionally, towards the end of a long therapy or analysis, might I mention it, almost *en passant*, and perhaps provide the address of a Buddhist association. But I'd do so only if I felt this person to be on a search of his own, looking for information about a path to pursue, and only if I knew him well enough to know that Buddhism might prove suitable. But I wouldn't do more than that. I wouldn't start teaching Buddhist precepts, or anything like that at all.

As regards my own practice, and how Buddhism has affected my clinical work with patients, one of the earliest things I noticed was the deepening of attention. I'd written a paper on attention in my first book, where I refer to "bare attention," which is a very Buddhist phrase. Bare attention has a sort of purity about it. It's not a cluttered concept. It's that you simply become better, as any good analyst knows, at concentrating more and more directly, more purely, on what's going on in a session. You come to concentrate more and more fully on this person who is with you, here and now, and on what it is they experience with you: to the point that many sessions become similar to meditations. When this happens, I usually don't say very much, but am very, very closely attending to the patient, with my thought processes in suspension, moving towards what Bion called 'O': a state which I see as being "unthought out," involving a quality of intuitive apperception of another person's evolving truth. All this undoubtedly became easier to do, as a result of my Buddhist practice. Sessions became more frequently like meditations. That is about the most powerful effect Buddhism had on my clinical practice.

I can't help but wonder about the effects a Buddhist training might have on the countertransference sphere. What has your experience been along these lines?

It's an interesting way of looking at the relationship between the two paths. My immediate response, without having given your observation any prior thought, is that a Buddhist training might facilitate certain aspects of being oneself in a clinical situation. One of the things an analyst has constantly to learn to do – although with any luck we all do get better at it over time – is to sort out our own coutertransferences. Learning to sort out our own personal reactions to the patient, and to what's going on between us, from the insidiousness of projective identifications. Such an exercise, of course, is vital. I would say that Buddhism makes this process easier because it not only gives a person, by clearing one's mind of too many scrambling thoughts, the capacity to fade out of the picture temporarily; it also opens up the space for something which the patient is busily trying to lodge into you. To this end, I would have to think that an analyst with this kind of sensitivity would be less defended, and all the quicker to recognize the nature of such a dynamic ...

Although I've never reflected on this question before, I think what I'm saying is true. It feels right ... There are two main forms of meditation in Theravadin Buddhism. One is *samatha*, where you simply watch the breath until you imagine you'd be bored to death with it. And yet it's not actually boring; it's a very good way of quieting the mind. The other is called *vipassana*, which involves getting to a stage of quieting the breath whereby a sort of internal detachment occurs from one's own powers of observation. It's a sort of self-splitting really. You can observe your thoughts running past you. You're not trying to control them or squash them or anything like that, but let them run on, as they are, of their own accord. *Vipassana* is the art of studying the thought stream. Now, if you've done a lot of this kind of meditation, it can't but help in studying the counter-transference, because you do get to know all sorts of layers of your own thoughts by doing *vipassana*. I've not thought of this before, but it's fascinating to try and work it out here on the spot with you. If you've done a lot of *vipassana* and have managed to foster a split attitude of observation detached from thinking and reacting, yes, it's got to help the countertransference as well, hasn't it?

I'd like to end our discussion on Buddhism with one general question regarding what you've called the "religious temperament." Alongside Freud's many accomplishments, he also helped close the doors of psychoanalysis to such temperaments or sensibilities. Recently, however, people as different as the Jewish mystic Michael Eigen and the Marxist Joel Kovel have been advocating and encouraging a return of the spiritual within psychoanalysis. Even beyond the reaches of Buddhism, how do you view the relationship of psychoanalysis to spirituality?

I simply couldn't begin to address such a question! I don't know if even you have a sense of how simply colossal a question it is. I would have to sit and think about the question quite a bit more. It's not one I'd want to answer off the cuff. But I have read quite a lot of Michael Eigen. I'm a great admirer of his ...

What if I were to reframe the question, or refocus it for you?

Yes, please do.

From both your own practice and what you know of the British scene, is there a greater opening towards and acceptance of the religious and spiritual temperaments, or is there still a foreclosure operating against them?

There's still a foreclosure. Definitely. I have no doubt at all that the whole notion of spirituality, anything tainted with the very word *religion* creeping in under the cracks of the doors of psychoanalysis, is still very much a taboo subject. I would certainly say that in the British Society, you do get islands of interest ... odd people here and there who obviously have religious temperaments, or an interest in some form of spirituality. Joe Berke, for instance, has become a practicing orthodox Jew. One or two other friends of mine have also gone deeply into Judaism and its practice. I certainly know of at least one practicing Christian psychoanalyst ...

Neville Symington also seems to have opened up ...

Neville Symington has opened up a lot with his recent book, *Emotion and Spirit*, and he's done so very, very well. I mean, it's an immensely readable and thought-provoking book. Nevertheless, I think there's still a lot of foreclosure in the field at-large. Of course, the Kleinians are a religion in and of themselves, and operate as if they were a high church with the truth to proclaim. But we won't go any further into that ...

Since death isn't all that ominous a topic here, I'd like to close with a few questions regarding it. You actually do cite Eliot in your last book, and suggest: "In my beginning is my end ..." I connected this and certain other references in the book with a word of immense resonance for me and, I imagine, for other readers as well. You talk about the concern *of death. It's a word that stopped me in my tracks. There's such a serene gravity to it that it just focused my attention. What a lovely word:* concern. *It almost seems, in your usage, to be emptied of preoccupation, as if meant to suggest something other than preoccupation. Could you talk about the* concern *of death?*

I'm glad you used the word "emptied," because insofar as I had any message for people about death, it would be something like the sense you've picked up on. If you can use the word *concern* as an empty word, a serene word, for something which concerns us all because it's the one sure thing ahead of us all, then you might have managed to reduce worry for some people. You see, an awful lot of people worry about death, like that poor, old, bloody patient whom I discuss in "Endings," who spent his entire life worrying about his death. If ever there were a living hell, if ever there were death in life, one need look no further. I mean, I didn't like him and he didn't like me, but I felt profoundly sorry for him because his life was a waste, a desert waste. And I did little to help him ...

We need to be concerned to die, if we can, with grace. It may not be allowed to us. It may not be given to us to die with grace. But of course we all hope for such an end, without worry or fuss or anxiety. I've seen a lot of people dying one way and another. A year ago one of my dearest friends of fifty years died. She had cancer of the lung, and for several months she was very agitated about her death ... how it was going to happen, would she choke and become frightened ... We often talked about the prospect of death, and I often said that I had never seen anybody, at the actual moment of death, frightened or kicking against it, in spite of what Dylan Thomas says. Towards the end, she became really completely peaceful. She realized before she died that she needn't have been so agitated after all. But I think we'd be more likely to die with some grace if we were to have had death as a concern of ours in life. Does that speak to your question?

Yes. And it leads perfectly to the question with which I'd like to bring our conversation to a close. I recently found, in a book by Janet Malcolm entitled The Purloined Clinic, *an essay on Jacques Lacan and his noted American apologist, Stuart Schneiderman. In an essay called "The Seven-Minute Hour," Malcolm thus elaborates on Schneiderman's view of psychoanalysis: "Schneiderman firmly maintains that psychoanalysis ought to get out of the business of thinking about how people live their lives or about how they behave. What this means, perhaps, unexpectedly, is that psychoanalysis has as its major task the repairing of the relationships people have not with other people but with the dead."*

Really!

Your closing comments, on death and psychoanalysis ...

What comes to my mind immediately are two categories of the dead. Having listened to your question, I instantly saw my own dead, so to speak, of which by now I have a considerable number ... people pertaining to me and my life. For somebody who's still only in their sixties, I've really lost a relatively large number of close friends. I've been lucky, though, and as I've had a large number of close friends, perhaps that increases the chances of loss ... But still, several have died relatively young. One of my closest analytic friends died in her forties, when I was only in my forties ... So there's the category of one's own dead ...

In a different category are the patients to whom I referred earlier, of whom I've written – the patients I've known who have died. I was concerned with these patients in a particular way ... Personally, I don't think I believe in immortality – and the Buddha himself, of course, left open the question of reincarnation ... I suspect that the Buddha taught that life itself, as a force, cannot be extinguished completely ... To this end, you have to be concerned with the only posterity that dying people have: with what we, the living, can still give them. This is why the two categories – my own dead and my patients who have died – feel a bit separate for me. I'm not sure why I say this; I'd have to work out why. But I do believe that it was to keep the memory of a patient alive that I wrote, for example, the paper called "Paradoxes" in my middle book, *How to Survive as a Psychotherapist*. I remember her very vividly in that piece, with great color and great humor. I was very fond of her. She was the woman who, with a stroke of her arm, once swept everything off my mantlepiece, breaking a treasured ivory figurine and knocking one of my flower vases into my lap, soaking my skirt. She also brought a knife into a session with her one day, and sat twiddling it quite suggestively. Anyway, she was a great, great character. I was extremely fond of her, and as she didn't have many friends and her husband predeceased her, I feel that her immortality, if anywhere, is in my head. That's not much of an immortality, and it won't outlive me, but it's something ...

It will surely outlive you now ...

(*laughing*) Yes, now it will!

Is this a good place to end?

Yes, I think it is. I really do. I think you handled all this very skilfully, and I do thank you.

It's been my privilege and pleasure. Thank you.

WORKS CITED

Bollas, Christopher (1989). *Forces of Destiny: Psychoanalysis and Human Idiom.* London: Free Association Books.

— (1987). *The Shadow of the Object: Psychoanalysis of the Unthought Known*. London: Free Association Books.

Burgess, Anthony (1987). *Little Wilson and Big God: Being the First Part of the Confessions of Anthony Burgess* London: Penguin.

Keizer, Bert (1994). *Dancing with Mr. D*. London: Doubleday.

Khan, M.R. Masud (1974). *The Privacy of the Self*. London: The Hogarth Press.

King, Pearl and R. Steiner. (1992). *The Freud–Klein Controversies, 1941–1945*. London: Routledge/Tavistock.

Malcolm, Janet (1992). *The Purloined Clinic: Selected Writings*. New York: Knopf.

Newby, Eric. (1995). *A Merry Dance Around the World*. London: HarperCollins.

Philips, Adam (1996). *Monogamy*. London: Faber & Faber.

— (1993). *On Kissing, Tickling and Being Bored*. London: Faber & Faber.

Symington, Neville (1994). *Emotion and Spirit*. London: Cassell.

Winnicott, D.W. (1965). *The Maturational process and the Facilitating Environment*. London: The Hogarth Press and the Institute for Psychoanalysis.

NINA COLTART: Selected Bibliography

The Baby and the Bathwater (1996). London: Karnac Books; Madison: International Universities Press.

How to Survive as a Psychotherapist (1993). London: Sheldon Press; Northvale: Jason Aronson, Inc.

Slouching Towards Bethlehem (1992) London: Free Association Books; New York: Guilford Press.

PUBLISHER'S POSTSCRIPT

It is so hard to read those final words in Nina Coltart's interview – her thoughts on death – without a terrible sense of poign-
ancy. It is even harder to absorb the realization that the vigour,
so evident and transparent in that interview, has gone. Nina,
who understood only too well the hammer blow of sudden loss,
would know how we feel but would lose no time in telling us to
get on with our lives. She was a realist and she possessed a
diffidence often found in the truly able.

Several publishers have worked with Nina. My own experience has been one of everlasting pleasure. She was prompt, effi-
cient, appreciative and diligent, thoughtful of the needs of the
person with whom she was working. Her intelligence was pierc-
ing; her sense of humour blazing. She wrote like a dream. I
often sent manuscripts to her for assessment and would wait
with relish for her reports. The speed and almost brutality with
which she dissected evidence of muddle and, especially, self-
regard, often took my breath away. She would have none of it.
But there was not the slightest hint of spite or point scoring. I
had given her a job to do and she was going to give it her full
intellectual and professional concentration. She dragged in no
extraneous matter. Conversely, she gave generous praise when
she discovered something of merit and was happy to make her
encouragement public. Her reports were educational documents
in the best sense. Her arguments and her knowledge were
broadly informed. She could make connections. Like all people
of real stature, she was also able to stand back and be occasionally critical of her own profession – a strength born of integrity,
individualism and truthfulness.

I am glad that her final contribution to psychoanalytic literature is through her conversation with Anthony Molino because
here we are able to approach the person in a more direct way.
Many readers who did not know her will have already formed an
impression of her through her books, simply because her writing
is so lucid. But in this conversation, we can see and hear the
Nina some of us knew – direct, funny, open and honest, entertaining and penetrating, and still hell-bent on getting something
out of everything in which she became involved. It is a treat, but
we should not allow it to become a sad treat. At a time when
the word 'distinguished' is bandied around, often in the direction

of people who have simply lasted the course, she deservedly earns the epithet. She lasted the course and then she had the courage and the strength of character to walk away from the work that had brought her great praise. I shall miss her wisdom, her hilarious stories, her kindness. She was great fun. My only regret is that she did not have the chance to spend more time in her beloved garden.

Gill Davies
Free Association Books
July 1997